Smart Electric and Hybrid Vehicles

This book presents an analysis of the existing surveys in the literature of batteries, chargers, control systems, battery management systems, plugs, sockets, drives, and fuel-cell-based and plug-in smart electric and hybrid vehicles. It provides detailed comparative analysis of parameters of intelligent electric and hybrid vehicles with conventional vehicles and in-depth knowledge of power electronics tools in smart electric and hybrid vehicles. This book compiles the research work and findings in advancements of smart electric and hybrid vehicles from automobile, mechanical, electronic, electrical, computer science, and allied engineering domains and explains how smart electric and hybrid vehicles can be utilized without harmful emissions over the entire lifecycle of a vehicle and how reliance on fossil fuels can be reduced.

Features:

- Discusses different types of lightweight and robust materials for the fabrication of smart electric and hybrid vehicles.
- Presents computational models, emerging technologies, numerical techniques, and environmental and economic benefits applicable to electric vehicles.
- Highlights the applications of smart and hybrid vehicles in diverse sectors including aerospace, agriculture, defense, and medical.
- Covers electromechanical drives, storage systems, wireless charging, and component design for smart electric and hybrid vehicles.
- Showcases a detailed comparative analysis of parameters of intelligent electric and hybrid vehicles with conventional vehicles.

It is primarily written for senior undergraduates, graduate students, and academic researchers in the fields of electrical engineering, electrical and electronics engineering, computer engineering, and automotive engineering.

Industrial and Manufacturing Systems and Technologies: Sustainable and Intelligent Perspectives

Series Editors: Ajay Kumar and Parveen Kumar

This book series provides a platform of single and multidisciplinary advance research on industrial and manufacturing engineering to introduce a requirement for a synergy from management and engineering. It provides the readers paradigms and systems of intelligence and sustainability in industrial and manufacturing engineering. It will contribute towards dissemination of 5.0 industrial revolution techniques towards academia, industry, and various practical communities involved in mechanical, industrial, computer science, automobile, electrical, electronics, aerospace engineering, supply chain, logistics, banking, finance management, circular economy, medical, pharmaceuticals, and healthcare industries. It will focus on important topics such as additive manufacturing, virtual reality in industrial engineering, industrial internet of things, intelligent engineering asset management system, and modeling of intelligent industrial engineering systems.

Smart Electric and Hybrid Vehicles
Fundamentals, Strategies and Applications
Edited by Ajay Kumar, D. K. Rajak, Parveen Kumar and Sarita Rathee

Smart Electric and Hybrid Vehicles
Design, Modeling, and Assessment by Industry 4.0 Approaches
Edited by Ajay Kumar, D. K. Rajak, Parveen Kumar and Sarita Rathee

For more information about this series, please visit: www.routledge.com/Industrial-and-Manufacturing-Systems-and-Technologies-Sustainable-and/book-series/CRCIAMSAT

Smart Electric and Hybrid Vehicles

Fundamentals, Strategies and Applications

Edited by Ajay Kumar, D. K. Rajak,
Parveen Kumar, and Sarita Rathee

CRC Press
Taylor & Francis Group
Boca Raton London New York

CRC Press is an imprint of the
Taylor & Francis Group, an **informa** business

Designed cover image: Shutterstock

First edition published 2025
by CRC Press
2385 NW Executive Center Drive, Suite 320, Boca Raton FL 33431

and by CRC Press
4 Park Square, Milton Park, Abingdon, Oxon, OX14 4RN

CRC Press is an imprint of Taylor & Francis Group, LLC

ISBN: 9781032600369 (hbk)
ISBN: 9781032814261 (pbk)
ISBN: 9781003495574 (ebk)

DOI: 10.1201/9781003495574

Typeset in Sabon
by Newgen Publishing UK

Contents

Preface

The automotive industry has become one of the most important world-wide industries, not only at the economic level, but also in terms of research and development. Increasingly, more technological elements are introduced on vehicles for the improvement of both passenger and pedestrian safety. In addition, there are a greater number of vehicles on the roads, which allows us to move quickly and comfortably. However, this has led to a dramatic increase in air pollution levels in urban environments [i.e., pollutants, such as PM, nitrogen oxides (NO_x), CO, sulfur dioxide (SO_2), etc.].

According to a report by the European Union, the transport sector is responsible for nearly 28% of total carbon dioxide (CO_2) emissions, while road transport is accountable for over 70% of the transport sector emissions. Therefore, authorities of most developed countries are encouraging the use of smart electric and hybrid vehicles to avoid the concentration of air pollutants, CO_2, as well as other greenhouse gases. More specifically, they promote sustainable and efficient mobility through different initiatives, mainly through tax incentives, purchase aids, or other special measures, such as free public parking or the free use of motorways. Smart electric and hybrid vehicles offer the advantages of lower emissions, simplicity, reliability, cost effective, better comfort, better efficiency, accessibility, lightweight structure, and fatigue-free driving mode over traditional vehicles.

This book offers handy data concerning application of smart electric and hybrid vehicles in several knowledge domain areas like automobile, mechanical, electrical and electronics, computer science and information technology and engineering, and environmental impact assessment and much more. All the book's chapters contain prime quality pictures to create better visuals for readers. Together they will provide universal coverage of the technologies used for smart electric and hybrid vehicles. This book acts as a perfect textbook or reference guide for course of automobile, mechanical, industrial, electrical, electronic engineering at UG and PG levels also conjointly act as a reference for academicians, researchers, and professionals of allied domains.

The book consists of 12 chapters that describe perspectives of smart electric and hybrid vehicles. Chapter 1 'An overview on electric vehicles: technologies, emissions, and challenges' presents a review on the different types of electric vehicles, batteries, charging type, and electric motors used in EV. In addition, the greenhouse gas emissions of the different electric vehicles are discussed in this chapter. Chapter 2 'A comprehensive review on rechargeable batteries: technologies, advancements, and comparative analysis' covers historical development, battery chemistries, and emerging technologies like solid-state and lithium-sulfur batteries and also highlights rechargeable batteries' imperative responsibility while addressing global energy challenges and promoting sustainable energy solutions. Chapter 3 'Fabrication of test rig to analyze the effects of variable belt tension in a CVT system' explains how a CVT system can improve the efficiency, enhance the torque and speed delivery to the drive wheels of the vehicle. Chapter 4 'Analysis of a start-stop system for an energy-efficient micro-hybrid two wheeler' aims to analyze a two-wheeler engine start and stop system for efficient fuel utilization by two wheelers on Indian roads. Chapter 5 'Optimization of electric vehicle lithium-ion battery parameter by using Taguchi methodology' focused on determining the optimum combination of lithium-ion battery parameters for the EV range. Chapter 6 'Energizing the future: electric vehicle charging infrastructure, integration, and policy perspectives' covers the important considerations to make while building infrastructure for electric vehicle charging. It offers details on current technological advancements and strategic planning, which can help with the infrastructure design and building of charging stations. Chapter 7 'Modeling of electronic-waste recycling intentions among Generation Z' aimed to study major influential factors for e-waste recycling intention among Generation Z in India and results found that information received, knowledge, convenience, government regulations, and environmental concerns were the major drivers of e-waste recycling intention. Chapter 8 'Vision-based target tracking for UAVs using YOLOv2 deep algorithms' proposed a vision-based target tracking and following system for UAVs using YOLOv2. Chapter 9 'Flight delay prediction: a comprehensive review of models, methods, and trends' highlights the benefits of using machine learning to predict flight delays, including improved airline and passenger planning and scheduling. Chapter 10 'Selection of electric car using multi-attribute decision-making methods' aims to choose the best electric car among five alternatives using a multi-criteria approach and taking into account a selected five crucial and essential attributes such as top speed, battery charging, battery capacity, mileage, and price. Chapter 11 'People's perception of electric vehicles in developing countries: a case study of Jaipur city' involved understanding people's perception towards electric vehicles (EVs) in Jaipur city of state Rajasthan, India and aimed to find out consumer's perception, sentiments, awareness of electric vehicles and concern about the environment and having knowledge about various government policies to fight with this depleting climate condition and willingness to purchase the electric vehicles to attain environmental sustainability again. Chapter 12 'Significance of AI in automobiles' focuses on the core aspects of artificial intelligence like the real-life implementations, the working, the constraints, and viable solutions and discusses the future scope and implementation of artificial intelligence in the automobile industry.

This book is intended for both academia and industry. The postgraduate students, Ph.D. students, and researchers in universities and institutions, who are involved in the areas of smart electric and hybrid vehicles, will find this compilation useful.

The editors acknowledge the professional support received from CRC Press and express their gratitude for this opportunity.

Reader's observations, suggestions and queries are welcome,

Ajay Kumar
D.K. Rajak
Parveen Kumar
Sarita Rathee

Editors

Ajay Kumar is a Professor in the Mechanical Engineering Department, School of Engineering and Technology, JECRC University, Jaipur, Rajasthan, India. He earned his Ph.D. in the field of Advanced Manufacturing from Guru Jambheshwar University of Science & Technology, Hisar, India, after B.Tech. (Hons.) and M.Tech. (Distinction) from Maharshi Dayanand University, Rohtak, India. His areas of research include artificial intelligence, intelligent manufacturing, incremental sheet forming, additive manufacturing, intelligent vehicles, advanced manufacturing, Industry 4.0, waste management, and optimization techniques. He has over 60 publications in international journals of repute including SCOPUS, Web of Science, and SCI indexed database and refereed international conferences. He has co-authored/co-edited several books including the folowing:

- *Incremental Sheet Forming Technologies: Principles, Merits, Limitations, and Applications*, CRC Press, Taylor and Francis, ISBN 9780367276744, https://doi.org/10.1201/9780429298905
- Managing Guest Editor of Journal Proceedings, Ajay Kumar, Journal of Physics: Conference Series, Volume 1950, International Conference on Mechatronics and Artificial Intelligence (ICMAI) 2021 27 February 2021, Gurgaon, India, https://iopscience.iop.org/issue/1742-6596/1950/1
- *Advancements in Additive Manufacturing: Artificial Intelligence, Nature Inspired and Bio-manufacturing*, ISBN: 9780323918343, ELSEVIER, https://doi.org/10.1016/C2020-0-03877-6
- *Handbook of Sustainable Materials: Modelling, Characterization, and Optimization*, CRC Press, Taylor and Francis, ISBN: 978-1-032-28632-7, https://doi.org/10.1201/9781003297772
- *Waste Recovery and Management: An Approach Towards Sustainable Development Goals*, CRC Press, Taylor and Francis, ISBN: 9781032281933, https://doi.org/10.1201/9781003359784

- *Smart Manufacturing: Forecasting the future of Industry 4.0*, CRC Press, Taylor and Francis, ISBN: 9781032363431, https://doi.org/ 10.1201/9781003333760
- *Handbook of Flexible and Smart Sheet Forming Techniques: Industry 4.0 Perspectives*, ISBN: 9781119986409, WILEY. https://onlinelibr ary.wiley.com/doi/book/10.1002/9781119986454
- *Modeling, Characterization, and Processing of Smart Materials*, IGI Global, and ISBN: 9781668492246. DOI: 10.4018/ 978-1-6684-9224-6

D.K. Rajak is a scientist at CSIR-Advanced Materials and Processes Research Institute, Bhopal, Madhya Pradesh, India. He completed his Ph.D. from the Indian Institute of Technology (ISM), Dhanbad, Jharkhand. He received many prestigious awards and was recognized in the World Top 2% Scientists by Sanford University in 2022 & 2023. He has published over 100 peer-reviewed journal papers and has three books, 16 book chapters, 18 patents, two designs, and one copyright. His recent work involves developing lightweight alloy composite foams and composites for applications requiring low density and high specific energy absorption in automobile, aerospace, marine, noise, and thermal management sectors.

Parveen Kumar is currently an Assistant Professor and Head of the Department of Mechanical Engineering at Rawal Institute of Engineering and Technology, Faridabad, Haryana, India. Currently, he is pursuing a Ph.D. from the National Institute of Technology, Kurukshetra, Haryana, India. He completed his B.Tech. (Hons.) from Kurukshetra University, Kurukshetra, India and M. Tech. (Distinction) in Manufacturing and Automation from Maharshi Dayanand University, Rohtak, India. His areas of research include intelligent manufacturing systems, materials; die less forming, design of automotive systems, additive manufacturing, CAD/ CAM and artificial intelligence, machine learning and Internet of Things in manufacturing, multi-objective optimization techniques. He has over 20 publications in international journals of repute including SCOPUS, Web of Science, and SCI indexed database and refereed international conferences. He has eight national and international patents in his credit. He has supervised more than ten M.Tech. scholars and numerous undergraduate projects/theses. He has 13 years of experience in teaching and research. He has co-authored/co-edited several books including the following:

- Waste Recovery and Management: An Approach Towards Sustainable Development Goals, CRC Press, Taylor and Francis, ISBN: 9781032281933, https://doi.org/10.1201/9781003359784

- *Handbook of Sustainable Materials: Introduction, Modelling, Characterization and Optimization*, CRC Press, Taylor and Francis, ISBN: 9781032295874, https://doi.org/10.1201/9781003297772
- *Handbook of Smart Manufacturing: Forecasting the future of Industry 4.0*, CRC Press, Taylor and Francis, ISBN: 9781032363431, https://doi.org/10.1201/9781003333760
- *Handbook of Flexible and Smart Sheet Forming Techniques: Industry 4.0 Perspectives*, ISBN: 9781119986409, WILEY. https://onlinelibrary.wiley.com/doi/book/10.1002/9781119986454
- *Modeling, Characterization, and Processing of Smart Materials*, IGI Global, and ISBN: 9781668492246. DOI: 10.4018/978-1-6684-9224-6

Sarita Rathee is an Assistant Professor in the Department of Electrical and Electronics Engineering, School of Engineering and Technology, JECRC University, Jaipur, Rajasthan, India. She earned her M.Tech (Distinction) in Electrical and Electronics Engineering from Maharshi Dayanand University, Rohtak, India after a B.Tech. (Hons.) in electrical engineering. Her areas of research include artificial intelligence, IOT, cloud computing, Industry 4.0, waste management, and optimization techniques. She has over ten publications in international journals of repute including SCOPUS, Web of Science and SCI indexed database and refereed international conferences. She has more than five national and international patents to her credit. She has supervised more than four M.Tech scholars and numerous undergraduate projects/theses. She has five years of experience in teaching and research. She has won several proficiency awards during his career, including merit awards, best teacher awards, and so on. She is co-adviser of QCFI, Delhi Chapter student cell at JECRC University and has also authored many in-house course notes, lab manuals, monographs, and invited chapters in books. She has attended a series of Faculty Development Programs, International Conferences, workshops, and seminars for researchers, Ph.D, UG, and PG level students. She teaches the following courses at the graduate and postgraduate level: instrumentation engineering, IOT, FACTS devices, power electronics, electric vehicles, and so on. She is associated with many research, academic, and professional societies in various capacities.

Contributors

S.K. Abdul Kareem
Department of Electronics and
Communication Engineering,
Ramireddy Subbarami Reddy
Engineering College, Kavali,
India

Asif Ahmad
Pranveer Singh Institute of
Technology, Kanpur, India

Akhil Ajith
Department of Automobile
Engineering, Chandigarh
University, Gharuan, India

A. Akshitha
Department of Electronics and
Communication Engineering,
Ramireddy Subbarami Reddy
Engineering College, Kavali,
India

Momin Altaf Itoo
Department of Automobile
Engineering, Chandigarh
University, Gharuan, India

Gaydaa AlZohbi
Prince Mohammad Bin Fahd
University, Al Khobar, Saudi
Arabia

Eklavya Gupta
Department of Mechanical
Engineering, Medi-caps
University, Indore, India

Mukkisa Indhu
Department of Computer Science
& Engineering, Chandigarh
University, Mohali, India

A.G. Kamble
School of Mechanical Engineering,
MIT Academy of Engineering,
Alandi, Pune, Maharashtra,
India

Rohit Kaushik
Department of Computer Science
& Engineering, Chandigarh
University, Mohali, India

N. Krishna Chaitanya
Department of Electronics and
Communication Engineering,
Ramireddy Subbarami Reddy
Engineering College, Kavali,
India

Aman Kumar Upadhyay
Department of Computer Science
& Engineering, Chandigarh
University, Mohali, India

Anupam Kumar
Department of Computer Science
& Engineering, Chandigarh
University, Mohali, India

Parveen Kumar
Department of Mechanical
Engineering, Rawal Institute of
Engineering and Technology,
Faridabad, India

Ajay Kumar
Department of Mechanical
Engineering, School of
Engineering & Technology,
JECRC University, Jaipur, India

S. Rankesh Laxman
Department of Aeronautical
Engineering, Hindustan Institute
of Technology and Sciences,
Chennai, India

Mallhar Maitra
Department of Automobile
Engineering, Manav Rachna
International Institute of
Research and Studie, Faridabad,
India

Ankit Mittal
Department of Automobile
Engineering, Manav Rachna
International Institute of
Research and Studie, Faridabad,
India

Raja Munusamy
Hindustan Institute of Technology
and Sciences, Chennai, India

Mahjabeen Naz
Department of Civil Engineering,
JECRC University, Jaipur, India

Gourav Patel
Department of Mechanical
Engineering, Medi-caps
University, Indore, India

Ravi Patel
Department of Mechanical
Engineering, Medi-caps
University, Indore, India

Chand Prakash
School of Management and
Liberal Studies, The North Cap
University, Gurugram, India

P.V. Ram Kumar
Department of Electrical and
Electronics Engineering,
Ramireddy Subbarami Reddy
Engineering College, Kavali,
India

Sarita Rathee
Electrical and Electronics
Department, School of
Engineering and Technology,
JECRC University, Jaipur,
India

Kunal Rawal
Department of Mechanical
Engineering, Medi-caps
University, Indore, India

K.R. Ritu
Electrical and Electronics
Engineering Department, UIT
RGPV Bhopal, India

Neelesh Sahu
Department of Artificial Intelligence
and Robotics, Gyan Ganga
Institute of Technology &
Science, Jabalpur, India

Sumit Saini
Department of Mechanical
  Engineering, Chandigarh
  University, Gharuan, India

A.S. Sanap
School of Mechanical Engineering,
  MIT Academy of Engineering,
  Alandi, Pune, India

Gaurav Saxena
Department of Automobile
  Engineering, Manav Rachna
  International Institute of
  Research and Studie, Faridabad,
  India

Richa Sharma
Department of Computer Science
  & Engineering, Chandigarh
  University, Mohali, India

Avinash Sharma
Department of Mechanical
  Engineering, Medi-caps
  University, Indore, India

Areeb Shazli
Department of Automobile
  Engineering, Chandigarh
  University, Gharuan, India

Ankit Singh Beniwal
Department of Civil Engineering,
  JECRC University, Jaipur,
  Rajasthan, India

V. Suneel Reddy
Department of Electronics and
  Communication Engineering,
  Ramireddy Subbarami Reddy
  Engineering College, Kavali,
  India

Devendra Vashist
Department of Automobile
  Engineering, Manav Rachna
  International Institute of Research
  and Studies, Faridabad, India

Divam Vats
Department of Automobile
  Engineering, Chandigarh
  University, Gharuan, India

Ram Vilas Meena
Department of Civil Engineering,
  JECRC University, Jaipur, India

A.K. Wadhwani
Electrical and Electronics
  Engineering Department, MITS
  Gwalior, India

Amit Yadav
Department of Automobile
  Engineering, Chandigarh
  University, Gharuan, India

Ritu Yadav
Department of Management,
  Gurugram University,
  Gurugram, India

Acknowledgments

The editors are grateful to CRC Press for publishing this book *Smart Electric and Hybrid Vehicles: Fundamentals, Strategies and Applications.* The editors express their personal gratitude to Mr. Gauravjeet Singh Reen, Executive Editor, CRC Press, for giving consent to publish our work. He undoubtedly imparted great and adept experience with his systematic and methodical staff that have helped the editors to compile and finalize the manuscript. The editors also extend their gratitude to Ms. Mehnaz Hussain, CRC Press, for her support.

The editors, wish to thank all the chapter authors for contributing their valuable research and experience to compile this volume. The chapter authors, and corresponding authors in particular, deserve special acknowledgements for bearing with the editors, who persistently kept bothering them for deadlines, and with their remarks.

Dr. Ajay also wishes to express his gratitude to his parents, Sh. Jagdish and Smt. Kamla, and his loving brother Sh. Parveen for their true and endless support. They have made him able to walk tall before the world regardless of sacrificing their happiness and living in a small village. He cannot close these prefatory remarks without expressing his deep sense of gratitude and reverence to his life partner Mrs. Sarita Rathee for her understanding, care, support, and encouragement to keep his moral high all the time. No magnitude of words can ever quantify the love and gratitude he feels in thanking his daughters, Sejal Rathee and Mahi Rathee, and son Kushal Rathee who are the world's best children.

Finally, the editors dedicate this work to the divine creator and express their indebtedness to the "ALMIGHTY" for gifting them power to yield their ideas and concepts into substantial manifestation. The editors believe that this book will enlighten readers about each feature and characteristic of smart electric and hybrid vehicles.

Ajay Kumar
D.K. Rajak
Parveen Kumar
Sarita Rathee

Chapter 1

An overview on electric vehicles
Technologies, emissions, and challenges

Gaydaa AlZohbi
Prince Mohammad Bin Fahd University, Saudi Arabia

1.1 INTRODUCTION

The transportation sector accounts for one-fifth of total CO_2 emissions. Road travel contributes three-quarters of transport emissions and 15% of total CO_2 emissions [1]. The contribution of vehicles, cars, and buses is the biggest accounting for 45.1% and trucks carrying freight amounts to 29.4%. The transport sector is predicted to increase due to fast population growth. According to the *Energy Technology Perspectives* report [2], global transport is expected to double, with a 60% rise of car ownership and demand tripling for passenger and freight aviation by 2070. Thus, a large rise of emissions from transportation is expected in the coming decades.

The enormous future increase in carbon emissions from the transportation sector has a huge impact on socio-economic development. Technological advancement could play a significant role in recouping the growth of transportation demand and lessening greenhouse gas (GHG) emissions. Electric vehicles are one of the eco-friendly options that could be a feasible option to minimize the emissions from vehicles and decarbonize the whole economic system by reducing the carbon footprint.

Two main models of engine-driven vehicles existed at the initiation of automobiles: internal combustion engines (ICEs) and electric drive trains. The first electric car was invented in 1834 by the American Thomas Davenport. In the 1900s, electric cars were a substantial part of all engine-driven cars, and the first hybrid electric car equipped with a wheel hub electric motor and an ICE range extender was invented by F. Porsche. Thus, the EV technology is not new, it has a simple technical approach that has been available for more than 110 years. The conversion of used or new ICE vehicles into electric vehicles can be easily performed. However, the technology of lithium-ion batteries, which are essential for the feasibility of most EVs, is new and related to recent technical development. The most popular manufactures of electric vehicles are Test (Model 3 and Model X), Nissan (Leaf), Chevrolet (Bolt), and Toyota (Prius PHEV).

DOI: 10.1201/9781003495574-1

EVs have many benefits compared to traditional vehicles:

- Simplicity: the number of components in EV engines is lower, resulting in less maintenance. The engines are simpler, without a need for a cooling system and for integration of gearshift, or any components to minimize engine noise.
- Comfort: EVs are more comfortable since they do not generate vibrations.
- Efficiency: compared to traditional vehicles, EVs are more performant. The overall well-to-wheel (WTW) efficiency of gasoline vehicles is in the range of 11–27%, and between 25–37% for diesel vehicles [3]. However, the WTW efficiency of EVs powered by natural gas ranges between 13–31%, while EVs powered by renewable energy can reach a WTW efficiency of 70%.
- Reliability: the smaller number of components and their simplicities lead to a reduction of EV breakdowns. Besides, EVs do not face inherent wear and tear caused by fuel corrosion, engine fire.
- Attainability: EVs are allowed to enter urban areas with strict restriction regarding the GHG emissions since EVs do not emit tailpipe pollutant, CO_2, and nitrogen dioxide. However, according to a study conducted by Organisation for Economic Cooperation and Development (OECD), EVs are not able to enhance the air quality in terms of particulate matter emissions [4, 5].
- Cost: the cost of electricity needed to power EVs, and the maintenance costs are cheaper compared to traditional vehicles. Figure 1.1 shows the cost saving per km of different types of vehicles.

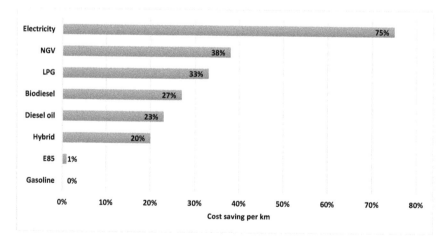

Figure 1.1 Cost saving per km of different types of vehicles.

Source: [5].

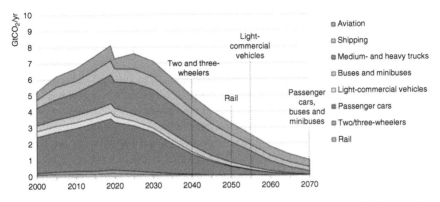

Figure 1.2 Global CO_2 emissions in the transportation sector in the IEA Sustainable Development Scenario 2000–2070.

An examination study on the challenges and opportunities of several industrial processes and energy services that are specifically hard to decarbonize, such as air travel, long-distance freight transport, and highly reliable electricity has been conducted by [6, 7]. These services are difficult to decarbonize due to the quickly growing demand, and the long time required for energy infrastructure and technology development. The study pointed out that the use of hydrogen as a fuel cell, and the battery to store electricity and power ships, cars, and planes is restricted by the range and power needed. The emissions resulting from the use of these services will still account for the biggest GHG emissions from the transport sector in 2070 (Figure 1.2). Thus, these emissions should be neutralized by negative emissions such as the capture and storage of carbon from other parts of the energy system to attain a net-zero energy sector. According to the net-zero scenario of International Energy Agency (IEA), the amount of emissions lessening, around two-thirds, will be executed by technologies that are not yet available in the market [2]. The IEA mentioned that minimizing the CO_2 emissions from the transportation sector during the next half-century will be a complicated and enormous mission.

The current chapter aims at presenting an overview of electric vehicles in terms of types, components (battery, charger, electric motor), and their environmental impacts. In addition, the challenges and opportunities of EVs are summarized in this chapter.

1.2 TYPES OF EVS

Electric vehicles can be classified intro five classes: hybrid electric vehicles, battery electric vehicles (BEVs), hydrogen fuel cell electric vehicles, plug-in hybrid vehicles (PHEVs), and solar energy vehicles (SEV). Fully electrified vehicles are a combination of the four categories of electric vehicles.

- Hybrid electric vehicles

These are the most popular electrified vehicles. This type of electric vehicle has an internal combustion engine connected to at least one electric motor and a battery pack. An electric motor is employed in the case of inefficient use of internal combustion, mainly in starting and low speed. However, the combustion engine and the electric motor are used together in the case of higher speeds. Hybrid electric vehicles do not connect and energize from the electric grid. The combustion engine operates on gas, and the battery is recharged either through a regenerative braking in condition of braking or from recovering electricity from the combustion engine and the electric motor operates as a generator. In some hybrid cars, there is a generator linked to the combustion engine to energize the battery. The main advantages of hybrid electric vehicles are the lower greenhouse gas emissions compared to traditional vehicles, lower gas consumption resulting in extra driving range, and cost savings. In addition, there is no need for a frequent replacement of electric batteries thanks to the smaller use of batteries compared to electric vehicles, resulting in cost savings. In contrast, hybrid vehicles have many drawbacks related to high cost due to the complex architecture, costly maintenance, and higher weight of batteries and smaller fuel tanks. Moreover, riders might be subjected to high voltage wires in the case of accidents.

There are three kinds of hybrid vehicles: parallel hybrids, series hybrids, and combined hybrids presented in Figure 1.3.

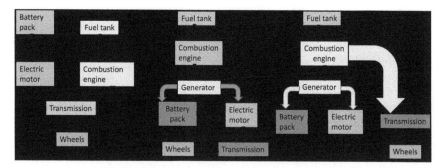

Figure 1.3 Architecture of (a) parallel hybrid car; (b) series parallel car; (c) combined hybrid car.

Source: [7].

In parallel hybrid vehicles, the transmission wheel is attached to the electric motor and combustion engine. The operation of parallel hybrid vehicles in electric mode is not possible since the internal combustion engine is the primary source of power. The battery used in this type has a lower capacity and is used in high speeds.

In series hybrid vehicles, the transmission wheels are connected only to the electric motor and the combustion engine is used to run a generator to power the electric motor and recharge the batteries. This type of hybrid vehicle is more performant in the case of low speed and under conditions of stopping and starting the car with frequency.

The benefits of the series and parallel hybrid vehicles are used in the combined hybrid vehicles. Most hybrid vehicles in the market are combined. They can run in combustion and electric modes and batteries can be energized in a recharging station in some combined hybrid cars.

- Plug-in hybrid electric vehicles

A diesel or gasoline engine with an electric motor are integrated with a big rechargeable battery in plug-in hybrid electric vehicles (Figure 1.4). This type of vehicle might be connected and recharged from an electricity grid, resulting in extending the driving distance using only an electric motor, within the range of 20 to 50 miles prior to the need for a gas engine to power and operate the vehicle. The diesel or gasoline engine is used to power the vehicle in the case of run-down battery. Regenerative braking stores some of the lost energy in the batteries.

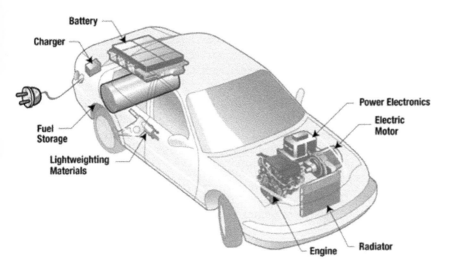

Figure 1.4 Plug-in hybrid electric vehicle.

The benefit of PHEVs is the ability to completely operate in electric mode, resulting in saving gas, in addition to its flexibility since it can operate in two modes based on the availability of a gas station or electric charge. Moreover, PHEVs emit less GHGs, and any tailpipe pollution compared to a conventional vehicle when operating on electricity. Since the electric motor supplies the engine's power, the engines needed should be smaller, resulting in improved vehicle fuel efficiency. Idle-off deactivates/stops the engine during idling at lights or in a traffic jam, reducing fuel consumption. Also, hundreds of dollars could be saved since less gas is required.

Many light-duty PHEVs are available in the market, and medium-duty cars have recently entered the market. Despite the fact that PHEVs are more costly compared to conventional and hybrid vehicles, fuel saving with tax credit could recover their high cost.

There are two different configurations of PHEVs: series PHEVs and parallel PHEVs. In series PHEVs, the wheels are turned by an electric motor powered by electricity generated by the gasoline engine. However, the wheels are powered by both an electric motor and gasoline engine. The series PHEVs can operate only on electric mode for short trips however, the electric mode can be used only in parallel PHEVs at low speeds.

- Battery electric vehicles (BEVs)

A battery electric vehicle (BEV) is the simplest kind of electric vehicle, using energy from a single-source battery, to perform one or more electric motors. The battery could be energized by a charging station by regenerative braking. The components of BEVs are electric motors with controllers, and the battery pack (Figure 1.5). The battery is formed of many cells that are organized into modules and are assembled into packs. The groups of cells or modules could be connected in series and parallel. BEVs require a few hundreds of volts to be operated, that can be ensured with a minimum of 100 cells. The number of cells could be bigger but with a smaller size, connected in series and in parallel. A 'balance of point' of thermal management is needed to avoid overcharging and to detect deterioration or failure of cells. The biggest and the most expensive component of BEVs is the battery pack, mainly thanks to it being essential and the single power source to generate power and energy.

BEVs are simple, lightweight, and eco-friendly since they do not rely on fossil fuels to power them and the high cost is offset by the tax breaks and credits. Also, they are relatively quick and controllable, and pilotable. The drawbacks of EVs are the required time for a complete recharge of their batteries, which is longer than the time required to refuel a gasoline car. Also, the distance traveled by EVs is shorter than gasoline cars before

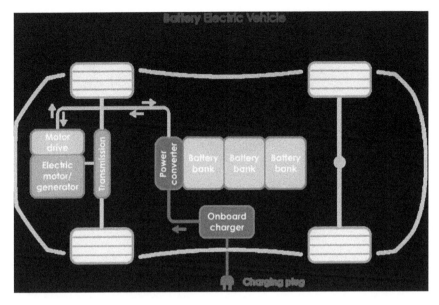

Figure 1.5 Architecture of battery electric vehicle.

charging. Besides, the cost of EVs is more expensive compared to gas cars. In addition, a replacement of batteries is required frequently, resulting in rising its capital and maintenance cost.

- Hydrogen fuel cell electric vehicles

The hydrogen fuel cell electric car is classified as an electric car since it is powered by an electric motor supplied by electricity generated by itself. The working principle of hydrogen fuel cell electric vehicles is based on converting gaseous hydrogen into electricity to power the vehicle through an on-board fuel cell (Figure 1.6). Hydrogen, stored in one or more stored chamber in the car, reacts with oxygen from the ambient air. The electrons are removed from the hydrogen atoms, and then the hydrogen attaches to oxygen to form water. The electrons power the fuel cell's electric motor without any emissions. The electricity produced could directly supply the electric motor and drive the car and/or it is used to charge a battery so that electricity is stored to be used when needed to drive the car. The battery used in hydrogen fuel electric vehicles is smaller compared to other electric vehicles, signifying it is lighter. The electric motor in the hydrogen vehicle can recover barking energy and convert it into electrical energy to be stored in the battery.

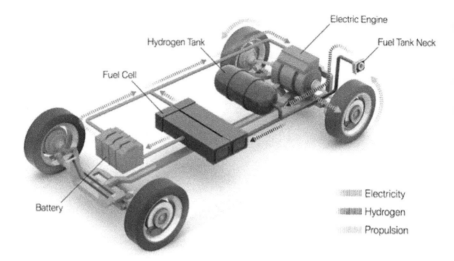

Figure 1.6 Hydrogen fuel cell car.

Source: [8].

The main advantage of hydrogen fuel cell vehicles is the required time to refuel the hydrogen fuel cell vehicles that is smaller compared to that required to recharge BEVs and plug-in hybrid electric vehicles. One kilogram of hydrogen can power a fuel cell car to travel around 100 km. Refilling the hydrogen tank of a BMW iX5 Hydrogen takes 3 to 4 min. In addition, it is eco-friendly since it does not rely on the electricity grid that might be generated from fossil fuel. Moreover, the external temperature does not affect hydrogen fuel cell vehicles. However, the costly fuel cell power train and its complexity are the main drawbacks. Besides, the hydrogen refueling stations are roughly restricted in amount.

- Solar electric vehicles (SEVs)
- The electricity needed to power this kind of vehicle is supplied by photovoltaic cells, used to convert solar energy into electricity. The electricity generated is used to charge the battery pack, benefiting from a longer range of travel comparing to BEVs. The free energy generated from the sun and used in SEVs is considered as its main benefit. However, if the sun is not out, SEVs become electric vehicles, that can be charged using any level of EV charger. Actually, some companies have already started manufacturing SEVs, such as Sono Motors, Aptera, and Lightyear.

1.3 COMPONENTS OF EVS

1.3.1 Batteries for EVs

Actually, several kinds of batteries are used in EVs. The different types of batteries used in EVs are presented in Table 1.1.

Lead acid batteries were innovated in 1859 and are known as the eldest rechargeable batteries. These batteries are used in conventional vehicles and employed in commercially electric-drive vehicles for the purpose of ancillary loads. The GM EV1 and the Toyota RAV4 EV use this type of battery.

The use of nickel-cadmium batteries started in the 1990s. The main benefit derives from its high energy density [9]. However, it faces many issues related to high memory effect, high cost due to the high cost of cadmium, and short lifetime.

The technology of nickel-metal hydride batteries is developed to replace the nickel-cadmium batteries. The use of nickel metal started at the beginning of the 1990s, during the re-electrification of vehicles. Hydrogen is utilized to substitute cadmium in the negative electrodes [10]. The main issues of nickel-metal hydride are the high cost, high self-discharge, production of heat under high temperatures, environmental impacts, and loss of hydrogen, which should be controlled. This kind of battery offers a higher self-discharge compared to nickel cadmium and is used in many hybrid vehicles mainly in HEVs, like the Toyota Prius, and the Toyota RAV4 EV, that has a nickel-metal hybrid battery beside a lead acid battery.

Zinc-bromine batteries: zinc-bromine solution is used in this kind of battery to be stored in two tanks. This kind of battery was utilized by a prototype.

Sodium-bromine batteries: this type of battery is known as Zebra, and it has identical properties as sodium-sulfur batteries. It can supply up to 30% more energy under low-temperature conditions. This technology is optimal to be used in EVs [11]. The Zebra cell is viewed as a promising alternative to Li-ion batteries. The sodium-sulfur batteries offer high energy density, high lifespan, high charging, and discharging efficiency (89–92%), and low cost. The disadvantage is the functioning temperature, which is in the range of 300–350 °C.

Li-ion batteries are considered as the first choice thanks to their high energy density, resulting in rising the wide spreading of electric cars. The cost of lithium-ion batteries has dropped thanks to the rise of production scale and to the cost-effective methods developed by manufacturers. Lithium-ion batteries are used by all electric vehicles and PHEVs. Many studies are going to lessen their cost, expand their lifetime, and deal with safety concerns in the case of overheating.

Ultracapacitors might supply extra power to vehicles throughout acceleration, hill ascending and retrieve energy from barking. Besides, it can be

Table 1.1 Batteries of EVs

Battery type	Active chemical components	Energy density (Wh/kg)	Advantages	Drawbacks	Reference
Lead acid	Pb/PbO_2 H_2SO_4	30–35 10–40	Cheap, long lifetime, operates well under different circumstances, no memory effect, low self-discharge rate	Minor risk of leakage, long charging time, temperature sensitive output, moderate energy, and power density	[12]
Nickel cadmium	NiOOH-KOH	50–75	Good performance under heavy discharge and low temperature	Expensive, losing of cell capacity in case of not being fully charged before recharging	[13]
Nickel-metal-hydride	various alloys, as e.g., LaNdNiCoSi	100	Average initial cost and round-trip efficiency, extremely quick charging excellent safety record	Memory effect, short cycle life, poor recovery, and high self-discharge rate	[14]
Zinc-bromine (Zn-Br$_2$).	$ZnBr_2$	60–85	relatively high energy density, deep discharge capability, and good reversibility	Material corrosion, dendrite formation, and relatively low cycle efficiencies compared to traditional batteries	[15]
Sodium chloride and nickel (Zebra)	NaCl-Ni	100–120	Light, quick reaction, strength to full discharge, and a high vitality density	Significant expense and self-discharge	[16]
Lithium-ion batteries (Li-ion).	Li-Ni-Co-Al Li-Ni-Mn-Co LiMn2 O$_4$ Li-titanate LiFePO$_4$ Li-Polymer (LiPo)	150–220 50–80 90–120	Light weight, high loading capacity, high loading and unloading cycles, reduced memory effect, operate at higher voltages	Risk of bursting, expensive, complete discharge causes a damage of the battery, highly sensitive to temperatures, advanced battery management system is required	[17]

used as a secondary energy-storage device in EVs since it assists electro-chemical batteries' level load power.

Recycling batteries are important to accomplish the sustainability approach of EVs. Thus, the design of batteries with a focus on the recycling, materials used, and cell design should be taken into consideration beside the standardization. Batteries' recycling aims to stop dangerous materials entering into the waste stream during its generation and at its end-of-life. More advantages could be accomplished from recycling batteries, such as reuse of the hazardous materials in the supply chain, resulting in rising the domestic sources for these materials. Currently, researchers are working on developing battery-recycling processes to reduce the lifetime impacts of using batteries in EVs. There are different recycling processes for batteries with different material separation methods to recover materials. These methods are categorized into the following [18]:

- Direct recovery: the separation of components is performed using chemical and physical processes to recover all materials and metals under low temperature using less energy. It could not be used for different kinds of batteries.
- Smelting: this method is actually workable and could recover only basic elements. This method requires high temperature to burn organic materials as fuel or reductant and recover the noble metals. The recovered noble materials should be refined such that the metal might be appropriate for any use. The other remaining components are comprised in the slag and could be used as an added ingredient to concrete.
- Intermediate processes: this method is between the two above methods. It can be used for different types of batteries, like smelting, but can recover more materials than the smelting method.

1.3.2 Charging of electric vehicles

The duration and properties of the charging method for batteries in electric vehicles are important aspects. Charging the battery in a quick and simple way is fundamental for successful use in EVs. Thus, an implementation of infrastructure that ensures a quick and simple charge is essential. The duration of charging electric vehicles ranges between 20 min to 40 h, depending on the size of the battery, the location, and the time of charging. There are three levels of charging electric vehicles:

Level 1: EV is connected to a 120-volt outlet, which is the same as a phone charge. The duration of charging at this level is slow, ranges between 40 to 50 h with a charging from empty. It is convenient for daily necessities.

Level 2: the charging at this level is from 220-volt outlet and it takes 4 to 10 h from an empty battery. Parking locations are popular for level 2 charging stations, such as commercial parking. Many EV owners install this charging level in their parking lot to charge their EVs at night.

Level 3: it is known as a direct current fast charger (DCFC charger), and it is the quickest charging. The charging of EV takes 20 min for an empty battery. Level 3 charging is costly compared to levels 1 and 2 but it offers a fast charging for time-conscious road-trippers with a charging power of 350 kW.

Table 1.2 presents the difference between the charger types in terms of voltage, output power, charging time, and locations for BEVs and PHEVs. Actually, there are three options of charging of BEV applications: inductive charging, conductive charging, and battery swapping. The characteristics, the benefits and the drawback of each option are summarized in Table 1.3. The simplest and cheapest option is the conductive charging, which is the most commonly used [20]. It is based on direct contact between the charge port and the EV connector. However, it suffers from many drawbacks, such as electric shocks due to the use of aging components, unsafe use in tough conditions (underwater and dust), and inapplicability of automatic operation. There are two ways to use a conductive option in the charging stations of EVs: on board charger (or AC chargers) and off-board chargers (DC chargers). DC charging use a devoted DC EV supply apparatus to provide energy from a connected off-board charger to EVs in public areas. The charging duration of DC chargers depends on the battery and vehicle conditions, it can charge a battery in 20 min from empty to 80% under normal circumstances. However, in the case of AC chargers, the vehicle should be connected to an ordinary electric outlet particularly anticipated for EVs. The charging duration of AV chargers is longer, and the vehicle

Table 1.2 Overview of available chargers for electric vehicles

Connector type	Level 1	Level 2	Level 3
Voltage	120 V AC	208–240 V AC	400–1000 V DC
Output power	1 kW	7–19 kW	50–350 kW
Estimated charging time for PHEV from empty	5–6 h	1–2 h	N/A
Estimated charging time for BEV from empty	40–50 h	4–10 h	20 min–1 h
Relevant location	Home	Public, workplace, home	Public

Source: [19].

Table 1.3 Overview on the different charging options

Charging method	Type	Electrical parameters	Time	Cost ($)	Benefits	Drawbacks
Conductive	Level 1	120 V, 15 A	>10 h	500–880	Simple installation, cheap	Required time for charging
	Level 2	208–240 V, up to 80 A	2–12 h	150–3000	Fast charging	A dedicated equipment and a connection installation are needed for household
	Level 3	400 V, 32 A	15–20 min	30000–160000	Faster charging time	Expensive, an off-board charger is required, influence of power grid
Inductive	Static wireless charging	2–15 kW	3–3.5 h	1500–3000		Misalignment tolerance, power received attached to the car is needed
	Dynamic wireless charging	0.3–25 kW	Depends on the length of charging track	1 million/km		Low efficiency
Battery swapping	Battery swap station	400 V 70–250 batteries	5 min	5–10 million	Fast	Special tools for battery swapping are needed

Source: [20–22, 26, 27].

should be provided with an on-board charging unit, resulting in rising the weight of the car.

The inductive charger is contactless (wireless) and the transfer of power is performed using a magnet. There are two methods of wireless charging: static wireless charging and dynamic wireless charging. It can ensure a higher security level, and a spark safe thanks to being touchless between the charging unit and the vehicle assemblage, and it is easily operated [21, 22]. However, inductive charging suffers from high cost, lower charging performance, lengthy charging time, and the need of drive electronic and coils on two sides [23]. Also, the rise of power transfer rates leads to a rise in the sophistication and the size of the power management electronics. The increase of power means that supplement parameters should be studied such as life the thermal management and the thermal losses. The rise of the power and the drop of efficiency cause a rise of heat losses, and thus more management is required to manage the heat losses. Dynamic wireless charging can charge the vehicles while driving it down the road up to 20 kW at highway speeds.

The shortest charging time is offered by battery swap thanks to the replacement of the discharged battery with a recharged one. Nevertheless, it is an expensive option and faces many challenges associated with the number of batteries and the number of the needed charged batteries in conformity of different periods, the moving method of batteries between stations, recovering and rehabilitation of the swapped batteries, and the number of charging ports that should be displayed in the facility [24, 25]. Besides, the difficulty related to changing heavy batteries and the unavailability of standardization for power batteries are considered as challenges of this option.

1.3.3 Electric motors

The electric motor is an essential component of EVs, used to transform the electrical energy stored in the battery into mechanical energy to run the vehicles. It requires special properties, such as high performance, robustness, high power and torque, small size, reduced price, bit noisy, toughness, ease of control, and a broad range of speed [28, 29]. Many kinds of electric motors have been already developed and used in electric vehicles. The three main types of electric motor are permanent magnet (PM), induction motors (IM), and switched motors (SRMs).

- Induction motor: it is known as an asynchronous motor. An electromagnetic induction from the rotating magnetic field is used to induce an electric current in the rotor and this generates a torque. The rotor might be a wound type rotor or squirrel cage rotor. The kind of electric motor is used in General Motor EV1 and in Tesla EVs (Model S and Roaster). The induction motor is a mature technology and has many benefits such as being cheap, reliable, robust, and requiring less maintenance [30]. However, its drawback is the low performance at light loads [31]. Direct torque control (DTC) is used to enhance the use of IM in EV applications, thanks to its ability to control the instantaneous torque in the stable state or transient operation moments [32, 33]. Thus, DTC can ensure a reliability and a quick torque response to IM with low cost. In addition, field-oriented control (FOC), known also as vector control, is used to adapt IMs for a successful use in EVs. FOC is able bring a crucial variation in the control of the IM by giving a broad range of speed up to 3–4 times base speed, and thus minimizing the losses under any loading circumstances through managing the current of the rotor and stator [34]. However, the drawback of FOC is the impact on speed range performance.

- Permanent magnet brushless DC motor: it is a DC motor that employs a permanent magnet to generate the magnetic field needed to power a DC motor. This type of electric motor has many advantages such as high performance and high-power density. There is no rotor copper loss since the rotor does not have winding [30]. The commutation of the PMBLDC is accomplished by electronic switches that ensure a synchronous current to the motor winding with the rotor location [35]. The position of rotor plays an important role in controlling the PMBLDC and is observed by optical encoders or Hall sensors [36]. However, the use of a position sensor leads to a raise in the cost and size of motor. Thus, a control technique without a sensor is usually used to minimize the total cost of propulsive devices [37]. A new control technique without the need for a sensor has been developed and is based on the use of H function (not coupled to speed) to determine the commutation moments [38]. Also, a method based on obtaining the rotor position from the productivity of the motor and measure the speed of the rotor in a closed-loop speed control scheme utilizing the position [39]. The back electromotive force could be also used to accomplish sensor-less control for the PMBLDC motor [40]. It is a simple and profitable method, and it is able produce commutation pulses in the absence of phase shift and filtering. Thanks to the numerous advantages of PMBLDC, such as safety, high performance, controllability, and a broad range of speed, PMBLDC is viewed as an ideal option to be used in EVs.
- Permanent magnet synchronous motor (PMSM): this type of electric motor has many advantages compared to other electric motors like simplicity of structure, high efficiency, and high power density [41]. There are two types: interior permanent magnet synchronous motor (IPMSM) and surface mounted permanent magnet synchronous motor (SM-PMSM). Thanks to simple structure, easier control, and

the lower inertia of the rotor, SM-PMSM has been already used in EVs [42]. Many control methods are studied in the literature, like adaptive structures [43], DTC [44], and predictive control [44], beside FOC, which is the most common method for PMSM drives [45]. The effect in the speed on the FOC structure has been studied in [46], the authors suggested an adaptive control algorithm to enlarge speed operation. An approach to minimize electromagnetic torque ripple and copper losses in SM-PMSM has been suggested by [47]. Results showed that this approach can boost the efficiency of the SM-PMSM. In contrast, PMSM has some drawbacks in terms of cost and demagnetization of permanent magnet materials in tough environment, like intense heat and oscillation. Moreover, the scarcity of permanent magnet materials in many countries is a considerable challenge for using PMSMs in propulsion systems [48].

- Switched reluctance motor (SRM): it is known as a variable-reluctance motor. It has many benefits such as simple and rugged construction, insensitivity to intense heat, high-speed functioning capability, and its feature redundancy. SRM motors have been employed on clocks and are actually, with improving of its energy efficiency, used in industrial application and electric vehicles. Moreover, rare-earth materials are not needed in this type of motor, meaning less price and less environmental impact caused by excavation and refining [47]. The acoustic noise generated from radial vibration and torque ripple is the main drawbacks of SRM [29]. Many studies have been conducted to alleviate the noise of SRM through a developed control strategy design and an enhancement of motor topology. A new kind of motor with the aim of reducing the torque ripple of the SRM has been designed by [49] and a viscoelastic resin to enclose an SRM stator to minimize the sound in operation has been optimized by [50]. A new remodeled method established on the two-stage commutation analysis to minimize the oscillation and sound that are not associated to the functioning condition has been suggested by [51].

1.4 GREENHOUSE GAS EMISSIONS OF ELECTRIC CARS IN OPERATION

The GHG emission of EVs is assessed based on the electricity mix utilized in the charging and on the emissions from vehicle generation and scrappage. The positive effect of using EVs, mainly a renewable-dominated electricity system, on the climate charge compared to ICE has been confirmed and demonstrated by many studies [52, 53]. However, the extra electricity required by EVs and the charging time that depend on the charging strategies have not been considered in the estimation in those studies.

The estimation of GHG emissions of BEVs is performed based on the amount of electricity consumed and the GHG emitted for the electricity generation [54]. There are many studies conducted to estimate the GHG emissions from electric cars. The street conditions and the size of car play an important role in the amount of electricity consumption, and thus on the amount of GHG emission. According to [55], which reviewed 21 studies on the amount of GHG emission from electric vehicles between 1999 and 2009, the mean amount of electricity consumption by BEVs and PHEVs is 17.5 kWh/100 km. Some studies quantify the lifecycle assessment (LCA), which assesses the environmental impacts of all stage of the lifecycle of the product. The amount of electricity consumed based on LCA quantification is higher. Based on a modeling study conducted by [56], electricity consumption of 20.4 kWh/100 km, 20.8 kWh/100 km, and 24.9 kWh/100 km in urban areas, in extra-urban areas, and on the highway, consecutively. Regarding the size of car, [57] estimated the electricity consumption for different sizes of BEVs. The electricity consumption is 18.7 kWh/100 km and 22.9 kWh/100 km for a mini-class BEV (736 kg curb weight) and compact class BEV (specified curb weight 1,115 kg), respectively.

Despite the fact that EVs could minimize GHG emissions, a lifecycle assessment is needed to assess the whole carbon emissions of EVs. Lifecycle assessment aims to assess the whole environmental effects, thus preventing problem shifting. Many studies have been conducted to estimate the LCA of EVs and Li-ion batteries for small to medium sized EVs and batteries. An assessment study on the lifecycle of batteries in the generation stage was conducted by [58]. Results showed that the energy used in manufacturing accounts for the highest global warming with 50%, followed by electronic with 30%, the cathode with 30%, and the lowest in the raw materials transportation with 30%. The authors of [59] conducted a study on the lifecycle assessment of three types of batteries of electric vehicles: ion-phosphate lithium-ion, nickel-metal hydride, and nickel-cobalt manganese lithium-ion. Results pointed out that the NiMH batteries recorded that largest environmental impact while LFP recorded the lowest environmental impact on a per-storage basis. An environmental and economic assessment of electric vehicles and internal combustion engine vehicles based on lifecycle assessment and well-to-wheel has been performed by [60]. It has been shown that the GHG emissions of BEVs are half of that of ICEVs. The authors of [61] performed a transparent lifecycle assessment on electric and conventional vehicles for different impact types. Results revealed a significant global warming potential (GWP) for electric vehicles compared to gasoline and diesel vehicles for a vehicle lifetime of 200,000 km. However, the GWP decreases as the vehicle lifecycle decreases to 100,000 km. The authors of [62] estimated the lifecycle GHG emissions for four different sizes and range penalty of EVs (from segment A to F). This study demonstrated that the EVs with smaller battery packs have less environmental impact compacted to heavier EVs with larger battery packs. Also, the conventional vehicles have less environmental impacts during generation phase compared to EVs. Moreover, the study pointed out that the lifecycle GHG emissions of larger EVs is bigger compared to smaller conventional vehicles.

1.5 CHALLENGES AND OPPORTUNITIES

1.5.1 Challenges

Despite that, EVs gain popularity on public roads, and there are many challenges that should be addressed to facilitate their uses. These challenges are in terms of infrastructure, pricing, the issues related to the installation of new charging stations and energy grid intensification, and the fast deterioration of road due to the rise of the weight of vehicles. The different challenges are presented below.

Infrastructure: EVs require electrical outlets to be charged that could be available in the garage through a special wall-mounted charger. This works for people since the average person drives 29 miles/day. Nevertheless, there are two raised issues. The first one is associated with people who live in apartments, the need of parking garages furnished with charging infrastructure is unusual/infrequent, and inauguration of such infrastructure is unaffordable and exorbitant for building supervisors.

Cost: the charging of EVs follows different pricing plans, resulting in unstable and variable pricing and expensive charging costs in some cases. The prices of home charging are stable rate per kWh determined by utility regulators. However, public charging prices depend on many factors, such as session fees, per-minute fees, and choice pricing that depends on vehicles' max charging speed. In addition, the charging fees are rarely displayed at charging stations. Thus, the inconsistent pricing and muckiness are obstacles to EV approbation/acceptance since they can result in displeasure, exasperation, and bad customer experiences.

Weight: the weight of EVs is higher than gas-powered vehicles due to the use of batteries. For instance, the weight of the Ford F-150 is 35% more than the gas-powered Ford F-150 truck. The increase of vehicle weight has a negative effect on the road due to the rise of stress that can result in defeating paved roads. Preventive maintenance will be an ideal solution to prevent any pavement issues. The real-time insights into the status/situation of roadways are fundamental in preventative maintenance. Currently, manual methods, which are exposed to delay and biases, are used to assess the pavement. Although, the use of AI and imagery could entirely automate the assessment process in a fast and accurate way, and without any objective insights. Photogrammetry is an example of detecting cracks and potholes with a high accuracy. Thus, money and time needed for the manual process could be used to repair issues before repaving is needed.

1.5.2 Opportunities

There are many opportunities offered by electric mobility. These opportunities are summarized below.

- Abrogation of ICE vehicles: the growing interest in EVs leads to a wane of interest in ICE vehicles, resulting in growing business opportunities for scrapping them. ICE vehicles will be forbidden on the road since they are pollutants and do not stratify with the global goal of minimizing GHG emissions, and thus they will fall out in scrapping centers. The components of ICE vehicles, metals and materials, will be recycled to manufacture eco-friendly products.
- Manufacturing opportunity: the growing of the EV market evidently leads to open more opportunities to the manufacturing industry. Many big companies, such as Amazon, have already shifted their traditional vehicle to electric vehicles. The rise in demand for electric vehicles will surely create an enormous pool for manufacturing opportunity.
- An enormous wave in B2B (business-to-business) opportunities: the rise of interest in EVs does not affect only the businesses, but also consumers. The global rise on media attention on the electric mobility has created a vast space for numerous opportunities in the business-to business market. The leaders have already constructed an excitement in fabricating facilities and services for a sustained prosper of the electric mobility sector.
- Battery technology: the battery is a fundamental component of EVs. Recently, the battery market has experienced huge changes with improving its technology. The battery market is predicted to grow in the coming year, resulting in opening numerous opportunities in battery technology.

1.6 CONCLUSIONS

The rising concern of GHG emissions and their effect on climate change, beside the quick exhaustion of fossil fuels led to an increased requirement to generate and adopt new environmentally safe sustainable alternatives to the internal combustion engine vehicles. Electric vehicles have experienced a massive advancement and development during the last 20 years in the matter of battery technology and cost, chargers, and electric motors. Electric vehicles have four times the efficiency compared to ICEVs; thus they can be a suitable option for a future sustainable mobility. The current chapter presented an overview of the different kinds of EVs, and on the different components of EVs, batteries, chargers, and electric motors.

Hybrid vehicles emit the highest amount of GHGs and the highest cost per km compared to the other EVs. BEVs and FCEVs have the highest fuel efficiency. The highest driving range could be achieved by HEVs and PHEVs when they are working with fuel. The highest charging or refuel time is for BEVs and PHEVs. Regenerative braking, which is the ability to collect electricity during deceleration, is possible in all types of EVs.

Moreover, the different challenges and opportunities are highlighted in the chapter. The main challenges facing the EVs are the infrastructure required for charging the electric batteries, and the public charging prices that depend on many factors, such as session fees, per-minute fees, and choice pricing that depends on vehicles' max charging speed. In addition, the weight of EVs is higher than gas-powered vehicles due to the use of batteries, resulting in defeating the paved roads.

A successful commercial integration of EVs requires a development of approaches to minimize vehicle production supply chain impact with reinforcing clean electricity sources. In addition, development and installation of advanced batteries and infrastructure to facilitate battery charging will lead to a rise in the accessibility and affordability of using EVs.

REFERENCES

1. Ritchie, H. Cars, planes, trains: where do CO2 emissions from transport come from? 2020. [cited 2023]; Available from: https://ourworldindata.org/co2-emissions-from-transport.
2. IEA, *Energy Technology Perspectives 2020*. 2020, IEA: Paris.
3. Albatayneh, A., M.N. Assaf, D. Alterman, & M. Jaradat, *Comparison of the overall energy efficiency for internal combustion engine vehicles and electric vehicles*. Rigas Tehniskas Universitates Zinatniskie Raksti, 2020. 24(1): p. 669–680. https://doi.org/10.2478/rtuect-2020-0041
4. Fulvio Amato, A.D.-K.F. & Walid Oueslati, *Non-Exhaust Particulate Emissions from Road Transport*. 2020, OECD: Paris. p. 142.
5. Blázquez,J. & J.M.M.Moreno, Eficiencia energética en automoción: el vehículo eléctrico, un reto del presente. *Economía Industrial*, 2010. 377: p. 76–85.
6. Davis, S.J., N.S. Lewis, M. Shaner, S. Aggarwal, D. Arent, I.L. Azevedo, S.M. Benson, T. Bradley, J. Brouwer, & Y.-M. Chiang, Net-zero emissions energy systems. *Science*, 2018. 360(6396): p. eaas9793. DOI: 10.1126/science.aas9793
7. Stroski, P.N. Operation of hybrid vehicle. 2019. [cited 2023 July 2023]; Available from: www.electricalelibrary.com/en/2019/02/13/operation-of-hybrid-vehicle/.
8. Arnold, N. *Hydrogen fuel cell cars: everything you need to know*. 2013. [cited 2023; Available from: www.bmw.com/en/innovation/how-hydrogen-fuel-cell-cars-work.html
9. Haschka, F. & D. Schlieck. *High power nickel-cadmium cells with fiber electrodes (FNC). in Proceedings of the 32nd international power sources symposium*. 1986.

10. Maggetto, G. & J. Van Mierlo, *Electric and electric hybrid vehicle technology: A survey*. 2000. https://doi.org/10.1016/j.est.2016.03.005

11. Sessa, S.D., G. Crugnola, M. Todeschini, S. Zin, & R. Benato, Sodium nickel chloride battery steady-state regime model for stationary electrical energy storage. *Journal of Energy Storage*, 2016. 6: p. 105–115. https://doi.org/10.1016/j.est.2016.03.005

12. Yang, J., C. Hu, H. Wang, K. Yang, J.B. Liu, & H. Yan, Review on the research of failure modes and mechanism for lead–acid batteries. *International Journal of Energy Research*, 2017. 41(3): p. 336–352. https://doi.org/10.1002/er.3613

13. Rahangdale, D. & A. Kumar, Acrylamide grafted chitosan based ion imprinted polymer for the recovery of cadmium from nickel-cadmium battery waste. *Journal of Environmental Chemical Engineering*, 2018. 6(2): p. 1828–1839. https://doi.org/10.1016/j.jece.2018.02.027

14. Young, K.-h. & S. Yasuoka, Capacity degradation mechanisms in nickel/metal hydride batteries. *Batteries*, 2016. 2(1): p. 3. https://doi.org/10.3390/batteries2010003

15. Lex, P. & B. Jonshagen, The zinc/bromine battery system for utility and remote area applications. *Power Engineering Journal*, 1999. 13(3): p. 142–148. https://doi.org10.1049/pe:19990307

16. Longo, S., V. Antonucci, M. Cellura, & M. Ferraro, Life cycle assessment of storage systems: the case study of a sodium/nickel chloride battery. *Journal of Cleaner Production*, 2014. 85: p. 337–346. https://doi.org/10.1016/j.jclepro.2013.10.004

17. Zubi, G., R. Dufo-López, M. Carvalho, & G. Pasaoglu, The lithium-ion battery: State of the art and future perspectives. *Renewable and Sustainable Energy Reviews*, 2018. 89: p. 292–308. https://doi.org/10.1016/j.rser.2018.03.002

18. Elwert, T., D. Goldmann, F. Römer, M. Buchert, C. Merz, D. Schueler, & J. Sutter, Current developments and challenges in the recycling of key components of (hybrid) electric vehicles. *Recycling*, 2015. 1(1): p. 25–60. https://doi.org/10.3390/recycling1010025

19. Alternative Fuels Data Center. *Developing Infrastructure to Charge Electric Vehicles*. 2023. Available online: https://afdc.energy.gov/fuels/electricity_infrastructure.html

20. Rahman, I., P.M. Vasant, B.S.M. Singh, M. Abdullah-Al-Wadud, & N. Adnan, Review of recent trends in optimization techniques for plug-in hybrid, and electric vehicle charging infrastructures. *Renewable and Sustainable Energy Reviews*, 2016. 58: p. 1039–1047. https://doi.org/10.1016/j.rser.2015.12.353

21. Miller, J.M., O.C. Onar, C. White, S. Campbell, C. Coomer, L. Seiber, R. Sepe, & A. Steyerl, Demonstrating dynamic wireless charging of an electric vehicle: The benefit of electrochemical capacitor smoothing. *IEEE Power Electronics Magazine*, 2014. 1(1): p. 12–24. 10.1109/MPEL.2014.2300978

22. Muneret, X., M. Coux, & P. Lenain. Analysis of the partial charge reactions within a standby VRLA battery leading to an understanding of intermittent charging techniques. in *INTELEC. Twenty-Second International*

Telecommunications Energy Conference (Cat. No. 00CH37131). 2000. IEEE. https://doi.org/10.1109/INTLEC.2000.884264

23. Budhia, M., G. Covic, & J. Boys. A new IPT magnetic coupler for electric vehicle charging systems. in *IECON 2010-36th Annual Conference on IEEE Industrial Electronics Society*. 2010. IEEE. https://doi.org/10.1109/IECON.2010.5675350

24. Sarker, M.R., H. Pandžić, & M.A. Ortega-Vazquez. Electric vehicle battery swapping station: Business case and optimization model. in *2013 International Conference on Connected Vehicles and Expo (ICCVE)*. 2013. IEEE. https://doi.org/10.1109/ICCVE.2013.6799808

25. Yan, J., M. Menghwar, E. Asghar, M.K. Panjwani, & Y. Liu, Real-time energy management for a smart-community microgrid with battery swapping and renewables. *Applied Energy*, 2019. 238: p. 180–194. https://doi.org/10.1016/j.apenergy.2018.12.078

26. Ban, M., J. Yu, Z. Li, D. Guo, & J. Ge, Battery Swapping: An aggressive approach to transportation electrification. *IEEE Electrification Magazine*, 2019. 7(3): p. 44–54. https://doi.org/10.1109/MELE.2019.2925762

27. Mahoor, M., Z.S. Hosseini, & A. Khodaei, Least-cost operation of a battery swapping station with random customer requests. *Energy*, 2019. 172: p. 913–921. https://doi.org/10.1016/j.energy.2019.02.018

28. Lee, H.-K. & K.-H. Nam, An overview: Current control technique for propulsion motor for EV. *The Transactions of the Korean Institute of Power Electronics*, 2016. 21(5): p. 388–395. https://doi.org/10.6113/TKPE.2016.21.5.388

29. Rajashekara, K., Present status and future trends in electric vehicle propulsion technologies. *IEEE Journal of Emerging and Selected Topics in Power Electronics*, 2013. 1(1): p. 3–10. https://doi.org/10.1109/JESTPE.2013.2259614

30. Sutikno, T., N.R.N. Idris, & A. Jidin, A review of direct torque control of induction motors for sustainable reliability and energy efficient drives. *Renewable and Sustainable Energy Reviews*, 2014. 32: p. 548–558. https://doi.org/10.1016/j.rser.2014.01.040

31. Kumar, M.S. & S.T. Revankar, Development scheme and key technology of an electric vehicle: An overview. *Renewable and Sustainable Energy Reviews*, 2017. 70: p. 1266–1285. https://doi.org/10.1016/j.rser.2016.12.027

32. Le-Huy, H. Comparison of field-oriented control and direct torque control for induction motor drives. in *Conference record of the 1999 IEEE industry applications conference. Thirty-forth IAS annual meeting (Cat. No. 99CH36370)*. 1999. IEEE. https://doi.org/10.1109/IAS.1999.801662

33. Farasat, M. & E. Karaman. Speed sensorless electric vehicle propulsion system using hybrid FOC-DTC induction motor drive. in *2011 International Conference on Electrical Machines and Systems*. 2011. IEEE. https://doi.org/10.1109/ICEMS.2011.6073516

34. Ameid, T., A. Menacer, H. Talhaoui, & Y. Azzoug, Discrete wavelet transform and energy eigen value for rotor bars fault detection in variable speed field-oriented control of induction motor drive. *ISA Transactions*, 2018. 79: p. 217–231. https://doi.org/10.1016/j.isatra.2018.04.019

35. Singh, B. & S. Singh, State-of-art on permanent magnet brushless DC motor drives. *Journal of Power Electronics*, 2009. 9(1): p. 1–17.
36. Kim, T., H.-W. Lee, L. Parsa, & M. Ehsani. Optimal power and torque control of a brushless DC (BLDC) motor/generator drive in electric and hybrid electric vehicles. in *Conference Record of the 2006 IEEE Industry Applications Conference Forty-First IAS Annual Meeting*. 2006. IEEE. https://doi.org/10.1109/IAS.2006.256695
37. Gamazo-Real, J.C., E. Vázquez-Sánchez, & J. Gómez-Gil, Position and speed control of brushless DC motors using sensorless techniques and application trends. Sensors, 2010. 10(7): p. 6901–6947. https://doi.org/10.3390/s100706901
38. Sundeep, S. &B. Singh, Robust position sensorless technique for a PMBLDC motor. *IEEE Transactions on Power Electronics*, 2017. 33(8): p. 6936–6945. https://doi.org/10.1109/TPEL.2017.2759761
39. Kumar, M., B. Singh, & B. Singh, *DSP based sensorless control of permanent magnet brushless DC motor*. IETE Journal of Research, 2003. 49(4): p. 269–275. https://doi.org/10.1080/03772063.2003.11416346
40. Singh, S. &S. Singh, Position sensorless control for PMBLDC motor drive using digital signal processor. *Journal of Circuits, Systems and Computers*, 2016. 25(07): p. 1650077. https://doi.org/10.1142/S0218126616500778
41. Chaoui, H., M. Khayamy, & O. Okoye, MTPA based operation point speed tracking for PMSM drives without explicit current regulation. *Electric Power Systems Research*, 2017. 151: p. 125–135. https://doi.org/10.1016/j.epsr.2017.05.019
42. Fodorean, D., M.M. Sarrazin, C.S. Marțiș, J. Anthonis, & H. Van der Auweraer, Electromagnetic and structural analysis for a surface-mounted PMSM used for light-EV. *IEEE Transactions on Industry Applications*, 2016. 52(4): p. 2892–2899. doi 10.1109/TIA.2016.2537784
43. Niu, H., J. Yu, H. Yu, C. Lin, & L. Zhao, Adaptive fuzzy output feedback and command filtering error compensation control for permanent magnet synchronous motors in electric vehicle drive systems. *Journal of the Franklin Institute*, 2017. 354(15): p. 6610–6629. https://doi.org/10.1016/j.jfranklin.2017.08.021
44. Rocha-Osorio, C., J. Solís-Chaves, I.R. Casella, C. Capovilla, J.A. Puma, & A. Sguarezi Filho, GPRS/EGPRS standards applied to DTC of a DFIG using fuzzy–PI controllers. *International Journal of Electrical Power & Energy Systems*, 2017. 93: p. 365–373. https://doi.org/10.1016/j.ijepes.2017.05.033
45. Lara, J. &A. Chandra, Performance investigation of two novel HSFSI demodulation algorithms for encoderless FOC of PMSMs intended for EV propulsion. *IEEE Transactions on Industrial Electronics*, 2017. 65(2): p. 1074–1083. https://doi.org/10.1109/TIE.2017.2733500
46. Arias, A., E. Ibarra, E. Trancho, R. Griñó, I. Kortabarria, & J. Caum, Comprehensive high speed automotive SM-PMSM torque control stability analysis including novel control approach. *International Journal of Electrical Power & Energy Systems*, 2019. 109: p. 423–433. https://doi.org/10.1016/j.ijepes.2019.02.035

47. Monteiro, J.R.B., A. Oliveira Jr, M.L.d. Aguiar, & E.R. Sanagiotti, Electromagnetic torque ripple and copper losses reduction in permanent magnet synchronous machines. *European Transactions on Electrical Power*, 2012. 22(5): p. 627–644. https://doi.org/10.1002/etep.594

48. Miranda, R., E. Fernandes, C. Jacobina, A. Lima, A. Oliveira, & M. Correa. Sensorless control of a PMSM synchronous motor at low speed. in *IECON 2006-32nd Annual Conference on IEEE Industrial Electronics*. 2006. IEEE. doi 10.1109/IECON.2006.347910

49. Jing, L. & J. Cheng, Research on torque ripple optimization of switched reluctance motor based on finite element method. *Progress in Electromagnetics Research M*, 2018. 74: p. 115–123. doi:10.2528/PIERM18071104

50. Millithaler, P., J.-B. Dupont, M. Ouisse, É. Sadoulet-Reboul, & N. Bouhaddi, Viscoelastic property tuning for reducing noise radiated by switched-reluctance machines. *Journal of Sound and Vibration*, 2017. 407: p. 191–208. https://doi.org/10.1016/j.jsv.2017.07.008

51. Shin, S., N. Kawagoe, T. Kosaka, & N. Matsui, Study on commutation control method for reducing noise and vibration in SRM. *IEEE Transactions on Industry Applications*, 2018. 54(5): p. 4415–4424. doi: 10.1109/TIA.2018.2831173

52. Bauer, C., J. Hofer, H.-J. Althaus, A. Del Duce, & A. Simons, The environmental performance of current and future passenger vehicles: Life cycle assessment based on a novel scenario analysis framework. *Applied Energy*, 2015. 157: p. 871–883. https://doi.org/10.1016/j.apenergy.2015.01.019

53. Qiao, Q., F. Zhao, Z. Liu, X. He, & H. Hao, Life cycle greenhouse gas emissions of Electric Vehicles in China: Combining the vehicle cycle and fuel cycle. *Energy*, 2019. 177: p. 222–233. https://doi.org/10.1016/j.energy.2019.04.080

54. Helmers, E., Bewertung der Umwelteffizienz moderner Autoantriebe–auf dem Weg vom Diesel-Pkw-Boom zu Elektroautos. *Umweltwissenschaften und Schadstoff-Forschung*, 2010. 22(5): p. 564–578.

55. Hacker, F., R. Harthan, F. Matthes, & W. Zimmer, Environmental impacts and impact on the electricity market of a large scale introduction of electric cars in Europe-Critical Review of Literature. *ETC/ACC Technical Paper*, 2009. 4: p. 56–90.

56. Helms, H., M. Pehnt, U. Lambrecht, & A. Liebich. Electric vehicle and plug-in hybrid energy efficiency and life cycle emissions. in *18th International Symposium Transport and Air Pollution, Session*. 2010.

57. Held, M. &M. Baumann, Assessment of the environmental impacts of electric vehicle concepts, in *Towards Life Cycle Sustainability Management*. 2011, Springer. p. 535–546.

58. Zackrisson, M., L. Avellán, & J. Orlenius, Life cycle assessment of lithium-ion batteries for plug-in hybrid electric vehicles–Critical issues. *Journal of Cleaner Production*, 2010. 18(15): p. 1519–1529. https://doi.org/10.1016/j.jclepro.2010.06.004

59. Majeau-Bettez, G., T.R. Hawkins, & A.H. Strømman, Life cycle environmental assessment of lithium-ion and nickel metal hydride batteries for plug-in hybrid and battery electric vehicles. *Environmental Science & Technology*, 2011. 45(10): p. 4548–4554. https://doi.org/10.1021/es103607c

60. Faria, R., P. Moura, J. Delgado, & A.T. De Almeida, A sustainability assessment of electric vehicles as a personal mobility system. *Energy Conversion and Management*, 2012. 61: p. 19–30. https://doi.org/10.1016/j.enconman.2012.02.023

61. Hawkins, T.R., B. Singh, G. Majeau-Bettez, & A.H. Strømman, Comparative environmental life cycle assessment of conventional and electric vehicles. *Journal of Industrial Ecology*, 2013. 17(1): p. 53–64. https://doi.org/10.1111/j.1530-9290.2012.00532.x

62. Ellingsen, L.A.-W., B. Singh, & A.H. Strømman, The size and range effect: lifecycle greenhouse gas emissions of electric vehicles. *Environmental Research Letters*, 2016. 11(5): p. 054010. DOI: 10.1088/1748-9326/11/5/054010.

Chapter 2

A comprehensive review on rechargeable batteries

Technologies, advancements, and comparative analysis

P.V. Ram Kumar,[1] N. Krishna Chaitanya,[2]
V. Suneel Reddy,[2] S.K. Abdul Kareem,[1] and A. Akshitha[1]

[1]Department of Electrical and Electronics Engineering, Ramireddy Subbarami Reddy Engineering College, Kavali, India
[2]Department of Electronics and Communication Engineering, Ramireddy Subbarami Reddy Engineering College, Kavali, India

2.1 INTRODUCTION

Rechargeable batteries [1] have evolved as a fundamental technology in the modern era, facilitating the growth of basic electronics towards EVs, with renewable energy systems. These versatile energy storage strategies have revolutionized the way we power our daily lives, enabling increased mobility, reducing reliance on fossil fuels, and mitigating environmental impacts. In this era of growing energy demand and sustainability concerns, rechargeable batteries hold immense promise for addressing global challenges and shaping a cleaner future [2]. The limitations of traditional primary batteries [3], which are considered for single-use and disposable applications, have shown a path for the widespread adoption of modern batteries. Unlike their non-rechargeable counterparts, rechargeable batteries offer the ability to store and release energy multiple times, making them a cost-effective and environmentally friendly choice. By utilizing reversible electrochemical reactions, rechargeable batteries allow for the efficient conversion and storage of electrical energy.

The main discussion in this chapter is to provide a comprehensive review of rechargeable battery technologies [4], exploring their advancements, performance parameters, and conducting a comparative analysis. By examining the current affirm of batteries [5], we aim to shed light on their strengths, weaknesses, and potential areas for improvement. This review will serve as a valuable resource for researchers, engineers, and decision-makers seeking to comprehend the latest developments and select appropriate battery technologies for specific applications. Here, we will first discuss the chronological growth of rechargeable batteries. The journey began when Gaston Plante invented a lead-acid battery in 1859, which provided a breakthrough in energy storage technology. Subsequent advancements led to the commercialization of

DOI: 10.1201/9781003495574-2

nickel-cadmium (NiCd) batteries during the premature 20th century, marking the first rechargeable batteries [6] widely available to the public.

Over time, the demand for more compact, lightweight, and higher-energy-density batteries spurred further innovation. This led to the advent of lithium-ion (Li-ion) batteries [6], which were used by the electronics industry from 1990s. Li-ion batteries are the preferred choice for applications ranging from smart phones to EVs due their greater energy density, as well as long lifecycle and minimum discharge. However, Li-ion batteries [7–9] also present challenges, including safety concerns and limited resource availability, necessitating ongoing research and development. The emergence of solid-state batteries [10] holds tremendous promise, offering superior safety, elevated energy density, improved cycle life. By replacing liquid electrolytes with solid-state electrolytes, these batteries [11, 12] abolish the jeopardy of leakage and enhance thermal stability. Furthermore, other emerging technologies, such as flow batteries as Li-S batteries, demonstrate potential for even greater energy storage capabilities [13].

As the demand for rechargeable batteries [4] continues to rise, it is crucial to evaluate their performance parameters for effective decision-making. By conducting a comparative analysis, this review chapter aims to provide important insights keen on the strengths and weaknesses of various rechargeable battery technologies [6], enabling stakeholders to craft clued-up choices. Rechargeable batteries [7] have altered the landscape of energy storage, driving innovation and propelling sustainable development. This comprehensive review will explore the current state of rechargeable battery technologies, highlighting advancements, analyzing performance parameters, and providing a comparative analysis. By gaining a deeper consideration of rechargeable batteries and their potential, we can pave the way for a cleaner, more efficient energy future.

This study compares various batteries that are used in current scenarios. The types of materials used in the battery, their capacities, lifetime of the batteries, different battery technologies used by various countries, percentage of utilization of batteries in the global market. It is also discussed about the future market trend and types of batteries preferred in vehicles and their capacities. After this discussion, the major challenges are discussed in the next section.

2.2 LITERATURE REVIEW

This section provides an extensive examination of the existing body of knowledge regarding rechargeable batteries. It encompasses research articles, academic chapters, industry reports, and patents to provide a wide-ranging outline of the historical development, fundamental principles, and various battery chemistries employed in rechargeable systems.

The journey of rechargeable batteries [5] began with Gaston Planté's invention of the lead-acid battery in 1859. This seminal development marked a significant milestone in energy storage technology. Lead-acid batteries offered a reliable and rechargeable solution, making them widely adopted for applications such as automotive starting, backup power systems, and renewable energy storage. Building upon the success of lead-acid batteries [14–16], further advancements led to the commercialization of nickel-cadmium (NiCd) batteries during the early 20th century. NiCd batteries [17] offered improved parameters. These rechargeable batteries found extensive use in portable electronics, power tools, and early hybrid electric vehicles.

The next major breakthrough came with the progress of batteries in 1980 like NiMH-nickel-metal hydride [18]. NiMH batteries offered even higher energy density, reduced toxicity, and eliminated the necessity for hazardous cadmium [19]. These batteries quickly gained popularity in applications requiring lightweight and high-capacity energy storage, such as laptops, digital cameras, and electric vehicles. However, the most significant advancement in rechargeable battery technology came with the commercialization of Li-ion batteries [20–24] in the 1990s. Li-ion batteries revolutionized portable electronics, enabling the widespread use of smartphones, laptops, tablets, and other devices. The elevated energy density, higher cycle life, and minimal self-discharge of Li-ion batteries made them the preferred choice for many applications [24]. The use of various cathode materials [25–28], such as lithium cobalt oxide (LCO), lithium iron phosphate (LFP), and lithium nickel manganese cobalt oxide (NMC), enables customization of battery characteristics [29–32] to suit specific applications.

Despite their widespread adoption, Li-ion batteries [23] face certain challenges. Safety concerns, such as thermal runaway and the potential for lithium plating, have prompted extensive research in developing safer battery chemistries [33, 34] and improving the stability of electrode–electrolyte interfaces. In recent years, solid-state batteries have emerged as a promising alternative to overcome the limitations of traditional rechargeable battery technologies. Solid-state batteries [35] replace the liquid electrolytes of conventional batteries with solid-state electrolytes, offering enhanced safety, higher energy density, and improved cycle life. Solid-state [35] electrolytes, typically composed of ceramics or polymer-based materials, mitigate the risk of leakage, improve thermal stability, and enable the use of lithium metal anodes [36–38].

Another promising rechargeable battery technology is lithium-sulfur (Li-S) batteries [39–42]. Li-S batteries are more popular when compared over Li-ion batteries due to high capacity sulfur as the material for the cathode. However, challenges [43] with Li-s due to low cycle life and poor sulfur employment have limited their commercial viability. Ongoing study aims to address these challenges and unlock the full potential of Li-S batteries [41, 44] requiring lofty energy density for applications like electric vehicles. Flow batteries [45] represent another class of rechargeable battery gaining attention for their potential in applications where large energy is required.

Flow batteries store energy [46] in electrolyte solutions contained in separate tanks, allowing independent scaling of energy and power capacity. This technology offers advantages [45] in requisites of scalability, long life, and rapid response times. Vanadium redox flow batteries (VRFB) as well as zinc-bromine flow batteries are among the most extensively researched flow battery systems.

The literature review highlights the historical development and evolution of rechargeable battery technologies. The chapter has started discussion from the lead-acid to the advanced lithium-ion batteries; each advancement has brought about significant improvements in energy density, cycle life, and safety. Emerging technologies in batteries offer promising solutions for addressing the precincts. The knowledge and insights gained from the literature review serve as a foundation for further research and advancements in this crucial field of energy storage.

2.3 CURRENT RECHARGEABLE BATTERY TECHNOLOGY

The field of rechargeable batteries has witnessed remarkable advancements [7, 47] over a decade, due to the rise in demand for efficient storage solutions of energy across a range of applications. This section provides a discussion on rechargeable battery technologies, exploring their characteristics, advantages, limitations, and recent developments.

In the literature most commonly and widely used batteries are discussed. Every battery has its own advantages and disadvantages. The materials used in the batteries and the corresponding battery applications are also discussed in section 2.2. In the current section 2.3, we will discuss the current state of the art of various batteries.

(a) **Lithium-ion batteries (Li-ion):** these batteries [27] became very dominant in rechargeable battery technology owing to their elevated energy density, long cycle life, and reasonably low self-discharge rate. They are extensively used in electronics, EVs, and grid energy storage systems. Li-ion batteries employ lithium-based compounds as electrode materials, such as lithium cobalt oxide (LCO), lithium nickel manganese cobalt oxide (NMC), and lithium iron phosphate (LFP). Ongoing research focuses on improving the energy density, safety, and cost-effectiveness of Li-ion batteries. This includes the exploration of new cathode materials, solid-state electrolytes, and advancements in electrode engineering to enhance performance.

(b) **Nickel-metal hydride batteries (NiMH):** these batteries are the established technology used in hybrid electric vehicles, portable electronics, and other applications. They offer higher energy density compared to nickel-cadmium batteries while eliminating the use of toxic cadmium. However, NiMH batteries [18] have lower energy density than Li-ion batteries and suffer from self-discharge and memory effects. Research efforts aim to improve their concert by optimizing electrode supplies and exploring new electrolyte chemistries.

(c) **Lead-acid batteries:** these batteries are the most popularly used rechargeable battery technology [16], and continue to be widely used in automotive applications, backup power systems, and renewable energy storage. They are relatively low cost and have a high-power output, making them suitable for applications requiring large energy capacities. However, lead-acid batteries have limited energy density, short cycle life, and environmental concerns due to the use of lead and sulfuric acid. Ongoing research focuses on improving their efficiency, durability, and reducing environmental impacts through innovations in electrode design and electrolyte formulations.

(d) **Solid-state batteries:** solid-state batteries represent a promising avenue for future rechargeable battery technology [37]. These batteries replace liquid electrolytes with solid-state electrolytes, offering enhanced safety, increased energy density, and improved cycle life. Solid-state electrolytes eliminate the risk of leakage and enhance thermal stability, making them suitable for applications where safety is paramount. However, challenges remain in achieving high ionic conductivity and ensuring stable interfaces between solid-state electrolytes and electrode materials. Research efforts aim to address these challenges by exploring various solid-state electrolyte compositions, electrode architectures, and fabrication techniques.

(e) **Lithium-sulfur batteries (Li-S):** these [41] are gaining significant attention due to their high theoretical energy density, abundance of sulfur, and potential for low-cost production. Li-S batteries utilize sulfur as the cathode material, which has a high specific capacity. However, they face challenges such as low cycle life, poor sulfur utilization, and the formation of soluble polysulfides. Ongoing research focuses on developing advanced sulfur cathodes, electrolyte formulations, and electrode architectures to overcome these limitations and unlock the full potential of Li-S batteries.

(f) **Flow batteries:** these batteries are a distinct class of batteries that store energy in electrolyte solutions contained in separate tanks [46]. They offer advantages w.r.t. scalability, long cycle life, as well as rapid response times, making them suitable for large-scale energy storage applications. Ongoing research aims to improve their energy density, reduce costs, and enhance overall system efficiency.

(g) **Other emerging technologies:** various other rechargeable battery technologies [7] are being explored and developed. This includes sodium-ion batteries, which utilize sodium ions instead of lithium ions, offering potential advantages like cost and abundance. Additionally, a study over these efforts focus on developing new materials and chemistries such as metal-air batteries, Li-oxygen, and dual-ion batteries to enhance energy storage capabilities.

The current landscape of rechargeable battery technology offers a diverse range of options for energy storage across various applications. Li-ion batteries continue to dominate the market because of high energy density with proven performance. However, the ongoing studies are directed towards increasing the performance, safety, and cost-effectiveness of rechargeable batteries, as well as exploring alternative chemistries and emerging technologies. These advancements pave the way for a more sustainable and efficient energy.

Table 2.1 provides a comparison [4, 8] of different rechargeable battery technologies based on their chemistry, capacity, voltage, discharge rate, lifespan, and cost. These comparisons help in understanding the trade-offs and characteristics of each battery technology for different applications.

Table 2.2 shows the major countries and their utilization of different rechargeable battery [3, 7] technologies. The countries listed above are recognized for their significant contributions and involvement of production, studies, and deployment of these battery technologies.

Some of the Indian battery manufacturers who are manufacturing various batteries for various vehicles are listed in Table 2.3.

Table 2.4 shows the best batteries and technology of recharging.

The precise percentage of utilization for each battery technology globally can be challenging due to the lack of comprehensive data covering all applications and regions as shown in Table 2.5. But here the authors tried to keep the data, which is available [47].

The dominance of lithium-ion batteries is mainly because of widespread use in consumer electronics, EVs, and storing the energy. However, the market landscape is continually evolving, and emerging technologies like SS batteries, Li-sulfur, and also flow batteries have the potential to gain larger market shares in the future as their development progresses and commercialization expands.

The precise percentage of utilization for different battery technologies by 2040 [48] is highly speculative as it depends on several factors, including technological advancements, market demand, policy changes, and emerging trends. However, I can provide a speculative estimate of their potential market shares based on current projections and industry forecasts (see Table 2.6).

Li-ion batteries will continue to dominate the market [47] due to their established infrastructure, ongoing advancements, and wide adoption across industries. Solid-state batteries are anticipated to gain a significant market share, driven by their potential for higher energy density, improved safety, and compatibility with multiple applications. Emerging technologies like lithium-sulfur batteries and flow batteries are expected to make some

Table 2.1 Comparison of various battery technologies

Battery technology	Chemistry	Capacity	Voltage	Discharge rate	Lifespan	Cost
Lithium-ion batteries	Lithium cobalt oxide	150–200 Wh/kg	3.6–3.7 V	10–30 C	500–1000 cycles	$100–$200/kWh
Nickel-metal hydride	Nickel hydroxide/metal hydride	100–150 Wh/kg	1.2 V	1–10 C	500–1000 cycles	$50–$100/kWh
Lead-acid batteries	Lead dioxide/lead	40–100 Wh/kg	2.0 V	0.1–1 C	300–700 cycles	$20–$50/kWh
Solid-state batteries	Lithium metal/solid electrolyte	200–300 Wh/kg	2.5–3.5 V	10–30 C	1000–2000 cycles	$200–$300/kWh
Lithium-sulfur batteries	Lithium/sulfur	300–500 Wh/kg	2.1–2.3 V	1–10 C	1000–2000 cycles	$300–$500/kWh
Flow batteries	Vanadium redox	30–100 Wh/L	1.2–2.0 V	1–10 C	10000–20000 cycles	$100–$200/kWh

Table 2.2 Major countries and their utilization of different rechargeable battery technologies

Battery technology	Major countries
Lithium-ion batteries	China, United States, Japan, South Korea, Germany, Taiwan, Canada
Nickel-metal hydride	Japan, United States, China, Germany, South Korea
Lead-acid batteries	China, United States, India, Japan, Germany, Brazil
Solid-state batteries	United States, Japan, China, South Korea, Germany
Lithium-sulfur batteries	United States, United Kingdom, China, Japan, Germany
Flow batteries	United States, Germany, China, Japan, Canada, Australia

Table 2.3 Battery manufacturers in India

Manufacturer	Materials used	Vehicle types
Exide industries limited	Lead-acid	Cars, motor cycles and commercial vehicles
Amara raja Batteries limited	Lead-acid	Cars and two wheelers
Tata green batteries	Lead-acid	Passenger cars, commercial vehicles and two wheelers
HBL power systems limited	Lead-acid, lithium-ion	Electric vehicles and commercial vehicles
Luminous power technologies	Lead-acid	Cars and two wheelers
Su-Kam power systems	Lead-acid	Cars and two wheelers
Bharat power solutions	Lead-acid	Cars and two wheelers

inroads but may face challenges related to scale-up, cost, and commercial viability. These estimates should be interpreted as broad projections, and the actual market shares may differ based on the future dynamics of the industry.

Table 2.7 shows the preferred battery technology, and typical capacity for each vehicle type.

2.4 CHALLENGES

Here are some common challenges associated with rechargeable battery technologies [7]:

(a) **Energy density:** one of the key challenges is to increase batteries' energy density, which refers to an amount of energy stored per unit mass or volume [48]. Higher energy density allows for longer-lasting batteries and enables the use of batteries requires more energy demands, such as electric vehicles.

Table 2.4 Best batteries and technology of recharging

Battery	*Charging technology*
Lithium-ion batteries	These use dedicated charges that provide correct voltage and current levels. Fast charging stations are commonly used in electric vehicles (ex.: Tesla supercharges).
Nickel-metal hydride	Standard charging protocols are used in NiMH batteries and are charged using household charges.
Lead-acid batteries	Conventional lead-acid batteries are charged using constant voltage charging methods.
Solid-state batteries	These are similar to lithium-ion batteries, but are charged at a faster rate compared with lithium-ion batteries.
Lithium-sulfur batteries	These also use technology similar to lithium-ion batteries, but here in this battery the charge and discharge characteristics are improved.
Flow batteries	These are entirely different to store the energy in liquid electrolyte solutions. Here charging involves pumping charged electrolyte into the system.

Table 2.5 Current global market share of battery technologies

Battery technology	*Estimated global market share*
Lithium-ion batteries	80–90%
Nickel-metal hydride	5–10%
Lead-acid batteries	5–10%
Solid-state batteries	<1%
Lithium-sulfur batteries	<1%
Flow batteries	<1%

Table 2.6 Battery technology market estimation by 2040

Battery technology	*Estimated global market share by 2040*
Lithium-ion batteries	70–80%
Nickel-metal hydride	5–10%
Lead-acid batteries	5–10%
Solid-state batteries	5–15%
Lithium-sulfur batteries	1–5%
Flow batteries	1–5%

Table 2.7 Battery technology used in various vehicles, their capacity

Vehicle type	Preferred battery technology	Typical capacity
Electric cars	Lithium-ion batteries	40–100 kWh
Hybrid cars	Nickel-metal hydride batteries	1–2 kWh
Conventional cars	Lead-acid batteries	30–60 Ah
Electric bicycles	Lithium-ion batteries	250–750 Wh
Electric scooters	Lithium-ion batteries	1–3 kWh
Electric motorcycles	Lithium-ion batteries	5–15 kWh
Electric trucks	Lithium-ion batteries	100–300 kWh
Electric buses	Lithium-ion batteries	200–500 kWh
Electric boats	Lithium-ion batteries	20–200 kWh
Renewable energy systems	Flow batteries	Varies based on system

(b) **Cycle life and degradation:** batteries experience degradation over time that refers to a decrease in their capacity and performance [49]. Increasing cycle life, which refers to increasing the life of batteries before significant degradation occurs, is a challenge in battery technology. Prolonging the cycle life ensures the longevity and reliability of batteries.

(c) **Cost:** the cost of rechargeable batteries is a significant challenge [50–51], particularly in EV applications and storing the energy. The high cost is mainly due to the expensive materials and complex manufacturing processes involved. Reducing the cost of batteries is crucial for their widespread adoption and market competitiveness.

(d) **Safety and thermal management:** rechargeable batteries can generate heat during operation [52] and can be prone to thermal runaway, leading to safety hazards such as fires and explosions. Developing effective thermal management systems and implementing safety features is essential to mitigate these risks and ensure the safe use of batteries.

(e) **Environmental impact:** battery technologies [50] often involve the use of rare or toxic materials, which can have adverse environmental effects during mining, production, and disposal. Addressing the environmental impact of batteries through sustainable material sourcing, recycling programs, and environmentally friendly manufacturing processes is a challenge in the industry.

(f) **Charging infrastructure:** as the demand for electric vehicles and other battery-powered devices increases, establishing a widespread [53] and efficient charging infrastructure is a challenge. Ensuring convenient access to charging stations and reducing charging times are key areas of focus to promote the adoption and usability of battery-powered technologies.

(g) **Technological advancements:** continual technological advancements [7] are necessary to overcome the existing limitations and challenges in battery technologies. Innovations in materials, cell designs, manufacturing processes, and energy management systems are crucial to enhancing the performance, efficiency, and overall capabilities of rechargeable batteries.

Addressing these challenges requires collaborative efforts from researchers, manufacturers, policymakers, and other stakeholders in the field of battery technology.

2.5 CONCLUSIONS

The study of rechargeable batteries has provided valuable insights into various batteries and their applications. The analysis encompassed various battery types, such as Li-ion, NiMH, lead-acid, solid-state, lithium-sulfur, and flow batteries. Each battery technology exhibits its own unique characteristics, advantages, and limitations.

Li-ion batteries are popular for many devices due to their efficiency, but they need to be safer and more eco-friendly. Nickel-metal hydride and lead-acid batteries work well in some cars, but they are not as powerful. Newer solid-state and lithium-sulfur batteries are promising but still need some improvements. Flow batteries, like vanadium redox batteries, are good for storing a lot of energy for homes and cities, but they can be expensive.

Throughout the research, several common challenges in battery technologies were identified. These include the need to improve energy density, extend cycle life, reduce costs, enhance safety, address environmental concerns, and develop efficient charging infrastructure. In rechargeable batteries it is very essential to address the challenges and advancement of various industries, including transportation, electronics, and renewable energy.

Finally, rechargeable batteries play a vital role in powering the applications, starts with portable electronics to EVs. Understanding the strengths, limitations, and future prospects of different battery technologies is essential for informed decision-making and the development of sustainable energy storage solutions. Continued research and innovation in battery technologies will pave the way for more efficient, reliable, and environmentally friendly energy storage systems in the years to come.

REFERENCES

[1] Zhang, J., Li, H., & Sun, Q. (2019). Rechargeable batteries: A review of recent advancements and performance parameters. *IEEE Access*, 7, 2753–2772. doi: 10.1109/ACCESS.2019.2908649

[2] Wang, Y., Zhang, D., & Sun, J. (2020). Rechargeable batteries: A review of recent advances and applications. *Journal of Energy Storage*, 26, 100858. doi: 10.1016/j.jes.2020.100858

[3]   Yu, M., Sun, W., & Zhang, H. (2020). Recent advances in rechargeable batteries for portable electronics. *Energies*, 13(2), 449. doi: 10.3390/en13020449

[4]   Zhang, W., Wang, X., & Zhang, J. (2020). Solid-state rechargeable batteries: A review of recent advances. *IET Energy*, 14(1), 4–15. doi: 10.1049/iet-en.2019.0680

[5]   Kim, D.-S., Lee, D.-H., & Park, J.-K. (2020). The literature review of rechargeable batteries: A historical perspective and emerging technologies. *IEEE Access*, 8, 1256–1272. doi: 10.1109/ACCESS.2020.2963529

[6]   Mishra, S., Kumar, R., & Kumar, S. (2022). Emerging rechargeable battery technologies for sustainable energy applications. *Journal of Power Sources*, 472, 228506. doi: 10.1016/j.jpowsour.2022.228506

[7]   Zhang, X., Wang, L., & Liu, Y. (2023). Current status and future trends of rechargeable batteries. *Springer Nature*, 13(1), 1–15. doi: 10.1007/s42452-022-00363-z

[8]   Zhao, Z., Wang, Y., & Zhang, X. (2023). Recent advancement in rechargeable battery technologies. *Wiley Interdisciplinary Reviews: WIREs Energy & Environment*, 12(1), e264. doi: 10.1002/wene.339

[9]   Liu, Y., Wang, L., & Zhang, W. (2022). A review of the recent advances in rechargeable lithium-ion battery safety. *IEEE Transactions on Electron Devices*, 69(3), 872–883. doi: 10.1109/TED.2022.3136873

[10] Zhang, W., Zhao, Z., & Li, J. (2022). Recent advances in rechargeable sodium-ion battery safety. *IET Power Electronics*, 15(3), 211–221. doi: 10.1049/iet-pel.20

[11] Liu, J., Bao, Z., Cui, Y., et al. (2020). Pathways for practical high-energy long-cycling lithium metal batteries. *Nature Energy*, 5(6), 526–537. doi: 10.1038/s41560-020-0614-3

[12] Li, W., Yao, H., Yan, K., et al. (2018). The synergetic effect of lithium polysulfide and lithium nitrate to prevent lithium dendrite growth. *Nature Communications*, 9(1), 1–10. doi: 10.1038/s41467-018-06256-8

[13] Wang, X., Zhang, J., & Wang, Y. (2020) Recent advances in lithium-ion batteries for electric vehicles. In *Advances in Battery Technology for Electric Vehicles*, Springer Nature, pp. 1–30. doi:10.1007/978-3-030-34767-3_1

[14] Dunn, B., Kamath, H., & Tarascon, J.-M. (2011). Electrical energy storage for the grid: A battery of choices. *Science*, 334(6058), 928–935. doi: 10.1126/science.1212741

[15] Scrosati, B., & Garche, J. (2010). Lithium batteries: Status, prospects and future. *Journal of Power Sources*, 195(9), 2419–2430. doi: 10.1016/j.jpowsour.2009.11.048

[16] Larcher, D., & Tarascon, J. M. (2015). Towards greener and more sustainable batteries for electrical energy storage. *Nature Chemistry*, 7(1), 19–29. doi: 10.1038/nchem.2085

[17] Armand, M., & Tarascon, J. M. (2008). Building better batteries. *Nature*, 451(7179), 652–657. doi: 10.1038/451652a

[18] Chen, X., Li, J., & Wang, Y. (2022). A review of recent advances in rechargeable battery technologies. *IEEE Transactions on Electron Devices*, 69(1), 1–10. doi: 10.1109/TED.2021.3123985

[19] Wang, Y., Zhao, Z., & Chen, X. (2022). High-performance rechargeable battery technologies: A review. *IET Power Electronics*, 15(1), 1–12. doi: 10.1049/iet-pel.2021.1007

[20] Kumar, Ajay, Hari Singh, Parveen Kumar, & Bandar AlMangour, eds. (2023). *Handbook of Smart Manufacturing: Forecasting the Future of Industry 4.0*. CRC Press. https://doi.org/10.1201/9781003333760

[21] Tarascon, J.-M., & Armand, M. (2001). Issues and challenges facing rechargeable lithium batteries. *Nature*, 414(6861), 359–367. doi: 10.1038/35104644

[22] Goodenough, J. B., & Kim, Y. (2010). Challenges for rechargeable Li batteries. *Chemistry of Materials*, 22(3), 587–603. doi: 10.1021/cm901452z

[23] Liu, P., Zhang, J., & Wang, Y. (2019). Recent advances in high-energy lithium-ion batteries. *Journal of Power Sources*, 427, 127–141. doi: 10.1016/j.jpowsour.2019.04.096

[24] Whittingham, M. S. (2012). Lithium batteries and cathode materials. *Chemical Reviews*, 104(10), 4271–4302. doi: 10.1021/cr020731c

[25] Kumar, Ashwini, Ravi Kant Mittal, & Rajesh Goel, eds. (2023). *Waste Recovery and Management: An Approach Toward Sustainable Development Goals*. CRC Press. doi:/10.1201/9781003359784

[26] Zhang, Y., Zhang, W., & Liu, Y. (2022). Cost-effective design of lithium-ion batteries for electric vehicles. *Journal of Power Sources*, 494, 230279. doi:10.1016/j.jpowsour.2022.230279.

[27] Zhang, Y., Zhang, W., & Liu, Y. (2022). Low-cost high-performance lithium-ion batteries for electric vehicles. *Journal of Energy Storage*, 35, 102762. doi:10.1016/j.jes.2022.102762

[28] Wang, Q., Xu, Y., & Wang, X. (2022). Thermal runaway of lithium-ion batteries: Causes, consequences, and mitigation strategies. *Journal of Energy Storage*, 34, 102709. doi:10.1016/j.jes.2022.102709

[29] Zhang, Y., Zhang, W., & Liu, Y. (2022). Thermal management of lithium-ion batteries for electric vehicles: A review. *Journal of Power Sources*, 497, 230362. doi:10.1016/j.jpowsour.2022.230362

[30] Rani, Sangeeta, Khushboo Tripathi, & Ajay Kumar. (2023). Machine learning aided malware detection for secure and smart manufacturing: a comprehensive analysis of the state of the art. *International Journal on Interactive Design and Manufacturing (IJIDeM)*, 17, 1–28.

[31] Nitta, N., Wu, F., Lee, J. T., & Yushin, G. (2015). Li-ion battery materials: Present and future. *Materials Today*, 18(5), 252–264. doi: 10.1016/j.mattod.2014.10.040

[32] Xu, K. (2014). Electrolytes and interphases in Li-ion batteries and beyond. *Chemical Reviews*, 114(23), 11503–11618. doi: 10.1021/cr500003w

[33] Huang, J. Q., Zhang, Q., Wei, F., & Xu, Z. (2018). Recent advances in flexible lithium-ion batteries: Materials, technologies, and perspectives. *Advanced Materials*, 30(37), 1801362. doi: 10.1002/adma.201801362

[34] Park, M., Zhang, X., Chung, M., Less, G. B., & Sastry, A. M. (2010). A review of conduction phenomena in Li-ion batteries. *Journal of Power Sources*, 195(24), 7904–7929. doi: 10.1016/j.jpowsour.2010.06.060

[35] Kumar, Amit, Vinod Kumar, Vikas Modgil, & Ajay Kumar. (2022).
      Stochastic Petri nets modelling for performance assessment of a manufac-
      turing unit. *Materials Today: Proceedings, 56,:* 215–219.
[36] Manthiram, A., Yu, X., & Wang, S. (2017). Lithium battery chemistries
      enabled by solid-state electrolytes. *Nature Reviews Materials,* 2(4), 16103.
      doi: 10.1038/natrevmats.2016.103
[37] Li, M., Lu, J., Chen, Z., Amine, K., & Goodenough, J. B. (2018). Progress
      and prospects of solid-state lithium batteries. *Advanced Materials,* 30(20),
      1800561. doi: 10.1002/adma.201800561
[38] Manthiram, A., Yu, X., & Wang, S. (2017). Lithium battery chemistries
      enabled by solid-state electrolytes. *Nature Reviews Materials,* 2(4), 16103.
      doi: 10.1038/natrevmats.2016.103
[39] Manthiram, A., Chung, S. H., & Zu, C. (2015). Lithium-sulfur
      batteries: Progress and prospects. *Advanced Materials,* 27(12), 1980–2006.
      doi: 10.1002/adma.201405115
[40] Bruce, P. G., Scrosati, B., & Tarascon, J. M. (2008). Nanomaterials for
      rechargeable lithium batteries. *Angewandte Chemie International Edition,*
      47(16), 2930–2946. doi: 10.1002/anie.200702505
[41] Zhang, W., Liu, Y., & Wang, Y. (2023). Recent advances in rechargeable
      lithium-sulfur batteries. *Wiley Interdisciplinary Reviews: WIREs Energy &
      Environment,* 12(2), e265. doi: 10.1002/wene.340
[42] Li, J., Wang, L., & Zhang, W. (2022). A review of the recent advances in
      rechargeable lithium-ion batteries. *IEEE Transactions on Electron Devices,*
      69(2), 512–521. doi: 10.1109/TED.2021.3131450
[43] Wang, Y., Yang, J., & Zhang, Y. (2023). Recent advances in lithium-ion
      battery cycle life improvement. *Journal of Power Sources,* 493, 230242.
      doi:10.1016/j.jpowsour.2022.230242
[44] Li, M., Lu, J., Chen, Z., Amine, K., & Goodenough, J. B. (2018). Progress
      and prospects of solid-state lithium batteries. *Advanced Materials,* 30(20),
      1800561. doi: 10.1002/adma.201800561
[45] Skyllas-Kazacos, M., Chakrabarti, M. H., & Hajimolana, S. A. (2011).
      Progress in flow battery research and development. *Journal of the
      Electrochemical Society,* 158(8), R55–R79. doi: 10.1149/1.3599565
[46] Kim, J.-W., Kim, M.-J., & Lee, H.-J. (2022). The economics of recharge-
      able batteries. *Renewable and Sustainable Energy Reviews,* 167, 109943.
      doi:10.1016/j.rser.2022.109943
[47] Wang, X., Zhang, J., & Wang, Y. (2020). A review of rechargeable battery
      technologies for electric vehicles. In *Advances in battery technology for elec-
      tric vehicles* (pp. 1–30). Springer Nature. doi: 10.1007/978-3-030-34767-3_1
[48] Dunn, B., & James, C. (2010). Electrochemical capacitors: Challenges
      and opportunities for real-world applications. *Electrochemical Society
      Interface,* 19(4), 53–57.
[49] Liu, Y., Yang, J., & Zhang, Y. (2021). Solid-state batteries: Recent advances
      and challenges. *Journal of Energy Storage,* 33, 102721. doi:10.1016/
      j.jes.2021.102721
[50] Chaitanya, N. Krishna, & S. Varadarajan. (2016). Load distribution
      using multipath-routing in wired packet networks: A comparative study.
      Perspectives in Science, 8, 234–236.

[51] Xu, Y., Wang, Q., & Wang, X. (2022). Safety of lithium-ion batteries: Recent advances and challenges. *Journal of Power Sources*, 492, 230210. doi:10.1016/j.jpowsour.2022.230210

[52] Liu, Y., Wang, Y., & Zhang, W. (2022). Rechargeable batteries: Technological advancements, challenges, current and emerging applications. *Science Direct*, 378, 135610. doi: 10.1016/j.energy.2022.135610

[53] Chu, S., & Majumdar, A. (2012). Opportunities and challenges for a sustainable energy future. *Nature*, 488(7411), 294–303. doi: 10.1038/nature11475

Fabrication of test rig to analyze the effects of variable belt tension in a CVT system

Kunal Rawal,[1] Ravi Patel,[1] Eklavya Gupta,[1] Gourav Patel,[1] Avinash Sharma,[1] Neelesh Sahu,[2] Parveen Kumar,[3] and Ajay Kumar[4]

[1]Department of Mechanical Engineering , Medi-caps University, Indore, India
[2]Department of Artificial Intelligence and Robotics, Gyan Ganga Institute of Technology & Science, Jabalpur, India
[3]Department of Mechanical Engineering, Rawal Institute of Engineering and Technology, Faridabad, India
[4]Department of Mechanical Engineering, School of Engineering & Technology, JECRC University, Jaipur, India

3.1 INTRODUCTION

As the demand for economical and eco-friendly vehicles is increasing, automobile manufacturers are focusing their attention on an alternative to conventional gearbox transmission. In comparison to the conventional manual or automatic transmission, continuous variable transmissions (CVTs) can be used to achieve greater fuel economy and better drive performance. A CVT operated engine mostly operates in high combustion efficiency region, resulting in lower emissions and lesser power loss.

CVT is a type of transmission system that works by gradually shifting to any gear ratios between a set of maximum and minimum limits. Thus, it provides a smooth, noiseless drive with higher fuel economy. Most of the vehicles' transmissions are equipped with a 4–6 specific gear ratio that can be selected either manually or automatically. In contrast, in CVT, almost infinite variability of gear ratio is possible that allows the engine to maintain an almost constant speed as the vehicle increases its velocity.

CVT results in better performance output as the engine is held at RPM where it runs most efficiently and produces the most power, which can be utilized for vehicle driving. This also reduces the sudden load on the engine when a vehicle drives over obstacles like potholes or speed breakers. When wheels of such a vehicle roll over the potholes and speed breakers, CVT immediately responds by changing the gear ratio to provide high torque on wheels and low torque load on the engine shaft, thereby reducing the load on the engine. This is achieved in a much less time duration. Again, as the vehicle runs over smoother road, the CVT adjusts the gear ratio to increase the speed of the wheels, and thus, the vehicle can move at its top

DOI: 10.1201/9781003495574-3

Figure 3.1 CVT system (Honda Activa scooter).

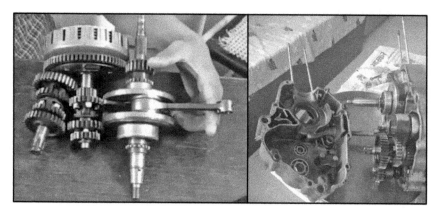

Figure 3.2 Conventional gear box (Hero Honda Glamour and Splendour Motorbike, respectively).

speed with lesser fuel consumption. As there are no steps or sets of gears in the CVT gearbox (as shown in Figure 3.1) unlike conventional manual gearbox transmission (as shown in Figure 3.2), it can operate smoothly, and no sudden jerk is experienced by the vehicle. Thus, CVT-driven vehicles are observed to have a longer engine life.

3.1.1 Literature review

In their chapter, Chaudhari et al. [1] reviewed a transmission system for performance of CVT using a single ball traction drive. They created a test rig for the analysis of performance characteristics and calculated design stress and velocity of the gear, and also determined the CVT pulley radius.

Srivastava et al. [2] reviewed state-of-the-art research on dynamic modeling and control of friction-limited continuously variable transmissions. The basic concepts, mathematical models, and computational schemes are extensively discussed. Challenges and critical issues for future research on modeling and control of such CVTs are also discussed.

Seelan [3] discussed in depth about the need for a transmission system and the working principle of CVT in his report. An attempt has been made to understand the contribution of hydraulic actuators, which is an integral part of a CVT. The materials used, constructional aspects and stress analysis of the belt has been discussed in detail.

Panda et al. [4] discussed the adoption of continuously variable transmissions in Indian cars with engines of 1000 CC or less. The primary goal is to provide a more comfortable and convenient driving experience, particularly for elderly and differently-abled individuals, in the face of increasing traffic congestion.

Shukla et al. [5] discussed the design of a CVT system for an Iranian automaker's manual transmission (MT) car. Their discussion revolved around the design of the CVT itself and the utilization of hydraulic mechanisms to control the pulleys within the CVT system.

Jha and Gandhi [6] worked on the research of friction-limited continuously variable transmissions. It suggests that as CVT technology advances, car performance will continue to improve while costs decrease. The chapter also highlights some critical issues and challenges associated with this system [6].

Willis [7] described a method for analyzing and designing a continuously variable transmission. A software package was employed to fine-tune a CVT for specific applications using kinematic principles and energy balance equations. The thesis primarily examines the Team Industries CVT as a case study applied to the Virginia Tech Mini Baja Team.

Arya [8] discussed the importance of automated evaluation of road damage in municipalities and road authorities, acknowledging the resource limitations and equipment challenges faced by many countries. The article further contributes by proposing a large-scale road damage dataset from multiple countries, presenting detection and classification models, and providing recommendations for adopting data and models from other countries, with enhanced accessibility through inclusion in the Global Road Damage Detection Challenge 2020 and availability on GitHub.

Ruan et al. [9] discussed how pure electric vehicles can achieve performance improvements by using multi-speed dual-clutch transmissions and continuously variable transmissions. The research indicates that incorporating multi-speed transmissions can bring substantial benefits to electric vehicles. Simulation results identify continuously variable and two-speed transmissions as the most promising options for different classes of pure electric vehicles.

Yildiz et al. [10] reviewed the control of a chain continuously variable transmission in electric vehicles. The process involves obtaining the transient power request for a specific velocity profile, selecting the electric motor's torque and angular speed, determining the CVT speed ratio, and implementing it in the control unit with a feedback PI controller considering CVT dynamics. The actual vehicle velocity is calculated using a dynamic formula that includes system dynamics and is then compared to the reference velocity profile. Simulation results confirm that the developed model aligns well with the reference, suggesting it can serve as a foundation for a sophisticated control algorithm.

Srivastava [11] worked on modeling and simulation of friction-limited continuously variable transmissions. The report presents a comprehensive one-dimensional transient dynamic model for a metal V-belt CVT, capturing its complex transient interactions. It also employs a detailed planar multibody model to account for the discrete structure dynamics in a chain CVT, particularly addressing polygonal excitations [3].

Wang et al. [12] worked on a magnetic continuously variable transmission device. They describe a magnetic CVT uses a stator and three concentric rotors (control, input, and output) with magnets on their surfaces to achieve variable gear ratios through magnetic interactions, allowing control of the gear ratio by adjusting the speed of the control rotor.

EID [13] had work on dynamic analysis and experimental evolution of the melt push belt CVT. The study emphasized understanding how loading conditions affect slip behavior and torque transmission in CVTs, investigating clamping force requirements for initiation and pressure compliance, with a focus on V-belt variator functional properties, including oil pressure control and reduction ratio.

3.1.2 Problem statement and objective

In current CVT-driven vehicles, the rotating masses decide the acceleration rate at no load or minimum load. The ball masses in CVT are selected such that they perform optimum in off-road and on-road conditions. However, even after careful considerations, a delay in time is observed when a vehicle reaches its top speed on the highway. Table 3.1 shows the comparison of different research work on CVT performance analysis. This delay does not allow the CVT to reach the top speed immediately, which affects the speed loss.

In the proposed chapter, at this moment, with the help of some actuator attached to the CVT system, the belt tension can be reduced to achieve the top gear ratio instantly to gain top speed as per the permitted speed limit on the highway.

Similarly, when the vehicle is riding off-road, CVT tends to accelerate the vehicle with fixed delay time period. When this delay time period is crossed, the CVT tries to achieve a higher speed at the output shaft. However, the higher speed of the vehicle is not desirable at all times, especially if the

Table 3.1 Comparison of different research work on CVT performance analysis

Author's (year)	Objective function	Performance charact-eristics or Analysis	Effect of belt on perfor-mance	CVT Review	Dynamic Modeling/ Analysis	Smart Vehicle	Force Analysis	Machine Learning
Chaudhari et al. (2015)	Multi-objective			Yes				
Srivastava et al. (2009)	Multi-objective				Yes			
Seelan (2015)	Multi-objective			Yes	Yes			
Panda et al. (2015)	Multi-objective	Yes						
Shukla et al. (2017)	Multi-objective	Yes						
Jha and Gandhi (2015)	Multi-objective	Yes		Yes				
Willis (2006)	Multi-objective			Yes				
Arya (2021)	Multi-objective							Yes
Ruan et al. (2018)	Multi-objective	Yes			Yes	Yes		
Yildiz et al. (2017)	Multi-objective	Yes			Yes	Yes		
Srivastava (2006)	Multi-objective	Yes		Yes				
Wang et al. (2011)	Multi-objective	Yes			Yes	Yes	Yes	
EID (2013)	Multi-objective	Yes					Yes	
This chapter	Multi-objective	Yes	Yes	Yes	Yes	Yes	Yes	Future work

vehicle is driving off-road. During off-road riding, the driver wishes to have more control on the vehicle with less speed, so that he can avoid jerks and discomforts in the off-road terrain. To attain low speed of the vehicle, the driver cuts the fuel supply to the engine by closing the throttle partially, and then opens the throttle when the speed nears the lower limit.

In this research work, an attempt is made to improve the performance of CVT by altering the belt tension. A lever will be provided in the vehicle that alters the belt tension of CVT. This change in the belt tension further decreases or increases the required wheel torque as per the terrain (highway or off-road riding), and can be achieved by installing an additional mechanism in the CVT drive system based on the driver's action on a manual lever.

For a smart vehicle of today's era, instead of using a manual lever for varying belt tension as per terrain, an automated system can be installed to detect the road conditions, specifically distinguishing between rough and smooth surfaces (highway or off-road) using machine learning and deep learning techniques. By analyzing data collected from various sensors, the belt tension can be adjusted by an actuator automatically to optimize the torque required for the smooth running of CVT operated vehicles. The design and working of this lever is a part of the future scope for this chapter. Following objectives are identified based on this problem statement:

1. Explain CVT function
2. Fabricate test rig for CVT performance testing
3. Analyze the effect of varying initial belt tension on the gear ratio of CVT

3.2 CVT SYSTEM COMPONENTS AND ITS WORKING

The main components of CVT are primary and secondary clutch, which are connected by the belt. Primary clutch is connected to the prime mover (engine or motor), while the secondary clutch is connected to the vehicle wheel. The power is transmitted from primary clutch to the secondary clutch with the help of the belt.

3.2.1 Components of CVT

3.2.1.1 Primary clutch

Primary clutch comprises of a fixed pulley sheave, movable pully sheave, roller masses, follower, and cover plate as shown in Figure 3.3.

3.2.1.2 Secondary clutch

Secondary clutch is attached to the driven wheel through a gear train with a fixed gear ratio. It comprises of movable pulley, sheave, and spring (as shown in Figure 3.4).

Figure 3.3 Primary sheave components.

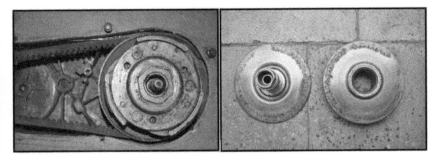

Figure 3.4 Secondary sheave components.

3.2.1.3 Belt

Belt transmits the power from the input clutch to the output clutch. The power is transmitted due to friction between the belt and pulleys. Usually, rubber belts are used for lower capacity CVTs, and steel or metal belts are used for higher capacity CVTs. General rubber V-belts cannot be used for this purpose as they cannot withstand the higher tension and force applied by the pulleys to shift the belt. So, specially manufactured rubber belts are used in CVTs (see Figure 3.5).

3.2.2 Working of CVT

As discussed above, the primary clutch of the CVT has five main components whose placements are shown in Figure 3.6. The assembly comprises of a fixed sheave, belt, movable sheave, roller mass, and the cover plate. This complete arrangement rotates about the center line as it is mounted on the shaft of the prime mover (engine or motor shaft).

When the engine is at lower RPM, the roller mass rotates at a lesser radius and the centrifugal force acting on roller mass is small, which causes the belt to move at smaller working diameter. In contrast, when the engine is at

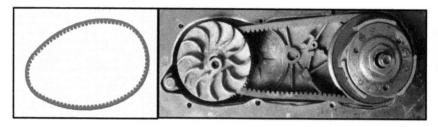

Figure 3.5 Belt in the CVT system.

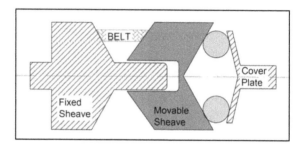

Figure 3.6 Primary clutch pulley system.

higher RPM, the roller mass rotates at larger radius and the centrifugal force acting on roller mass is large due to which the movable sheave is pushed towards the fixed sheave. This pushes the belt moving on larger working diameter on both the sheaves (fixed sheave and movable sheave together form the primary pulley).

The effect of centrifugal force on roller masses decides the equilibrium position of movable sheave, and thus decides the working diameter of belt on the primary clutch pulley.

Figure 3.7 shows how the variation in speed ratio can be achieved by varying the working diameter. When the engine is at ideal RPM, the belt is positioned with minimum diameter in the primary clutch and maximum diameter in the secondary clutch. This is shown in Figure 3.7(a) as the minimum speed position. Now, as the speed of the engine increases, due to throttling the belt changes and shifts its position in the clutches in such a way that it contacts the primary clutch with maximum diameter and secondary clutch at minimum diameter so it can achieve minimum speed reduction. This is shown in Figure 3.7(b) as the maximum speed position.

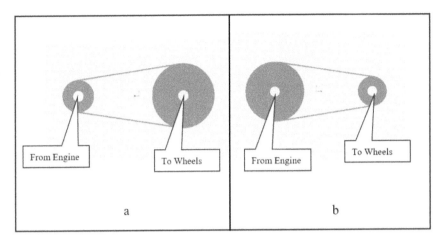

Figure 3.7 Position of belt during operation.

3.3 FABRICATION AND WORKING OF TEST RIG

The test rig is of paramount importance for evaluating and improving the performance of a CVT system. It enables the measurement of input and output shaft speeds to monitor the changes in gear ratio. Through experimentation with different ball masses, center distances, and belt tension variations, the test rig allows identification of the optimal parameters of the CVT system, and thus enhances CVT performance. Moreover, the test rig allows how the tension adjustments of the belt affect the gear ratio and torque to be understood, providing valuable insights for refining the CVT system.

The selection of ball masses is crucial for the optimal performance of a continuously variable transmission based on the terrain of the ride. Smaller ball masses offer higher output torque at low speeds, whereas heavier ball masses provide top speed and lower output torque. Ultimately, the acceleration of the vehicle is influenced by the selection of these ball masses. Therefore, determining the appropriate ball masses for achieving optimum torque is a practical task that can be determined through a test rig.

In a CVT system, the fixed length of the belt causes movement on the input and output pulleys, resulting in a balanced tug of war. Changing the radius of the input pulley affects the belt tension and force the output pulley to adjust its diameter accordingly. This adjustment compensates for the extra belt length. By adjusting the belt tension, the gear ratio and torque in the CVT system can be modified. Optimal added tension in the belt can also be determined through the use of a test rig.

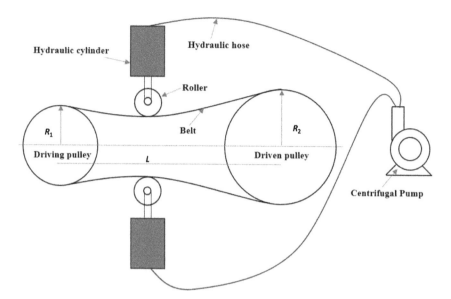

Figure 3.8 CVT test rig line diagram.

3.3.1 Fabrication of test rig

The test rig has been fabricated (as show in Figure 3.8) to adjust the belt tension of a continuously variable transmission while in running state. The rig includes a systematic arrangement of mechanisms that securely hold the bearings of the two shafts and allow for a slight modification of the center distance between them without disrupting the orientation of the shafts. The center distance is adjusted to vary the belt tension while the CVT is running. By increasing the tension from its present state, the diameters of both the input and output pulleys change. This alteration in pulley diameters cause change in the gear ratio without causing any abrupt impact on the drive system. The change in gear ratio can be determined by measuring the speeds of the input and output shafts.

A 4 mm thick steel sheet is selected as a stable frame to hold the shaft firmly at their places. Using gas cutting and wielding process, this frame along with the assembled CVT can be welded to a fabricated vehicle to arrange a drive unit. The drive unit used in this chapter is the 110 CC petrol engine as shown in Figure 3.9.

This drive unit has a pulley belt arrangement to transmit power to input shaft of the CVT assembly, which allows the easy engagement of engine with CVT. Input pulley of CVT is connected with the belt to operate at variable engine speed.

Figure 3.9 Assembled CVT on plate and frame.

Figure 3.10 Assembled CVT on frame with engine.

3.3.2 CVT performance on test rig

The CVT driving shaft is powered by an engine as shown within the experimental setup to conduct the tests at specific speeds and fixed time intervals by Figure 3.10.

The test rig is used to evaluate the gear ratios of the driving and driven shafts of a CVT system. It consists of various components such as the input shaft and output shaft of the CVT system, the drive pulley, which is connected to the engine, the engine control system, the carburetor, and throttle adjustments to allow the engine to operate at different speeds. By manipulating variables such as the belt length, ball mass, and belt tension, the test rig helps in the assessment of the CVT system performance and facilitates the observation of speeds on both the input and output shafts of CVT.

The power from the engine is transmitted to the CVT system through a belt and pulley arrangement as shown by Figure 3.10. The drive ratio is set at 3:1 to lower the speed of the CVT. The engine speed can be fixed at a constant value, and the RPM of the CVT relative to the engine can be adjusted using a preset pulley-to-pulley transmission with different pulley and belt sizes.

By setting the engine shaft speed at 3000, 4000, and 5000 RPM using the carburetor idle jet screw, the output speed at the CVT's output shaft is measured. This speed gradually increases over time with a fixed delay period under a constant load. The CVT increases the output speed when the load is low, and decreases the output speed to provide torque on the output shaft (under high load conditions). This automatic adjustment of speed and torque by the CVT ensures sufficient torque is delivered at the output shaft instantly.

3.3.3 Experimental procedure

In our work, keeping a fixed engine speed, the time taken by CVT to attain maximum output shaft speed is measured. Now, for all the experiment values, the delay time measurement must be done by keeping the fixed resisting torque on the output shaft.

This time taken will be initially increased if the belt tension is increased. In other words, the attainment of top speed will be delayed by CVT when belt tension is increased externally, and hence the torque at the output shaft will be greater in that delay period. Figure 3.11 shows the experimental setup.

3.4 ANALYZE EFFECT OF VARYING BELT TENSION ON GEAR RATIO OF CVT

3.4.1 Force analysis of the CVT primary clutch

Under operating conditions, the primary clutch of the CVT is continuously rotating with the prime mover. The belt runs on the pulley of the primary clutch. This pulley is divided into two parts, i.e., fixed sheave and the movable sheave.

Primary clutch shaft is running at engine speed, and hence complete assembly (as shown in Figure 3.12) rotates at this speed. The centrifugal force acting on the roller masses generates a net horizontal force F, which

Figure 3.11 Experimental setup during operation.

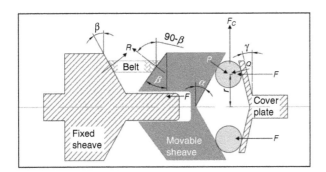

Figure 3.12 Primary sheave component with all forces.

is acting on the movable sheave. Under equilibrium conditions, there is a tendency of the belt to rotate at the possible minimum radius on this pulley. The net horizontal force 'F' acting on the movable sheave and the reaction force acting on the belt 'R' is balanced.

Now, if any change is there in the engine speed, it directly changes the centrifugal force on the roller masses, which results in the movement of movable sheave along the axis of rotation. This movement of sheave results in a change of contact diameter of the belt, and hence, at every instance, sheave tends to get a new equilibrium position resulting in a unique contact diameter of the belt on this pulley.

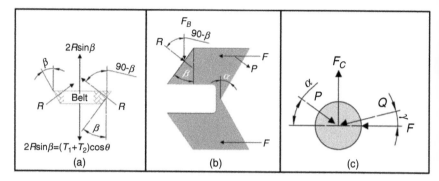

Figure 3.13 Free body diagram of belt, moveable sheave, and roller masses.

Here,

R is the reaction on the belt due to fixed and moveable sheave
β = side contact angle between sheave and belt =15°.
α and γ are the respective angle of roller guides on the movable sheave and cover plate.
F_c is the centrifugal force acting on roller masses when primary shaft is rotating.
Ω is the rotational speed of the primary shaft.
R is the instantaneous radius of rotation of roller masses.
P is the reaction force due to movable sheave on the roller masses.
Q is the reaction force due to cover plate on the roller masses.
F is the resultant horizontal force acting on the movable sheave due to roller masses.

3.4.1.1 Free body diagram of roller masses

From Figure 3.13, using Lami's theorem, we can write

$$\frac{P}{\sin(90+\gamma)} = \frac{Q}{\sin(90+\alpha)} = \frac{F_c}{\sin\{180-(\alpha+\gamma)\}} \tag{3.1}$$

By resolving the angles,

$$\frac{P}{\cos\gamma} = \frac{Q}{\cos\alpha} = \frac{F_c}{\sin(\alpha+\gamma)} \tag{3.2}$$

Therefore, from equation (3.2)

$$P = \frac{F_c \cos\gamma}{\sin(\alpha + \gamma)} \qquad (3.3)$$

3.4.1.2 Free body diagram of movable sheave

From Figure 3.13(b), when reaction force is in equilibrium

$$R\cos\beta = F \qquad (3.4)$$

3.4.1.3 Free body diagram of the belt

From Figure 13(a), reaction on the belt is equal to combine belt tension

$$2R\sin\beta = (T_1 + T_2)\cos\theta \qquad (3.5)$$

3.4.2 Calculation required for test rig experimentation and validation

3.4.2.1 Speed ratio calculation

Speed ratio for gear

$$\text{Speed ratio} = \frac{N_2}{N_1} = \frac{T_1}{T_2} \qquad (3.6)$$

Here,

N_1 = RPM at driving gear
N_2 = RPM at driven gear
T_1 = Teeth at driving gear
T_2 = Teeth at driven gear

Speed ratio for CVT

$$\text{Speed ratio} = \frac{N_2}{N_1} = \frac{D}{d} \qquad (3.7)$$

Here,

D = Diameter of driving pulley
d = Diameter of driven pulley

3.4.2.2 Gear ratio

$$\text{Gear ratio} = \frac{d}{D} \dots \tag{3.8}$$

Here,

D = Diameter of driving pulley
d = Diameter of driven pulley
Now, for the fabricated test rig,
Maximum working diameter of driving pulley (D_{max}) = 80 mm
Minimum working diameter of driving pulley (D_{min}) = 54 mm
Maximum working diameter of driven pulley (d_{max}) = 69 mm
Minimum working diameter of driven pulley (d_{min}) = 43 mm

Maximum gear ratio

$$(G.R)\,max = \frac{d_{min}}{D_{max}} \tag{3.9}$$

$$= \frac{43}{80} = 0.5375$$

Minimum gear ratio

$$(G.R)\,min = \frac{d_{max}}{D_{min}} \tag{3.10}$$

$$= \frac{69}{54} = 1.28$$

3.4.2.3 Angular velocity

$$\omega = \frac{2\pi N}{60} \tag{3.11}$$

Here,

N = RPM

Now, velocity at wheel

$$V = R_{wheel} * \omega \qquad (3.12)$$

At $V = 40$ Km/h or 11.11 m/s
& $R_{wheel} = 0.2$ m

$$11 = 0.2 * \left(\frac{2\pi N}{60} \right) \qquad (3.13)$$

$N_{wheel} = 525.21$ RPM or 530 RPM (atop speed)

$$(N)engine = \frac{(N)_{wheel}}{G.R} \qquad (3.14)$$

$$(N)engine = \frac{530}{0.53} = 1000\,RPM$$

$$(N)engine = \frac{530}{0.53} = 1000\ RPM \qquad (3.15)$$

3.4.2.4 Power and torque

CVT used for the test rig is chosen from the vehicle Kinetic Honda Zoom ZX, which has a maximum power output of 7.7 Bhp at 5600 RPM and maximum torque is 9.81 Nm.
Maximum power output at engine

$$(P)engine = 7.7 * 0.746\,Kw \qquad (3.16)$$

$$= 5.74 \ Kw \text{ or } 5740 \text{ watts}$$

Now, the power output of the engine when operating the test rig is equal to half of the maximum engine power capacity (for safety reasons while performing experiments)

$$(P)working = \frac{(P)engine}{2} = 2.87 \text{ Kw or } 2870 \text{ watts} \qquad (3.17)$$

Torque can be calculated by the following expression:

$$T = \frac{P*60}{2\pi N}$$

(3.18)

3.4.2.5 Length of belt

Length of belt while performing experiments for a specific center distance of driving and driven pulleys can be calculated keeping two assumptions for simplicity:

(1) No belt elongation occurs during operation
(2) Effective line is continuous along the pitch line

$$L = 2C + \frac{\pi(D_p + D_s)}{2} + \frac{(D_p - D_s)^2}{4C}$$

(3.19)

Here,

D_p – diameter of belt at primary pulley
D_s – diameter of belt at secondary pulley
C – pulley center distance

3.4.2.6 Tension in belt

Torque in the pulley depends on belt tension at tight side and slack side and the working diameter of the pulley, as mentioned by the expression

$$\text{Torque} = (T_1 - T_2)*R$$

(3.20)

Here,

T_1 – Tension at tight side
T_2 – Tension at slack side
R – Radius of pulley

From Figure 3.14, for known values of gear ratio, engine speed, center distance of belt, R_1 and R_2

$$\tan\theta = \frac{R_2 - R_1}{L}$$

(3.21)

$$e^{\mu\emptyset} = \frac{T_1}{T_2}$$

(3.22)

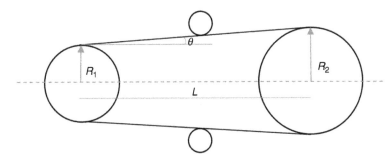

Figure 3.14 CVT working without external loads.

Here, $\varphi = 180 - 2\theta$

$$\text{Torque} = (T_1 - T_2)R \tag{3.23}$$

Note that the formulae and equations used in section 3.4 are referred from the books [14] and [15].

3.5 RESULT

When ideal rollers are pushing the belt in the inward direction, it generates added tension 't' in the belt. The contact angle θ of the belt is also increased. Due to change in these two parameters, the rotating masses in the CVT shift to smaller radius and speed ratio is decreased. This variation is explained further separately with the help of mathematical expression below.

3.5.1 Adding belt tension 't'

Figure 3.15 shows the belt pulley CVT arrangement when external loads F_1 and F_2 are applied on the belt to add extra tension.

If belt tension is increased by amount 't', then by equation (3.5), $[(T_1 + t) + (T_2 + t)]\cos\theta$ will increase in value compared to $[T_1 + T_2]\cos\theta$, i.e., $[(T_1 + t) + (T_2 + t)]\cos\theta$

Movable sheave was in equilibrium initially with the relation given in equation (3.4), i.e., $R\cos\beta = F$.

But now, with increased tensions ($T_1 + t$, and $T_2 + t$), the value of $R_1\cos\beta$ is greater than F. Hence, sheave will move towards right resulting in the belt rotating at lower working diameter.

Therefore, roller masses will start rotating at smaller radius (gear ratio will increase and speed will decrease), and also, when this applied tension 't'

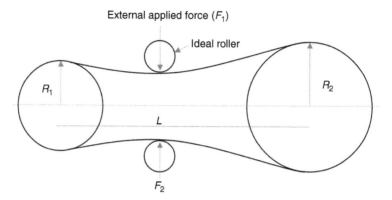

Figure 3.15 CVT working with external applied loads.

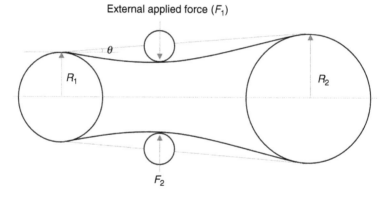

Figure 3.16 CVT working with external loads (θ).

is removed ($t = 0$) again, the sheave will shift to its initial position to regain the speed with decreased gear ratio.

3.5.2 Changing angle θ

Figure 3.16 represents the belt pulley CVT arrangement when external loads F_1 and F_2 are applied on belt to change belt angle.

If θ is reduced on pulley by an actuator, the tight side and slack side of belt come closer to each other. Then, $(T_1 + T_2) \cos\theta' = 2R \sin\beta$.

Again, R will change the equilibrium position and dominates to F, which results in the smaller radius (higher gear ratio and lower speed)

3.6 CONCLUSION

- If we change the belt tension at any instance, sheave equilibrium, i.e., equilibrium between the centrifugal force on the roller masses and belt tension force on sheave will break. Hence, the sheave will push the belt to a new position that will change the set of gear ratio.
- This concept can be used in automobiles equipped with CVT to vary the speed of vehicle riding on different terrains (highway or off-road) and simultaneously have more control on the vehicle torque and speed adjustments. This feature when incorporated in a smart vehicle will lead to a smoother ride and comfort drive in different terrains like highway, mountain trekking, and snow regions.
- This system controls speed and torque of prime mover (electric motor or IC engine) and hence improves vehicle performance like high torque and top speed in off-road and highway, respectively.

3.7 APPLICATIONS

- An automated system for varying belt tension based on the terrain nature can be installed on all-terrain vehicles (ATVs) that already have a CVT system.
- This setup would allow for multiple drive modes to be utilized for short intervals.
- In electric vehicles and smart vehicles, this system can optimize battery usage for improved efficiency and enhance the torque and speed delivery to the drive wheels through the motor.
- When this system is implemented in vehicles used for towing and carrying heavy loads, this system would provide smooth speed and torque adjustments in challenging road conditions, proving this system to be highly beneficial.

3.8 FUTURE SCOPE

- Actuators can be precisely designed to alter the belt tension and utilize these concepts in a CVT system.
- By harnessing the power of machine learning and deep learning techniques, a model can be trained to accurately identify the road conditions. This adaptive control of the CVT system will minimize the energy loss, reduce wear and tear, and provide a more comfortable driving experience.
- The system shall employ a combination of machine learning algorithms and deep learning models to analyze sensor data from a vehicle equipped with an accelerometer, gyroscope, and GPS sensors. Feature extraction techniques can be used to capture relevant

characteristics from the sensor data, which provide insights into the vehicle's behavior and dynamics under different road conditions.

REFERENCES

1. Dhanashree N. Chaudhari, and Pundlik N. Patil, "A Review of Transmission System for Performance of CVT," *International Journal of Engineering and Techniques* 1, no. 6(2015): 104–107.
2. Nilabh Srivastava, and Imtiaz Haque, "A Review on Belt and Chain Continuously Variable Transmissions (CVT): Dynamics and Control," *Mechanism and Machine Theory* 44, no. 1(2009): 19–41. https://doi.org/10.1016/j.mechmachtheory.2008.06.007
3. Vishnu Seelan, "Analysis, Design and Application of Continuously Variable Transmission (CVT)," *International Journal of Engineering Research and Applications* 5, no. 3(2015): 99–105.
4. Sanjog K. Panda, Abhirup Chatterjee, and Debkumar Chakrabarti, "Design of Continuously Variable Transmission Mechanism for Economy Cars in India," In *Ergonomics in Caring for People*. Springer (2015): 201–208. https://doi.org/10.1007/978-981-10-4980-4_25
5. Prakash C. Shukla, Prashant K. Tiwari, Yashwant K. Singh, Vikas Singh, and Rakesh K. Yadav, "Design and Performance Study of Continuously Variable Transmission (CVT)," *International Journal of Engineering Research & Technology (IJERT)* 6, no. 4(2017): 808–811.
6. Srishti Jha, and Amrutha G. Reddy, "Continuously Variable Transmission Control Strategy Review," *International Journal of engineering research & technology (IJERT)* 4, no. 4(2015): 1030–1034.
7. Christopher R. Willis, "A Kinematic Analysis and Design of a Continuously Variable Transmission," *Thesis submitted at Virginia Polytechnic Institute and State University* (2006).
8. Deeksha Arya, Hiroya Maeda, Sanjay K. Ghosh, Durga Toshniwal, Alexander Mraz, Takehiro Kashiyama, and Yoshihide Sekimoto, "Deep Learning-Based Road Damage Detection and Classification for Multiple Countries," *Automation in Construction* 132 (2021): 1–15.
9. Jiageng Ruan, Paul D Walker, Jinglai Wu, Nong Zhang, and Bangji Zhang, "Development of Continuously Variable Transmission and Multi-Speed Dual Clutch Transmission for Pure Electric Vehicle," *Advances in Mechanical Engineering* 10, no. 2(2018): 1–15. DOI: 10.1177/1687814018758223 journals.sagepub.com/home/ade
10. Ahmet Yildiz, and Osman Kopmaz, "A Study on the Basic Control of Speed Ratio of the CVT System Used for Electric Vehicles," *International Journal of Advances in Engineering & Technology* 10, no. 2(2017): 201–209.
11. Nilabh Srivastava, "Modeling and Simulation of Friction-Limited Continuously Variable Transmissions," *Thesis submitted at the Graduate School of Clemson University* (2006). https://tigerprints.clemson.edu/all_dissertations/29/
12. Jiabin Wang, Kais Atallah, and S.D. Carvley, "A Magnetic Continuously Variable Transmission Device," *IEEE Transactions on Magnetics* 47, no. 10(2011): 2815–2818. DOI: 10.1109/TMAG.2011.2157470

13. S. Mohamed EID, "Dynamic Analysis and Experimental Evaluation of the Metal Push Belt CVT," *International Journal of Engineering* 11, no. 3(2013): 41–50.

14. R.S. Khurmi, and J.K. Gupta, *A Text Book of Machine Design (S.I. Units)* Vol. 1, Eurasia Publishing House (Pvt.) ltd (2005): 68–713.

15. R.S. Khurmi, and J.K. Gupta, *A Text Book of Theory of Machine* Vol. 1, *S. Chand* (2005): 48–432.

Chapter 4

Analysis of a start-stop system for an energy-efficient micro-hybrid two wheeler

Devendra Vashist, Mallhar Maitra, Gaurav Saxena, and Ankit Mittal

Department of Automobile Engineering, Manav Rachna International Institute of Research and Studies, Faridabad, India

4.1 INTRODUCTION

4.1.1 Background

The vehicle design of a motorized scooter, which can automatically cut the fuel supply of the engine and start the engine as per the situation has always remained in the mind of designers for creating efficient vehicles. During the creation of such a vehicle, light weight, easy/smooth acceleration, easily manufactured parts, easy operation, and carrying capacity of 200 kg are a few parameters that are to be kept in mind for two wheelers. For proper implementation of emission norms and electric vehicle standards, the Government of India has established well-defined standards [1, 2, 3]. Tilt control for acceleration, deceleration, and steering are other parameters that are taken care of while preparing the new design [4, 5, 6]. The main objective of this study is to reduce the fuel consumption for reduced emissions and to prepare a design for a light weight vehicle, which can cut the cost of transportation for daily users of a two wheeler typically. The vehicle is a modified scooter propelled by an engine. The developed motorized scooter is small and light weight. It is designed for a ride in congested areas/streets. While designing the basic requirements of the end users are kept in mind. Short distance traveling and manufacturing cost are the two basic requirements that are taken care of by using economical and low-cost designs. Wheel belt drive is used to get maximum power output. The Indian companies who are working on motorized two-wheeler (MTW) start-stop technology are TVS, Jupiter 125, and Model 2023.

4.1.2 Two-wheeler engine start and stop system vehicle in India

Start-stop system shuts off the engine without human intervention when the vehicle is at rest to reduce fuel use and eliminate idle emissions. The

DOI: 10.1201/9781003495574-4

designed system restarts on its own with brake up movement or by usage of clutch. With this concept an automatic start-stop system helps in better fuel utilization with a check on emissions. By using this principle/technology, 3–8% of CO_2 emissions can be reduced [7]. Automobile manufactures and customers also find this technology to be interesting, which serves the two main challenging areas in an Indian context. Thus, this system is increasingly implemented by auto manufacturers in four wheelers but is still not getting momentum in two wheelers. This technology is also taking care of stringent EU and BS emission norms.

India currently consumes about 5 million barrels per day, which is growing at 3%. If it is compared with the average global growth rate of 1% [8], Indian figures are much higher. India is the third largest consumer of petroleum products in the world. The top 10 countries in the world that consume the most oil (2020) in barrels per day [9] is shown in Table 4.1

As per the current scenario India is one the largest MTW user with an estimated 37 million users [10] and the third largest fuel consumer of the world. With these figures, daily emission levels are the highest with 10 of the most polluted cities lying in India. Hence an immediate solution to overcome these challenges is required. Keeping all the traffic rules and regulations it should be a must for all the vehicle to turn off the vehicle while on red lights or standing at rest.

Proponents in the industry are developing connecting technologies that can intimate the rider about traffic jams and the status of traffic lights well in advance. This will empower the motorcycle control unit to configure itself for future start-stop cycles, ensuring the least possible wear of the battery, starter, and the engine. This will further improve the efficiency of the vehicle in terms of both fuel use and performance.

Table 4.1 Top 10 oil consumer countries of the world with consumption in barrels per day in 2020 (barrels per day)

Country	Oil consumption/day
US	17,178,000
China Republic	14,225,000
Bharat	4,669,000
Saudi Arabia	3,544,000
Japan	3,268,000
Russia	3,238,000
South Korea	2,560,000
Brazil	2,323,000
Canada	2,282,000
Germany	2,045,000

Source: [9].

The automotive industry is ever-evolving with a surge of new tech-based innovations, and the start-stop systems market is one of them that has captured the attention of vehicle owners across the world [11]. The application of these technologies has widened to motorcycles now and is expected to attain an extreme adoption rate soon.

The start and stop system fitted in two wheelers can make a lot of difference by contributing to oil saving and reducing emission levels. Start-stop technology is completely automatic and based on the lack of vehicle motion technology [12]. When the engine control unit (ECU) detects the brake pedal is pressed and the vehicle is out of gear, it cuts the fuel supply and switches the engine off.

In the proposed work, a 100 cc engine is mounted on a two-wheeled chassis and the start and stop system is retrofitted on it. The MTW is made to run on city roads and the time duration for which it remained in the stop mode is noted. A comparison is then made with a MTW using the start-stop system and without it. The proposed work is a small contribution in making the society pollution free with reduced fuel consumption. The designed vehicle can be used for daily working of common man. The vehicle can be driven on smooth city roads and will very well serve the purpose of office goers. While designing cost of the developed vehicle was also kept low so that people with less purchase capacity can use the motorized two wheelers.

4.1.3 Stop-start technology challenges

- People behavior: some people do not like the sensation part of the technology for which adaptation is required and requires some time to understand the system. [13]
- Extra cost: the cost of replacement components and fitting this technology is expensive. Stop-start technology requires extra components that requires energy to work.
- Extra fittings: for proper working of this system, extra fittings are to be applied in the existing system.
- Upgraded motor: a robust motor is required for proper functional operability of the system. Battery needs to have more energy density as the system has to work frequently on traffic lights.
- Engine parameters: engine operation should be smooth with reduced friction when the starting process is taking place. Good durability is another parameter that has to be taken care of [14].

4.2 PROPOSED DESIGN

4.2.1 Starting system of the vehicle

The starting system consists of a battery, starter motor, solenoid, ignition switch and starter relays. A neutral safety switch ensures that the system/motor do not function while the vehicle is in running mode. The starter's solenoid coil is energized through current once the ignition key is turned to the start position [15]. The plunger is pulled in the energized coil (that has become an electro magnet). High current operates the starter motor because of a set of contacts are closed by the plunger. The start-stop system detects when the MTW is stationary through different sensors. The engine is stopped once the driver has stopped at a traffic light (more than 30 seconds) and the transmission is in rest position. The same is explained with the help of the line diagram shown in Figure 4.1.

Start-stop technology works by detecting a lack of vehicle motion [16, 17]. The pressed brake pedal is detected by the sensors, which provides information that the vehicle is out of motion, the engine control unit (ECU) will cut the fuel and ignition to turn the engine off but when brakes are released, the vehicle is in running state or in pressed throttle condition, start-stop will send a message to the vehicle to start again. An automatic start-stop system is in communication from neutral gear sensor, wheel speed sensor and crankshaft sensor for collecting information about the status (MTW is moving or stationary) of the vehicle. The engine controller manages the start-stop operation and synchronizes them with the engine management system.

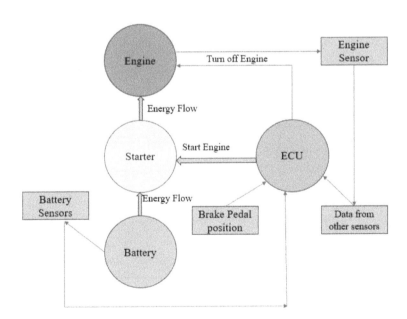

Figure 4.1 Line diagram of the working of the start-stop system.

4.2.2 ECE R40 drive pattern

ECE R40 is a drive pattern that is adopted by vehicle manufacturers across the world for emission tests. During this drive pattern, the vehicle is made to have variation in running, where it is made to accelerate, deaccelerate, have a uniform speed, and stopping phase. This pattern is repeated several times to calculate fuel consumption. One such pattern is shown in Figure 4.2. In the present work, city drive pattern is adopted, which has similar features as EE R-40 drive pattern.

4.3 TECHNOLOGY FEATURES

The electric energy is provided by the battery for starting. Battery provides power on turning the ignition switch. Starter solenoid on receiving power operates the starter motor, which makes the engine functional. The alternator produces electric energy for the supply to electrical components while the regulator controls the supply voltage going to different components [15]. The regulator takes care that alternator maintains the battery charged for smooth functioning. The diagram of the starter motor is shown in Figure 4.3.

While designing, optimization of the gear ratio of the pinion to the flywheel ring gear is made so that starter's motor turns more slowly. This feature helps in reduced starter-motor brush wear once the objective is over. Oil-impregnated bushings in the rotating assemblies, are replaced by needle bearings [12]. Stop/start motors have added technologies, which helps in identifying the piston position in cylinders at top-dead-center. This feature helps during starting. With this feature fuel injectors inject the fuel and

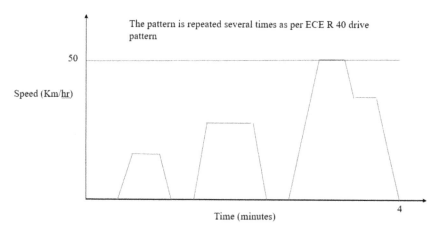

Figure 4.2 EE R-40 drive pattern used for emission test by vehicle manufacturers.

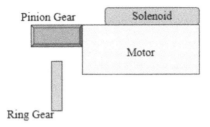

Figure 4.3 Starter motor for engine start and stop system.

Table 4.2 Specifications of the selected vehicle

Overall length 1530 mm	*Engine*
Overall width – 580 mm	Single cylinder, 4 stroke
Ground clearance – 220 mm	Displacement- 110 cc
Overall height – 1080 mm	Max. Power- 8.0 BHP @, 7000 RPM (5.88 KW)
Wheel base – 950 mm	Maximum Torque- 0.9 N-m @ 5000 RPM
Kerb weight – 50 kg	*Suspension*
Starting mechanism	Front – coaxial shock absorber & spring
Kick/electric start	Rear – shock absorber & coaxial spring
Tyre	Transmission type – CVT
Front: 3.50-10-4PR	*Suspension*
Rear: 3.50-10-4PR	Front – leading link with coaxial shock absorber & spring
Electricals – system voltage – 12, DC: head lamp amp – 12V, 35/35W	Rear – single shock absorber & coaxial spring
Fuel tank – capacity: 5.2 liters	*Brake system* – mechanical expanding shoe diameter 130 mm

firing is done in between the rotation of the crank, thus avoiding the wait for a complete revolution.

4.4 EXPERIMENTAL SET UP

The vehicle selected for test has the specifications as given in Table 4.2. The selected vehicle is shown in Figure 4.4 with dimensions in Figure 4.5.

4.5 METHODOLOGY ADOPTED

The system is a fitted two wheeler with a 109.7 cc engine. This type of two wheeler is chosen because a major percentage of two wheelers sold lies in this category. The vehicle is made to run in city conditions of NCR (National Capital Region) for one hour where in the duration of time is noted when

Figure 4.4 Selected vehicle on which the system is fitted.

Figure 4.5 Selected vehicle with dimensions.

the engine is in stop mode. Based on the data received, calculations were made. The complete process is explained with Figure 4.6.

4.6 RESULTS

The vehicle is made to run in the city conditions of Faridabad with moderate traffic. It was observed that during a continuation one hour journey an ideal

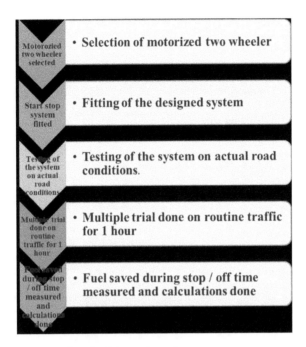

Figure 4.6 Flow diagram of methodology adopted.

average time for stoppage is 9 minutes where the system played its part. The same is presented in Table 4.2 and explained with a graph in Figure 4.7.

If it is assumed that it takes 0.14 liter/h [18] of fuel during idling then the amount of fuel saved is 0.021 liter/h as per the below calculation during idling.

$$= 0.14 * 9 / 60 = 0.021$$

And amount saved during this one hour is Rs 2.058 if the cost of petrol is considered to be Rs 98/litre

$$= 0.021 * 98 = 2.058$$

Now this amount will be directly proportional to the idling time duration for which the vehicle remained stranded in traffic. Although the saving seems to be small, the emissions related to consumption of 0.021 litres of fuel can be prevented [19]. If this system is applied in 50% of 21 Cr [18], MTW running on Indian roads for one hour per day then the saving will be 0.021*105000000 = 2205000 liters of fuel per day. If this is converted into

Table 4.3 Engine stop time measurement in a week when the vehicle was made to run for one hour

Week days	Time in minutes
Monday	12
Tuesday	10
Wednesday	10
Thursday	8
Friday	12
Saturday	6
Sunday	5
Total stop time in a week	63

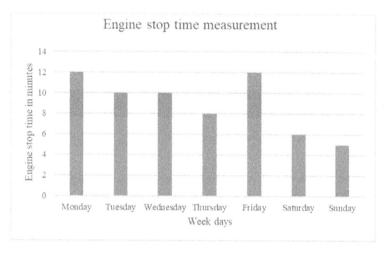

Figure 4.7 Engine stop time measurement in a week.

Rupees while considering the price of petrol to be Rs 98 per liter 21.609 Crore Rs saving for the Indian customers per day. During the complete journey of one hour, the fuel consumed is 0.5 liter by the MTW then the net saving of fuel is 4.2%.

4.7 DISCUSSION

The findings of the study clearly show that there is a reduced running cost for two wheelers using this system. The net saving of fuel is 4.2% when this system is used on the MTW during one hour of driving. This could have happened because of frequent stops on the road due to traffic congestion or traffic signals. When the results were compared with other case studies

[20–22] they are found to be comparable with their results. An improvement of 5.3% was found by Bishop et al. in their study. A lower value of performance is obtained because the developed system stops the MTW after 30 seconds of stoppage at a point.

Limitation of the systems is that, it is beneficial to have this system in the city drive conditions. Its performance values will decrease in countryside road operations because in that condition its usage will decrease.

4.8 CONCLUSION

The two-wheeler engine start and stop system for reducing fuel consumption and emissions is fitted in the MTW. The different systems that need to be redesigned because of this retrofitting were discussed. The designed vehicle was made to run on city roads for one hour and idle duration when the engine is in stop condition was noted. Based on the available data further associated cumulative calculations were done. Based on that it is concluded that although when savings were calculated on a single unit it appears to be small, when a combined effect of taking the MTW numbers on roads were analyzed, the significance of the usage of the start-stop system in two wheelers was found to be impactful. A net saving of 4.2% of fuel was seen with the application of this system. The application of the start-stop feature on MTWs will not only reduce the usage of gasoline but will also help in reducing emissions in Indian cities. Hence, fitting of the stop and start system in MTWs should be encouraged by the government since it will help in reducing country import of petroleum. Also the auto industry should decide and take a decision in making this feature compulsory in the new/future vehicle designs.

REFERENCES

1. Vashist, D., S. Pandey, S. Panwar and J. Nagar, "Analysis of Battery Fire Safety in Electric Vehicles: A Case Study in Indian Context," SAE Technical Paper 2023-28-0024. (2023), https://doi.org/10.4271/2023-28-0024
2. Malik, V. and D. Vashist, "An Analysis of Automotive Industry Standards for Electric Power Train Vehicles," SAE Technical Paper 2022-28-0394. (2022), https://doi.org/10.4271/2022-28-0394
3. Vashist, D and M. Bindra, "Development of a Novel Spiral Duct Particulate Matter Separator for Internal Combustion Engines," *Int. J. Automot. Mech. Eng.* 19(3): 9993–10001 (October 2022), https://doi.org/10.15282/ijame.19.3.2022.11.0771
4. Article HT Auto desk, "India has Over 21 Crore Two Wheelers Nearly 7 Crore Four Wheelers Registered" (4 August 2022), assessed on 25.10.2023 available at https://auto.hindustantimes.com/auto/news/india-has-over-21-crore-two-wheelers-nearly-7-crore-four-wheelers-registered-41659615998470.html

5. Kumar, Ajay, Hari Singh, Parveen Kumar, and Bandar AlMangour, eds. *Handbook of Smart Manufacturing: Forecasting the Future of Industry 4.0.* CRC Press (2023). https://doi.org/10.1201/9781003333760

6. Kumar, Ashwini, Ravi Kant Mittal, and Rajesh Goel, eds. *Waste Recovery and Management: An Approach Toward Sustainable Development Goals.* CRC Press (2023). https://doi.org/10.1201/9781003359784

7. Article, Varta Battery World, "How Automatic Start-Stop Works" (2022), assessed on 25.10.2023 available at https://batteryworld.varta-automotive.com/en-gb/what-is-automatic-start-stop-and-how-does-it-work

8. Article, Hindustan Times, "India's Daily Fuel Consumption Growing Faster Than Global Average" (14 October 2022), assessed on 25.10.2023 available at www.hindustantimes.com/india-news/indias-daily-fuel-consumption-growing-faster-than-global-average-puri-101665772050810.html

9. Article, World population Review (2023), "Oil Consumption by Country 2023" (2023), assessed on 25.10.2023 Available at https://worldpopulationreview.com/country-rankings/oil-consumption-by-country

10. Article, Motorcycling Wikipedia (2023), assessed on 25.10.2023 available at https://en.wikipedia.org/wiki/Motorcycling#:~:text=The%20four%20largest%20motorcycle%20markets,million%20motorcycles%2Fmopeds%20in%202002

11. Palwe, M.V. and P. Kanjalkar. "Development and Validation of Engine Start/Stop Strategy for P2 Hybrid Electric Vehicle" In: Smys, S., Bestak, R., and Rocha, Á. (eds.), *Inventive Computation Technologies.* ICICIT (2019). Lecture Notes in Networks and Systems, vol 98. Springer, Cham. https://doi.org/10.1007/978-3-030-33846-6_7

12. Tekin, M., and M. İhsan Karamangil, "Investigation of the Contribution of Deceleration Fuel Cut-off and Start/Stop Technologies to Fuel Economy by Considering New European Driving Cycle," *Transp. Res. Rec.* 2676(5): 388–397 (2022), https://doi.org/10.1177/03611981211066903

13. Kuang, M. L., "An Investigation of Engine Start-Stop NVH in a Power Split Powertrain Hybrid Electric Vehicle," SAE Technical Paper 2006-01-1500. (2006), https://doi.org/10.4271/2006-01-1500

14. Article, which Car, "How Auto Stop-Start Technology Works," (2018), assessed on 25.10.2023 available at www.whichcar.com.au/car-advice/how-auto-stop-start-technology-works

15. Bishop, J. "An Engine Start/Stop System for Improved Fuel Economy," SAE Technical Paper Series, 2007-01-1777. (2007), https://doi.org/10.4271/2007-01-1777

16. Chen, H. "Control Strategy Research of Engine Smart Start/Stop System for a Micro Car," SAE International, 2013-01-0585. (2013), http://dx.doi.org/10.4271/2013-01-0585

17. Wang, X. "Vehicle System Control for Start-Stop Powertrains with Automatic Transmissions," SAE International, 2013-01-0347. (2013), http://dx.doi.org/10.4271/2013-01-0347

18. Kumar, P.V.P. Anil Singh, Niraj Sharma and Ravi Sekhar Chalumuri, "Evaluation of Idling Fuel Consumption of Vehicles Across Different Cities," *Conference: Recent Advances in Traffic Engg* (2015), available at

www.researchgate.net/publication/318788877_Evaluation_of_Idling_Fuel_
Consumption_of_Vehicles_Across_Different_Cities

19. Mueller, N., S. Strauss, S. Tumback, G. Goh et al., "Next Generation Engine
    Start/Stop Systems: 'Free-Wheeling'," *SAE Int. J. Engines* 4(1):874–887
    (2011), https://doi.org/10.4271/2011-01-0712

20. Huff, S., S. Davis, R. Boundy, and R. Gibson, "Auto Stop-Start Fuel
    Consumption Benefits," SAE Technical Paper 2023-01-0346. (2023), https://
    doi.org/10.4271/2023-01-0346

21. Bishop, J., A. Nedungadi, G. Ostrowski, B. Surampudi et al., "An Engine
    Start/Stop System for Improved Fuel Economy," SAE Technical Paper 2007-
    01-1777. (2007), https://doi.org/10.4271/2007-01-1777

22. Zhang X., H. Liu, C. Mao, J. Shi, G. Meng, J. Wu et al., The Intelligent
    Engine Start-Stop Trigger System Based on the Actual Road Running
    Status. *PLoS One* 16(6): e0253201 (2021). https://doi.org/10.1371/journal.
    pone.0253201

DEFINITIONS/ABBREVIATIONS

MTW   Motorized Two wheeler

RPM   Revolutions per minute

Optimization of electric vehicle lithium-ion battery parameter by using Taguchi methodology

Asif Ahmad¹ and Parveen Kumar²

¹Pranveer Singh Institute of Technology, Kanpur, India
²Department of Mechanical Engineering, Rawal Institute of Engineering and Technology, Faridabad, India

5.1 INTRODUCTION

As greenhouse gas emissions increase, global warming concerns increase, and fossil fuel availability decreases, EVs have become a viable solution to address global environmental challenges and reduce CO_2 emissions. Today, electric vehicles are a focal point for research and development since they reduce atmospheric carbon emissions and play an important role in reducing atmospheric carbon emissions [1, 2]. Components of electric vehicles are shown in Figure 5.1.

A lithium-ion battery pack is the energy source of an electric vehicle, which stores electricity. The electric motor converts electrical energy from the battery into mechanical energy to drive the vehicle. Optimum performance and efficiency are achieved by controlling the flow of electricity between the battery and the motor. To recharge the battery, the charger converts AC power from the grid into DC power. The DC-DC converter adjusts the voltage of the battery to power auxiliary systems [3, 4]. The DC-DC converter adjusts the voltage of the battery to power auxiliary systems. EVs typically have a single-speed transmission, but some use multi-speed transmissions to maximize performance and efficiency. An effective thermal management system ensures that the battery and electric motor are operated at optimal temperatures for maximum efficiency and longevity. The ECU (electric vehicle control unit) is the component that controls and manages various aspects of the electric vehicle, such as the motor power, the battery state, and the charging process. Airbags, collision avoidance systems, stability control, and other safety features are included in the safety systems of the vehicle. With electric power steering, steering assistance is provided without relying on a hydraulic system. This battery pack is protected from environmental factors as well as collisions by the traction battery housing [5,6]. The wheels and tires of the vehicle are critical to the contact with the road and to the overall performance of the vehicle. A vehicle's body and frame make up its structural framework. The vehicle's body and frame are designed to maximize aerodynamics and safety. Visibility and safety are

      DOI: 10.1201/9781003495574-5

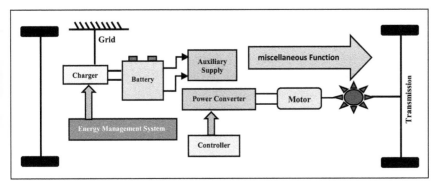

Figure 5.1 Component of electric vehicle.

ensured by exterior lighting, including headlights, taillights, and indicators. An onboard charger manages charging processes and can be connected to a variety of charging stations in the vehicle. Inverter: converts DC power from the battery into AC power for the electric motor, regenerative braking system: when braking, kinetic energy is captured and converted into electrical energy, which is stored in the battery. High-voltage wiring: connects the battery to various components, such as motors and power electronics. HVAC system: heat, venting, and air conditioning that provides passenger comfort and efficiency while being environmentally friendly, user interface: the dashboard, touchscreen, or digital display used by the driver to monitor and control the vehicle. This research study focused on the optimization of electric vehicle battery parameters by using Taguchi methodology to determine the performance of EVs. However, the performance of EVs mainly depends on the selection of input parameters. Some of these parameters are specific energy, specific power, and energy density are input parameters selected for this study. Taguchi methodology has been used for the optimization of input parameters to obtain the optimal combination of input parameters that gives a high range of EV per charge [7]. In the field of experimental design and statistics, particularly in the context of agricultural sciences, Sir Ronald A Fisher, a renowned British statistician and geneticist, made significant contributions. By developing the design of experiments (DOE) method, he revolutionized experimentation and laid the foundation for modern experimental design principles. Typically, DOE is a statistical method of investigating a system or process in which input variables are judged by the significance of their influences, the interactions between input variables, or none of the above [8]. The DOE method can be divided into full factorial design and fractional factorial design. While full factorial design is an important and thorough method of experimental design, it may be time-consuming, especially when a significant number of variables and levels are

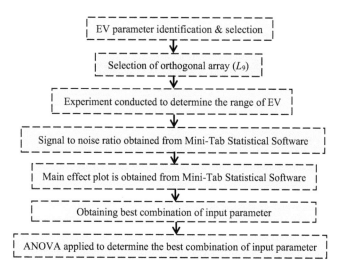

Figure 5.2 Steps of Taguchi methodology.

involved. Although fractional factorial design is generally recognized, it is too complicated, with no universal rules for its use [9]. Considering this difficulty, in the late 1940s, Dr. Genichi Taguchi created the Taguchi technique, a completely novel experimental approach that makes use of a simplified and standardized version of DOE. Various steps of the Taguchi methodology are shown in Figure 5.2 [10, 11].

5.2 OPTIMIZATION TECHNIQUES (TAGUCHI METHODOLOGY)

5.2.1 Selection of input parameter

The performance of EVs is based on the selection of input parameters. However, the selection of input parameters in this study is done after having proper brainstorming and literature [12, 13] review. Specific energy (Wh/kg), specific power (W/kg), and energy density (Wh/L) are three input parameters that were selected based on the literature review as shown in Table 5.1.

5.2.2 Selection of orthogonal array

Mathematical notation for OA is given in equation (5.1) and the formula to identify the number of experiments to be conducted is given in equation (5.2). For all possible iterations of the input parameter as shown in Table 5.2 standard orthogonal arrays give complete information [14,

Table 5.1 Input parameter with their levels

		Levels→		
Parameter ↓	Code	1	2	3
Specific energy (Wh/kg)	A	80	100	120
Specific power (W/kg)	B	1200	1400	1800
Energy density (Wh/L)	C	200	250	300
State of charge (%)	D	50	75	100

Table 5.2 Standard orthogonal array

			Maximum no. of columns at these levels			
Orthogonal array	Number of rows	Maximum no. of factors	2	3	4	5
N_4	4	3	3	–	–	–
N_8	8	7	7	–	–	–
N_9	9	4	–	4	–	–
N_{12}	12	11	11	–	–	–
N_{16}	16	15	15	–	–	–
N'_{16}	16	5	–	–	5	–
N_{18}	18	8	1	7	–	–
N_{25}	25	6	–	–	–	6
N_{27}	27	13	1	13	–	–
N_{32}	32	31	31	–	–	–
N_{32}	32	10	1	–	9	–
N_{36}	36	23	11	12	–	–
N_{36}	36	16	3	13	–	–
N_{50}	50	12	1	–	–	11
N_{54}	54	26	1	25	–	–
N_{64}	64	63	63	–	–	–
N_{64}	64	21	–	–	21	–
N_{81}	81	40	–	40	–	–

Source: [14].

15]. The appropriate orthogonal array may be chosen based on the number of parameters and levels. Four input parameters with three levels each are employed in this experiment, and the appropriate orthogonal array is L_9 is selected, as indicated in Table 5.3.

$$\text{No. of Experiment} = \text{Number of level}^{\text{Number of factor}} \quad (5.1)$$

$$\text{No. of Experiment} = (\text{Number of Level} - 1) \times \text{Number of factor} + 1 (5.2)$$

Table 5.3 L₉ orthogonal array

	Input response				Output response R
Experiment no.	Parameter A	Parameter B	Parameter C	Parameter D	
1	1	1	1	1	Response 1
2	1	2	2	2	Response 2
3	1	3	3	3	Response 3
4	2	1	2	3	Response 4
5	2	2	3	1	Response 5
6	2	3	1	2	Response 6
7	3	1	3	2	Response 7
8	3	2	1	3	Response 8
9	3	3	2	1	Response 9

Orthogonal arrays are fractional factorial designs for studies where just a portion of all potential combinations of variables are taken into account. An extensive range of operating conditions is covered by this fraction. Using fractional designs reduces the number of experiments and provides complete information about all variables that might affect performance. As per OA L₉, the range of electric vehicles is measured as shown in Table 5.3.

5.2.3 Signal-to-noise ratio

S/N ratio indicates the sensitivity of signal (quality characteristic) to noise (variation and deviation in factors) and, as a consequence, it is commonly used as an objective function to determine optimal operating conditions, since in this study we require the best combination of input parameter for the best range of the electric vehicle. Three types of S/N ratio are given in equation (5.3), equation (5.4) and equation (5.5), respectively [16]. The most suitable function for this study is the larger, the better as shown in equation (2.4). The S/N value for each factor is shown in Table 5.4. It is depicted that the highest value S/N ratio is at experiment number 3 as shown in Figure 5.3.

(a) **Smaller-is-better:** a quality characteristic value can range from zero to infinity, but it should be as small as possible.

$$\text{S/N Ratio}_{\text{smaller-is-better}} = -10\log.1/b\left[\sum_{i=0}^{n} x_1^2\right] \qquad (5.3)$$

Table 5.4 Output response as per L₉ orthogonal array

Experiment no.	Input response				Output response R	S/N ratio
	Parameter A	Parameter B	Parameter C	Parameter D		
I	80	1200	200	50	76	37.61
2	80	1400	250	75	86	38.69
3	80	1800	300	100	108	40.66
4	100	1200	250	100	106	40.51
5	100	1400	300	50	98	39.82
6	100	1800	200	75	102	40.17
7	120	1200	300	75	96	39.64
8	120	1400	200	100	103	40.25
9	120	1800	250	50	93	39.37

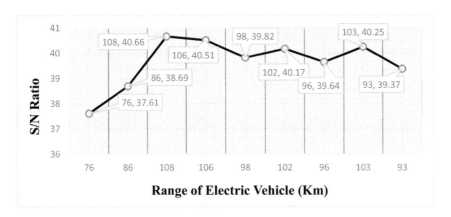

Figure 5.3 Range versus S/N ratio.

(b) **The larger-the-better:** a quality characteristic value can range from zero to infinity, but it should be as maximum as possible.

$$\text{S/N Ratio}_{\text{larger-the-better}} = -10\log.1/b\left[\sum_{i=0}1/x_1^2\right] \quad (5.4)$$

(c) **Nominal the best:** a quality characteristic value can range from zero to infinity, but it should be nominal.

$$\text{S/N Ratio} = -10\log.\left[\sum_{i=0}\bar{x}_i^2/s^2\right] \quad (5.5)$$

Here,

b = number of trials

x_i = measured value

$\bar{x}$ = mean of the measured value

s = standard deviation

5.2.4 Response table

After calculating the S/N ratio for each experiment, the average S/N value for each parameter and level is calculated, as shown in Table 5.5. To calculate the average response for parameter A, equations (5.6), (5.7), and (5.8) are used, respectively [16]. Similarly average response is calculated for parameters B, C, and D. Table 5.6 and Table 5.7 represent the response table for the S/N ratio and means. The delta value of each parameter is the difference between the maximum value and the minimum value of each response. The maximum delta value from the response table of the S/N ratio is 1.54 for parameter D, i.e., state of charge (%), therefore as per delta value state of charge (%) is at rank 1, specific energy (Wh/kg) at rank 2, specific power (W/kg) at rank 3 and specific density (Wh/L) at rank 4. This shows that the state of charge (%) influences the range of electric vehicles more as compared to the other three parameters.

$$S/N_{A1} = \frac{S/N\ 1 + S/N\ 2 + S/N\ 3}{3} \tag{5.6}$$

$$S/N_{A2} = \frac{S/N\ 4 + S/N\ 5 + S/N\ 6}{3} \tag{5.7}$$

$$S/N_{A3} = \frac{S/N7 + S/N\ 8 + S/N\ 9}{3} \tag{5.8}$$

Table 5.5 Average response

Levels	A	B	C	D
1	S/N_{A1}	S/N_{B1}	S/N_{C1}	S/N_{D1}
2	S/N_{A2}	S/N_{B2}	S/N_{C2}	S/N_{D2}
3	S/N_{A3}	S/N_{B3}	S/N_{C3}	S/N_{D3}
Deviation	$\Delta_{max} - \Delta_{min}$	$\Delta_{max} - \Delta_{min}$	$\Delta_{max} - \Delta_{min}$	$\Delta_{max} - \Delta_{min}$
Rank	**R1**	**R2**	**R3**	**R4**

Table 5.6 Response table for S/N ratios

Level	A	B	C	D
1	38.99	39.26	39.35	38.94
2	40.17	39.59	39.52	39.50
3	39.76	40.07	40.05	40.48
Delta	1.18	0.81	0.70	1.54
Rank	2	3	4	1

Table 5.7 Response table for mean

Level	A	B	C	D
1	90.00	92.67	93.67	89.00
2	102.00	95.67	95.00	94.67
3	97.33	101.00	100.67	105.67
Delta	12.00	8.33	7.00	16.67
Rank	2	3	4	1

5.2.5 Main effect plot

Figure 5.4 depicts the effect of the lithium-ion battery input parameter. Observations indicate that when the value of the specific energy (Wh/kg) increases, the range of an electric vehicle increases and then decreases as the value of the specific energy (Wh/kg) increases, indicating a high degree of impedance between the rider and the vehicle. An electric vehicle's range is significantly influenced by the specific energy of its battery, which is measured in watt-hours per kilogram (Wh/kg). Batteries are categorized according to their specific energy, which is the amount of energy they can store relative to their weight.

A battery with a higher specific energy can travel longer distances on a single charge, which can reduce the reliance on charging infrastructure, especially in areas with few charging stations. As a result, EVs with high-specific energy batteries can be used by a wider range of consumers. In addition, the specific energy of an electric vehicle also affects its overall weight and efficiency. Higher specific energy batteries can provide the same amount of energy while being lighter. The weight of the battery pack is reduced, resulting in a lighter vehicle, which is more efficient and maneuverable. By requiring less material, it can also reduce manufacturing costs. It is observed from Figure 5.4 that the range of electric vehicles increases with the increase in specific power (W/kg). As the specific power of the battery in an electric vehicle plays a significant role in determining the range of the vehicle and its overall performance, battery-specific power is an important aspect to consider. In batteries, specific power refers to how much power they can

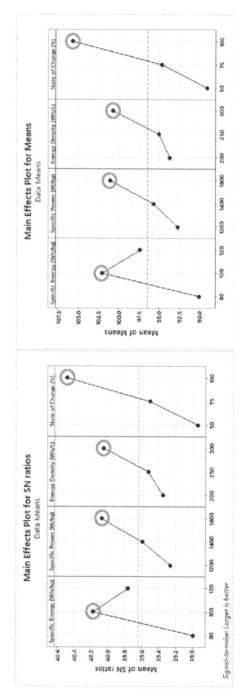

Figure 5.4 Main effect plot for S/N ratio and means.

deliver relative to their weight or volume. The unit of measurement is typically watts per kilogram (W/kg) or watts per liter (W/L). It is possible to accelerate rapidly and improve performance with batteries that have high specific power due to their ability to discharge energy quickly. For electric vehicles, instant torque is one of their key advantages. With higher specific power batteries, EVs can accelerate faster, making them more appealing to consumers. An electric vehicle's driving range is directly affected by its power. Higher specific power batteries can deliver more power per unit of weight or volume, meaning they provide the energy necessary to propel the vehicle farther. With higher specific power batteries, EVs can travel longer distances on a single charge. The performance, range, and overall usability of an electric vehicle depend on the specific power of its battery. Figure 5.4 indicates that the range of the electric vehicle increases with the increase in energy density (W/kg). When it comes to the significance of battery performance in electric vehicles, energy density, measured in watt-hours per kilogram (Wh/kg), is an important parameter. A battery's energy density is a measure of how much energy it can store to its weight. A higher energy density battery can reduce EVs' environmental impact over their lifetime. Potential EV buyers benefit from a longer range due to high energy density batteries. Consumer confidence in EVs increases when they know they can cover substantial distances without recharging. Batteries with a high energy density can store more energy than batteries with a low energy density. With high energy density batteries, EVs can travel further on a single charge. Electric vehicles are more appealing and practical when their range is longer.

Figure 5.5 indicates that the range of electric vehicle increases with the increase in state of charge (W/kg). In an electric vehicle, the state of charge (SOC) describes how much energy the battery currently has available compared to its maximum capacity. Whenever drivers encounter charging stations or opportunities to charge, the SOC helps them decide whether they should charge. They may choose to skip charging if the SOC is relatively high, saving time and energy.

As a result of its direct correlation with how much driving range the EV still has, the SOC is an essential indicator for drivers. Drivers can estimate how far they can travel before they need to recharge by checking their SOC. For battery packs to last longer, it is also crucial to manage the SOC. A battery can degrade faster if it is operated continuously at extremely high or low SOC levels. To preserve battery health, EVs typically have systems to prevent overcharging (at high SOC) and deep discharging (at low SOC). It is easier for drivers to plan their driving strategy when they know the SOC. It is up to them whether to drive more conservatively to extend the remaining range or to drive more freely if they have a larger SOC buffer. As a result of this flexibility, drivers can adapt to their particular needs and circumstances.

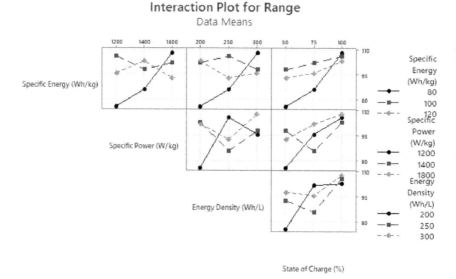

Figure 5.5 Intersection matrix between the significant parameter.

Table 5.4 indicates the average response for the S/N ratio for various parameters. At different levels of parameter, *A* (specific energy, Wh/kg), parameter *B* (specific power, Wh/kg), parameter *C* (energy density, Wh/L), and parameter *D* (state of charge, %), the highest S/N ratios are achieved. A S/N ratio of 40.17 is obtained at level 2 for parameter *A*, 40.07 at level 3 for parameter *B*, 40.05 at level 3 for parameter *C*, and 40.48 at level 4 for parameter *D*. Therefore, optimum combination of input parameter for electric vehicle range were found to be specific energy 100 Wh/kg, specific power 1800 Wh/kg, energy density 300 Wh/L and state of charge 100% by using Taguchi methodology. This predicted combination from the Taguchi methodology was represented as *A2B3C3D3*.

Figure 5.4 is the intersection matrix between the significant parameters. It is depicted from the intersection plot that the electric vehicle range is influenced by the state of charge of the battery. The intersection between specific energy and specific power is complex and has an impact on electric vehicle range, it is depicted that when specific energy is at 80 Wh/kg and as specific power is increasing range of electric vehicles is also increasing. The intersection of specific power and energy density shows that when specific power is at 1800 W/kg, an increase in energy density first decreases the electric vehicle range and then increases. The intersection between energy density and state of charge shows that when the energy density is at 300 Wh/L as energy density is increasing electric vehicle range slightly decreases then increases. Therefore, a significant impact of the state of charge on the electric vehicle range has been seen.

5.3 CONFIRMATORY TEST

After determining the ideal parameter values, the following step is to forecast and evaluate the quality performance characteristics using the best parametric combination. The estimated value of the electric vehicle range is calculated by using equation (5.9). The average value of the S/N ratio is 39.64, and the S/N ratio for A2, B3, C3, and D3 is 40.17, 40.07, 40.05, and 40.48, respectively, obtained from Table 5.6. The predicted S/N ratio value is 41.84. The experimental value S/N ratio is 40.66 obtained from Table 5.8.

$$\Delta = \Delta_m + \sum_{i=0}^{0}\Delta_{im} - \Delta_m \tag{5.9}$$

Here,

Δ – predicted S/N value

Δ_m – is the total average S/N ratio

Δ_m – is the S/N ratio at the optimal level

5.4 ANOVA

ANOVA was first introduced by Sir Ronald A. Fisher in the early 20th century. Analysis of variance is used to determine the percentage contribution of each input parameter. This is based on the calculation of the S/N ratio. ANOVA is also used to quantify significant and non-significant parameters based on F value. Table 5.9 and Figure 5.6. Summarizes the ANOVA table and ANOVA result, respectively. The parameters included in ANOVA are probability value (P-value), statistical value (F), mean squares (MS), sum of squares (SS), and degree of freedom (DF) [17, 18]. In this study, the parameters used were specific energy (Wh/kg), specific power (W/kg), energy density (Wh/L), and state of charge (%). The effect of this parameter on the range was investigated using the ANOVA test [19]. The ANOVA test results are presented in Table 5.10. Based on the ANOVA test, the percentage contribution of each parameter was determined. The parameter that has the highest effect on the range of electric vehicles is the state of charge (%) because it has the highest value P-value of 48.07. The next parameter with significant effect was specific energy (Wh/kg) having a P-value of 28.21, followed by specific power (W/kg) having a P-value of 13.26, and energy density (Wh/L) having a P-value of 10.45.

Table 5.8 Confirmation test for range of electric vehicles

Parameters					S/N ratio		Range	
					Predicted	Experiment	Predicted	Experiment
Code	A	B	C	D				
Name	Specific energy (Wh/kg)	Specific power (W/kg)	Energy density (Wh/L)	State of charge (%)				
Optimum level	2	3	3	3				
Optimum value	100 Wh/kg	1800 W/kg	300 Wh/L	100 %	41.84	40.66	108	107

Table 5.9 ANOVA (analysis of variance)

	SS	df	MS	F	Significance
Group between	$SS_{between}$	$df_{between}$	$MS_{between}$	$\dfrac{MS_{between}}{MS_{within}}$	P-value
Group within	SS_{within}	df_{within}	MS_{within}		
Total	$SS_{between} + SS_{within}$	$df_{between} + df_{within}$			

Source: [17,18].

Notes:

$$SS = \text{square deviation} = \frac{\sum(x_i - \bar{x})2}{n-1}$$

$$MS = \text{mean square} = \frac{SS}{df}$$

df = degree of freedom = $k - 1$
k = level of parameter

Table 5.10 ANOVA result to determine significant input parameter

Source	DF	Adj SS	Adj MS	F-value	P-value
Specific energy (Wh/kg)	2	2.13754	2.13754	1.06877	28.21
Specific power (W/kg)	2	1.00469	1.00469	0.50235	13.26
Energy density (Wh/L)	2	0.79187	0.79187	0.39593	10.45
State of charge (%)	2	3.64240	3.64240	1.82120	48.07
Total	8	7.57651			

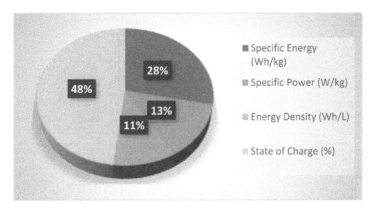

Figure 5.6 ANOVA result.

5.5 REGRESSION MODELING

We developed predictive mathematical models for the dependent variables of electric vehicle range based on specific energy, specific power, energy density, and state of charge using linear regression analysis in Minitab 19.0 software. Equation (5.10) shows the predicted equation obtained from regression analysis [20], where A, B, C, and D represent specific energy, specific power, energy density, and state of charge, respectively.

Range = 15.4 + 0.183 specific energy (Wh/kg) + 0.01381 specific power (W/kg) + 0.0700 energy density (Wh/L) + 0.333 state of charge (%) (5.10)

The fitness and adequacy of the model were verified by the determination coefficient (R^2), which varies from 0 to 1. The R^2 is close to 0, which suggests that independent variables only explain a small part of the variance. Whenever the R^2 is close to 1, it means that the independent variables account for a large portion of the variance in the dependent variable. In this study R^2 was calculated to be 0.8065, indicating that 80.65% of the sample variation in the electric vehicle range was attributed to independent variables. Figure 5.7 shows a normal probability plot where residual is the difference between the observed response and predicted response.

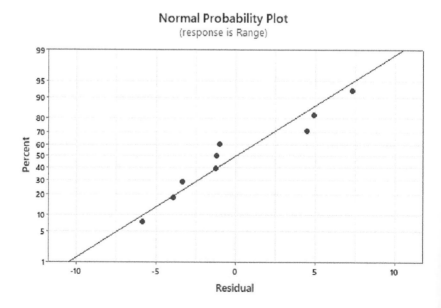

Figure 5.7 Normal probability plot.

Table 5.11 Confirmation result from the developed model

A	B	C	D	Ex. value (range)	Predicted value	Residual	% Error
80	1200	200	50	76	77.2619	−1.2619	1.6604
80	1400	250	75	86	91.8571	−5.8571	6.8106
80	1800	300	100	108	109.214	−1.2143	1.1243
100	1200	250	100	106	101.095	4.90476	4.62713
100	1400	300	50	98	90.6905	7.30952	7.4587
100	1800	200	75	102	97.5476	4.45238	4.36508
120	1200	300	75	96	99.9286	−3.9286	4.0923
120	1400	200	100	103	104.024	−1.0238	0.994
120	1800	250	50	93	96.381	−3.381	3.6354

It is depicted from the figure that all the points are well distributed along the straight line, which is known as a line of perfect fit. The normal probability plot of the residuals shows that the errors are distributed normally in a straight line. Therefore, there is adequate correction between predicted values and the experimental value, which indicates that the data is well-fitted with the model [20]. The adequacy of the model was further checked by conducting the experiment and the result of the experiment is shown in Table 5.11.

5.6 RESULT AND DISCUSSION

1. This work investigated the applicability of the Taguchi method to determine a set of battery parameters to produce an effective electric vehicle range.
2. The Taguchi methodology was suitable to determine the most effective parameter that influences electric vehicle range.
3. The optimum combination of input conduction for obtaining more electric vehicle range was found to be state of charge (%) at rank 1, specific energy (Wh/kg) at rank 2, specific power (W/kg) at rank 3, and specific density (Wh/L) at rank 4.
4. From the ANOVA table, it has been determined that the state of charge is the most influencing parameter giving a percentage contribution of 48.07%. From the regression mathematical model, a close agreement was found between predicted values and experimental values.
5. The adequacy of the mathematical model was validated by the normal probability plot, which shows that predicted values and experimental values are close to the line of perfect fit.

6. Future scope, Genichi Taguchi developed a robust optimization technique known for its applications in quality improvement and robust design. Taguchi's method is powerful on its own, but combining it with other optimization methods can enhance its effectiveness. Numerical simulation, gray relational analysis (GRA), principal component analysis (PCA), and genetic algorithms are some of these approaches.

REFERENCES

[1] Annamalai, M. C., and N. Amutha Prabha. "A Comprehensive Review on Isolated and Non-Isolated Converter Configuration and Fast Charging Technology: For Battery and Plug in Hybrid Electric Vehicle." *Heliyon* 9, no. 8 (2023): e18808. https://doi.org/https://doi.org/10.1016/j.heliyon.2023. e18808.

[2] Lee, Jae Hyun, Minyoung Cho, Gil Tal, and Scott Hardman. "Do Plug-in Hybrid Adopters Switch to Battery Electric Vehicles (and Vice Versa)?" *Transportation Research Part D: Transport and Environment* 119 (2023): 103752. https://doi.org/https://doi.org/10.1016/ j.trd.2023.103752.

[3] Nabi, Md Nurun, Biplob Ray, Fazlur Rashid, Wisam Al Hussam, and S. M. Muyeen. "Parametric Analysis and Prediction of Energy Consumption of Electric Vehicles Using Machine Learning." *Journal of Energy Storage* 72 (2023): 108226. https://doi.org/https://doi.org/10.1016/ j.est.2023.108226.

[4] Theilen, Bernd and Françeska Tomori. "Regulatory Commitment Versus Non-Commitment: Electric Vehicle Adoption under Subsidies and Emission Standards." *Resource and Energy Economics* 74 (2023): 101388. https:// doi.org/https://doi.org/10.1016/j.reseneco.2023.101388.

[5] Dwivedi, Pankaj Prasad, and Dilip Kumar Sharma. "Evaluation and Ranking of Battery Electric Vehicles by Shannon's Entropy and Topsis Methods." *Mathematics and Computers in Simulation* 212 (2023): 457–74. https://doi. org/10.1016/j.matcom.2023.05.013.

[6] Sarvaiya, Shradhdha, Sachin Ganesh, and Bin Xu. "Comparative Analysis of Hybrid Vehicle Energy Management Strategies with Optimization of Fuel Economy and Battery Life." *Energy* 228 (2021). https://doi.org/10.1016/ j.energy.2021.120604.

[7] Sun, Jinghua and Josef Kainz. "Optimization of Hybrid Pulse Power Characterization Profile for Equivalent Circuit Model Parameter Identification of Li-Ion Battery Based on Taguchi Method." *Journal of Energy Storage* 70 (2023). https://doi.org/10.1016/j.est.2023.108034.

[8] Park, Keun and Jong-Ho Ahn. "Design of Experiment Considering Two-Way Interactions and Its Application to Injection Molding Processes with Numerical Analysis." *Journal of Materials Processing Technology* 146, no. 2 (2004): 221–27. https://doi.org/https://doi.org/10.1016/j.jmatpro tec.2003.10.020.

[9] Fei, Ng Chin, Nik Mizamzul Mehat, and Shahrul Kamaruddin. "Practical Applications of Taguchi Method for Optimization of Processing Parameters for Plastic Injection Moulding: A Retrospective Review." *ISRN Industrial Engineering* 2013 (2013): 462174. https://doi.org/10.1155/2013/462174.

[10] Garud, Kunal Sandip, and Moo-Yeon Lee. "Grey Relational Based Taguchi Analysis on Heat Transfer Performances of Direct Oil Spray Cooling System for Electric Vehicle Driving Motor." *International Journal of Heat and Mass Transfer* 201 (2023): 123596. https://doi.org/https://doi.org/10.1016/j.ijh eatmasstransfer.2022.123596.

[11] Thakre, Sachin, Achal Shahare and G. K. Awari. "Performance Optimization of the Disc Brake System of Electric Two-Wheeler Using Taguchi Approach." *Materials Today: Proceedings* 62 (2022): 1861–67. https://doi.org/https:// doi.org/10.1016/j.matpr.2022.01.010.

[12] Chavan, Santosh, B. Venkateswarlu, R. Prabakaran, Mohammad Salman, Sang Woo Joo, Gyu Sang Choi, and Sung Chul Kim. "Thermal Runaway and Mitigation Strategies for Electric Vehicle Lithium-Ion Batteries Using Battery Cooling Approach: A Review of the Current Status and Challenges." *Journal of Energy Storage* 72 (2023): 108569. https://doi.org/https://doi.org/ 10.1016/j.est.2023.108569.

[13] Selvaraj, Vedhanayaki and Indragandhi Vairavasundaram. "A Comprehensive Review of State of Charge Estimation in Lithium-Ion Batteries Used in Electric Vehicles." *Journal of Energy Storage* 72 (2023): 108777. https://doi. org/https://doi.org/10.1016/j.est.2023.108777.

[14] Ahmad, Asif. *Application of Taguchi Method in Optimization of Pulsed TIG Welding Process Parameter.* Intechopen Limited (2020), http://dx.doi. org/10.5772/intechopen.93974

[15] Kacker, R. N., E. S. Lagergren, and J. J. Filliben. "Taguchi's Orthogonal Arrays Are Classical Designs of Experiments." *Journal of Research of the National Institute of Standards and Technology* 96, no. 5 (Sep-Oct 1991):– 91. https://doi.org/10.6028/jres.096.034.

[16] Ahmad, Asif, and Shahnawaj Alam. "Parametric Optimization of Tig Welding Using Response Surface Methodology." *Materials Today: Proceedings* 18 (2019): 3071–79. https://doi.org/https://doi.org/ 10.1016/j.matpr.2019.07.179.

[17] Başar, Canan Akmil, Aydan Aksoğan Korkmaz, Yunus Önal, and Tuğba Utku. "Evaluation of Optimum Carbonization Conditions of the Blended Domestic Polymeric Waste, Biomass and Lignite in the Presence of Catalyst by Taguchi and Anova Optimization Analysis." *Journal of Hazardous Materials Advances* 8 (2022): 100164. https://doi.org/https://doi.org/ 10.1016/j.hazadv.2022.100164.

[18] Chaudhary, Neeru and Sarbjit Singh. "Multi-Objective Optimization of Friction Stir Spot Welded Al 6061-T6 Incorporated with Silicon Carbide Using Hybrid Grey Rational Analysis-Taguchi Technique." *Materials Today: Proceedings* (2022). https://doi.org/https://doi.org/10.1016/ j.matpr.2022.12.086.

[19] Anggoro, P. W., Y. Purharyono, Abet A. Anthony, M. Tauviqirrahman, A. P. Bayuseno, and Jamari. "Optimisation of Cutting Parameters of New

Material Orthotic Insole Using a Taguchi and Response Surface Methodology Approach." *Alexandria Engineering Journal* 61, no. 5 (2022): 3613–32. https://doi.org/10.1016/j.aej.2021.08.083.

[20] Ezekannagha, Chinyere B., Callistus N. Ude, and Okechukwu D. Onukwuli. "Optimization of the Methanolysis of Lard Oil in the Production of Biodiesel with Response Surface Methodology." *Egyptian Journal of Petroleum* 26, no. 4 (2017): 1001–11. https://doi.org/10.1016/j.ejpe.2016.12.004.

Chapter 6

Energizing the future
Electric vehicle charging infrastructure, integration, and policy perspectives

K.R. Ritu,¹ A.K.Wadhwani,² Ajay Kumar,³ and Parveen Kumar⁴

¹Electrical and Electronics Engineering Department, UIT RGPV Bhopal, India
²Electrical and Electronics Engineering Department, MITS Gwalior, India
³Department of Mechanical Engineering, School of Engineering & Technology, JECRC University, Jaipur, India
⁴Department of Mechanical Engineering, Rawal Institute of Engineering and Technology, Faridabad, India

6.1 INTRODUCTION

The transition to electric vehicles (EVs) has emerged as a critical transformation in the ever-changing environment of modern transportation, with the potential to improve daily commutes while reducing emissions. The complicated network of electric vehicle charging infrastructure—a complex interaction of sustainability, policy, and technology—lies at the core of this significant development. As seasoned professionals in this area, we set out on an academic investigation to carefully examine and analyze the many aspects of EV charging infrastructure.

Without a doubt, the goal of our research is to perform a thorough evaluation and analysis of all the different aspects of EV charging infrastructure are unequivocal: to conduct an exhaustive examination and analysis of the various dimensions of EV charging infrastructure.

This includes delving deeply into the classification of charging stations, the complexities of charging technologies, the seamless integration of electric cars (EVs) with the power grid, as well as the governmental stances that encourage this rapidly altering environment.

We start our foundational work with a thorough examination of the literature, gleaned from scholarly studies, industry reports, and other publications. This thorough analysis forms the basis upon which our analytical framework is laboriously constructed [1].

Using a strict comparative analytical approach, we dissect important subtopics. These include a categorization of charging stations, an extensive analysis of charging technologies—ranging from wireless power transmission to conductive and inductive power transfer—and a look at the novel idea of battery swap stations [2, 3].

DOI: 10.1201/9781003495574-6

We explore the subtleties of legislative incentives, the critical importance of control and communication infrastructure, and the difficulties of connection types for both direct current (DC) and alternating current (AC) charging [4].

We continue our exploration of the topic of sustainable transportation by looking into how EVs and renewable energy sources may work together harmoniously. In the context of EV charging, we carefully examine power interface modes and their cooperative interaction with renewable energy. In addition, we evaluate the extensive effects of EV integration on the grid, highlighting the urgent requirement for renewable energy sources.

We routinely examine the nuances of policy analysis as perceptive observers of policy environments.

This involves identifying relevant laws and regulations, doing a thorough assessment of how well they work to promote EV charging infrastructure, and having a thoughtful conversation about the implications of these policies for future legislation.

We conclude our academic journey with a look ahead at new developments in the field of EV charging infrastructure. We thoroughly investigate market trends, technology developments, and sustainability programs, compiling our results into a coherent and perceptive story.

Essentially, our chapter functions as a carefully constructed introduction, offering an academic starting point for the subsequent investigation—a voyage that portrays an all-encompassing picture of EV charging infrastructure, filtered via the sophisticated lens of seasoned professionals. When taken as a whole, these observations provide not just a picture of the current state of affairs but also a calculated path towards an electric future in which information drives the change in our transportation system.

6.2 LITERATURE REVIEW

For an in-depth understanding of EV charging infrastructure, we reviewed academic chapters, industry reports, and relevant publications.

The use of a passive balancer in the energy sector oversight of contemplating EVs is discussed in [5]. EVs and charge points are assessed to examine the output strength of PVs as well. We consider the architecture in topology, EV-PVs that convert, and the five amplification methods in relation to enhancement of the program. Charge levels are shown, along with the range of emotions they portray and the car coil detection technique. In this chapter there is a description of the V2G technology along with the intelligent grid system for transportation.

The characteristics of 17 EVs [6] are compared and an analysis was carried out regarding the countries using the most popular EVs. Five aspects were considered and three charging techniques were investigated for finding the optimum site of charging stations, the infrastructure of charging stations, including decentralized and centralized architectures and their control, are presented. The three charging methods are BSS, CC, and WPT and its various connector protocols are investigated. In this chapter, the positive and negative impacts of integrating EVs with the grid along with the role of aggregators and the role of distributors on EVGI are also discussed.

In this chapter [7], the investigation of converted topology's comprehensive analysis of the EV manufacturing projects as well as patents is performed; there is also a detailed analysis on the charging station standard. For fast charging and discharging, the application of GaN and SiC in the converters is presented.

In this chapter [8], the role of DER is discussed and the integration of the grid with the distributed energy resources along with the data analysis is dealt with. Distributed resources are considered challenges and their solutions are discussed: the challenges that the EVs are facing, which include the economic, the social, and the different policies, are compared. The market shares from 2015 to 2019 of the various countries using EVs are shown. Charging standards are listed from the 13 articles in this chapter and a discussion on the different aspects of control, including disharmonic and harmonic methods, and the architecture of charging controls was carried out. The highlight of the study was the integration of a distributed network with the distributed resources.

The technical characteristics of EV models are compared in this chapter [9], and an improvement is investigated for the off-board charger (EVs and IPT), as the specific protocols for each EVs is addressed. Description of DC-to-DC converter and AC-to-DC converter topologies is presented to stage on-board charger power factor characters, and integrated on-board chargers were discussed. The effect of the charging stations on the grid, the stability of the current and the harmonics, and the demand/supply and assets are discussed in this chapter. Charging standards are also discussed and we address a few cases on which researchers focus, such as vehicle to grid technology off wood charging.

6.3 TYPE OF ELECTRIC VEHICLE CHARGING STATION (EVCS)

It is great to see that you are familiar with the three main categories of electric vehicles (EVs) based on their source of propulsion, as mentioned by [10] and [11]. Let us discuss these categories in more detail:

Hybrid electric vehicles (HEVs): HEVs combine an internal combustion engine (ICE) with an electric propulsion system. These cars may run solely on electricity, solely on gasoline, or a mix of the two. In comparison to conventional gasoline-powered cars, the combination of the electric motor and the gasoline engine improves fuel economy, lowers pollutants, and, in certain circumstances, extends driving ranges. If you are not ready to go entirely to electric vehicles, HEVs are an excellent intermediate technology.

Plug-in electric vehicles (PEVs): Plug-in hybrid electric vehicles (PHEVs) and battery electric vehicles (BEVs) are the two main subcategories of PEVs.

Battery electric vehicles (BEVs): BEVs are entirely electric automobiles that run on electric motors and rechargeable batteries. They only use energy for propulsion and have zero tailpipe emissions. The car must be recharged at an electric charging station or at home with a home charger when the battery runs low. BEVs are renowned for being environmentally friendly and sustainable.

Plug-in hybrid electric vehicles (PHEVs): PHEVs combine a gasoline engine and an electric propulsion system. Their driving range is restricted while using solely electricity; beyond that, the gasoline engine takes over to increase range. PHEVs provide a balance between traditional gasoline and electric power by having the option to run on electricity for short trips and convert to gasoline for longer ones.

Fuel cell electric vehicles (FCEVs): Fuel cell electric vehicles, or FCEVs, produce power internally using a fuel cell system. These cars run on hydrogen fuel, which is chemically mixed with oxygen to create electricity. The only byproducts that these cars release are heat and water vapor. Like BEVs, FCEVs are thought of as a zero-emission substitute and are especially promising for heavy-duty and long-range applications.

6.4 CHARGING TECHNOLOGY FOR ELECTRIC VEHICLES

6.4.1 Different levels of charging EV

6.4.1.1 Level 1

This charging, also referred to as '110V charging,' is the most basic and gradual way to charge an electric car (EV). A 110–120-volt AC common home electrical outlet is used for this purpose. The major features of level 1 charging are as follows: In [12]

1. Charging rate: level 1 charging has a sluggish rate of delivery, usually achieving a range of two to five miles per hour. This implies that, depending on the efficiency and battery capacity of the car, you may get an extra 10 to 30 miles of range if you keep your EV plugged in overnight.
2. Equipment: a typical home electrical outlet is all that is needed for level 1 charging. No further equipment is needed.

To connect the EV to the outlet, use the portable charging wire that usually comes with it. Sometimes, these cables are referred to as 'trickle chargers.'

3. Accessibility: since conventional electrical outlets are present in almost every home, level 1 charging is fairly accessible. This makes it a practical choice for EV owners who want a simple and straightforward method of charging their cars.

4. Charging at home: level 1 charging is mostly meant for usage at home. To guarantee that their EVs have a full or almost full battery every morning, the majority of EV owners use level 1 charging to top off their vehicles overnight. This technique works well for everyday commutes, but it is not the best for quickly replenishing a severely down battery.

5. Charging time: depending on the size of the EV's battery, the amount of time needed for a complete charge using level 1 charging might vary greatly. For instance, a standard EV with a 200-mile range may require 20 to 40 hours for a level 1 charge to be completed.

6. Limitations: level 1 charging is impractical for those who need a fully charged battery rapidly or for extended excursions. Those who can charge their cars overnight and travel short distances on a daily basis are the greatest candidates. Furthermore, not all EV models may be able to utilize level 1 charging, therefore it is important to review the specs of the EV and the included charging cable.

7. Cost: since level 1 charging does not require any new infrastructure and just utilizes regular household outlets, it is quite economical. However, because of its sluggish charging rate, if used frequently, it can result in increased power expenses.

6.4.1.2 Level 2

Electric vehicle owners frequently choose level 2 charging, whether at home or at public charging stations, as it is a major improvement over level 1 charging in terms of charging speed. The specifics of level 2 pricing are as follows [12,13]:

1. Charging rate: 240 volts AC is the operating voltage for level 2 charging, which offers a quicker charging rate than level 1. Depending on the EV and the charger's power output, it usually provides 10 to 20 miles of range each hour.

   Because of its significantly higher charging speed compared to level 1, it is a viable choice for both home and public charging.

2. Equipment: an electrician is needed to install a wall-mounted or specialized EV charging station for level 2 charging. These units come

with specific connections that work with the majority of EVs, such as type 2 in Europe and J1772, in North America. You will also want a properly fitted 240-volt circuit in addition to the charging station.

3. Accessibility: there are many places to find level 2 charging stations, including as public charging networks, businesses, and home installations. They are becoming more and more frequent to see at retail malls, parking garages, and along roads.

   This means that it is considerably faster than level 1, making it a practical option for both home and public charging.

4. Equipment: level 2 charging requires a dedicated EV charging station or wall-mounted unit, which is installed by an electrician. These units are equipped with specialized connectors, such as J1772 in North America or type 2 in Europe, which are compatible with most EVs. In addition to the charging station, you will need a professionally installed 240-volt circuit.

5. Accessibility: level 2 charging stations can be found in various locations, including public charging networks, workplaces, and residential installations. They are an increasingly common sight in parking garages, shopping centers, and along highways.

6. Installing level 2 chargers in their homes is a popular choice for EV owners. You may fully recharge your EV over night or throughout the working day thanks to the expediency of quicker charging that this offers. To ensure a safe and correct installation, installing a level 2 charger at home usually involves hiring a professional electrician.

7. Charging time: the amount of time needed for a complete charge with level 2 charging is contingent upon the EV's battery capacity and the power output of the charging station. Generally speaking, level 2 charging is appropriate for daily charging needs and can take several hours to overnight.

8. Cost: depending on the manufacturer, features, and installation requirements, a level 2 charging station's price might change. Because it is quicker and more energy-efficient than level 1 charging, it could save money over time.

9. Advantages: since level 2 charging strikes a compromise between convenience and speed, it is feasible for the majority of EV owners. It is ideal for regular commutes, and finding a location to top off your EV while on the road is made simple by the abundance of public charging stations that provide level 2 charging.

10. Compatibility: because level 2 charging ports are standardized, they are generally compatible with the majority of electric cars.

But you must make sure your EV is compatible with the connector that is used in your area (J1772, for example, in North America, and type 2, in Europe).

In conclusion, most EV owners choose level 2 charging as it provides a quicker and more useful charging option than level 1. It is the best choice for regular charging requirements, and the abundance of level 2 charging stations throughout town makes it a practical method to top off your electric car when you are not at home.

6.4.1.3 DC fast charging at level 3

The most potent and rapid EV charging option is DC fast charging, also referred to as level 3 charging. Because of its quick-charging architecture, it is especially helpful for long-distance trips and other scenarios when you need to fast charge your electric vehicle. The specifics of DC rapid charging are provided here [14].

1. Rate of charging: comparing DC rapid charging to level 1 or level 2 charging, the former uses a far lower voltage and current. Depending on the particular charger and the EV's compatibility, it can provide a quick charging rate of 60 to 80 miles of range in approximately 20 to 30 minutes.
2. Equipment: DC fast charging stations are not the same as level 1 and level 2 chargers. They operate on DC and have distinctive connectors that vary based on the region and standards. Common DC fast charging connectors include CHAdeMO, CCS (combined charging system), and Tesla's Supercharger system. These stations are larger and more potent, and they require a significant electrical connection.
3. Accessibility: DC fast charging stations are typically found in urban areas, next to roads, and in close proximity to major thoroughfares. They are positioned to provide quick top-ups for long trips and are commonly seen in public charging networks. A few automakers, like Tesla, have also established their own networks of DC fast chargers.
4. Charging time: the primary advantage of DC fast charging is its speed of operation. A typical DC fast charging session may fully charge an EV's battery in as little as 20 to 30 minutes. For long-distance drivers who want to make as few stops as possible along the trip, this is very beneficial.
5. Cost: the cost of DC fast charging may vary depending on the source and location. Certain stations are free, but others require payment through a smartphone app, credit card, or subscription. The quantity of time or energy expended, or the combination of the two, can be used to calculate costs.
6. Compatibility: not every electric vehicle can utilize DC quick charging. The specific connector type on the charging station needs to match the one on your vehicle. Various locations have different

standards, so be sure your EV has the correct connector for the charging infrastructure in your area.

7. Benefits: the primary benefit of DC quick charging is speed. It allows electric vehicle owners to quickly extend their driving range, which increases the viability of long journeys. These stations are especially helpful for electric automobiles with larger batteries since they may benefit from the faster charging rates.

8. Restrictions: despite its speed, DC fast charging might not be suitable for regular charging needs. It can be more expensive per mile and perhaps more stressful on an EV's battery than level 2 charging, which might have long-term effects on the battery's health. It therefore functions well for charging batteries throughout extended travels.

Table 6.1 shows the EV charging station types and Figure 6.1 shows the charging station level and connectors. In conclusion, DC fast charging is a game-changer for owners of electric cars that need to charge quickly while they are on the road. Because of its speed and accessibility along major travel routes, it is a vital component of the EV charging infrastructure, ensuring that electric vehicles can compete with conventional vehicles for long-distance travel.

6.4.2 Charging technologies (battery swapping stations, inductive/wireless power transfers, and conductive charging)

To charge an EV battery, there are essentially three methods. Firstly, the batteries need to be changed. Charging can be accomplished by either conductive or inductive charging. The vehicle control unit, charging cable, and charger control unit make up the EV charging system. The two primary categories of chargers are conductive and inductive. The electricity

Table 6.1 EV charging station types

S. no	Voltage	Current rating	Charging time
Level 1	120V AC, 1-Phase 250V AC, 1-Phase 480V AC, 3-Phase	12A-16A(32A for 3-Phase)	8–12 hours
Level 2	208V-240V AC, 1-Phase 250V AC, 1-Phase 480V AC, 3-Phase	12A-80 A	4–6 hours
Level 3	380V-600V AC, 3-Phase	DC output up to 4000 A	15–30 mins

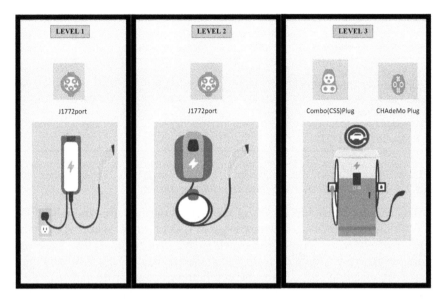

Figure 6.1 EV charging station levels and their connectors.

is transferred using a magnet, and the inductive charger has no touching surface. While this connection is convenient for drivers, it is still not at the level of high efficiency. A common gadget that creates electricity by touch is the conductive charger.

6.4.2.1 Conductive charging system

6.4.2.1.1 Electric vehicle automated conductive charging system

Direct contact between the charge inlet and the EV connection is required for conducting charging. A charging station or a regular electrical socket can provide the cord. Because the conductive charger for EVs only uses plugs and sockets to transport electrical energy via actual metallic contacts, it has the maturity, simplicity, and affordability benefits. EV charging stations use two different conductive methods: AC chargers, also known as on-board chargers, and DC chargers, also known as off-board chargers.

Energy is transferred between two electronic devices via a conductor in a process known as "conductive power transfer."

When it comes to charging electric vehicles, there are three main components: cables, connectors, and batteries. Off-board and on-board charging are separated based on the same conductive charging method [15].

Table 6.2 Summary of research and development of dynamic WEVCS

Research and development	Pick up power (KW)	Operating frequency (kHz)	Efficiency (%)	Air gap (mm)
Oak Ridge National Laboratory(ORNL)(25)	20	22–23	90	125–175
Japan Railway Technical Research Institute (26)	50	10	TBA	7.5
EV System Lab and Nissan Research Centre (27)	1	90	>90	100

6.4.2.1.2 Electric vehicle conductive DC charging system

A DC charger is used to do DC charging off-board. It uses specialized DC EV supply equipment to deliver energy to EVs in public spaces via suitable off-board chargers. Fast DC charging is the term for it. Unlike on-board chargers, there is flexibility in the power level. It has a 50 KW maximum capacity, meaning that a fully charged battery can go from empty to 80% full in 20 minutes. However, this figure might occasionally change based on the vehicle's quality and battery state.

Table 6.2 displays the chargers that have been utilized up to this point to connect the car to an external power source.

CCS US
CCS Europe
Chademo
Tesla US/Eu
China GB/ T Standard

Each of them is utilized in accordance with the power input in the car and has varying pin counts, voltage powers, and phases. The DC charging mechanism still has a few restrictions even though it is the quickest option and has no power supply restrictions.
Here is a list of the restrictions:

- Greater battery and charger losses
- Battery: reduced lifespan; quick charging is only possible for batteries that have 70–80% SOC.
- Cable: maximum current limit for readily lifted cable
- Hefty outlay
- Negative effect on the grid
- Exclusive to public charging stations
- Temperature control

6.4.2.1.3 Electric vehicle conductive AC charging system

The majority of regular power outlets charge their devices with AC electricity. All that is needed to charge the car is to plug it into a standard electrical outlet or an outlet with higher power meant for electric vehicles. As you can see, not much room or material is required for this kind of charging station. However, the process of charging takes longer, and the automobile has to have an on-board charging device, which increases the weight of the vehicle. The one exception is that on-board chargers have a restricted power supply. However, the fundamental principle of charging an electric car is power flexibility.

An AC charging system's entire charging procedure is a little bit different. As the charging inputs are installed within the car, there are two types of proximity pilots: those that continuously monitor the connection between the infrastructure plug and the electric vehicle, and those that regulate the maximum current that may be pulled. Therefore, under these kinds of circumstances, monitoring the maximum current supplied becomes essential. Infrastructure plugs, charging cables, and car nets are the three primary equipment kinds utilized.

Table 6.2 lists the many kinds of chargers that are utilized in AC charging systems.

US/Japan SAE
Europe Mannekes/ Tesla
EV Plug Alliance
Tesla US

The primary advantages of an AC charging system are its universal compatibility with common electrical outlets and its easy-to-communicate battery monitoring system (BMS). However, because of the fitted input unit, it has several significant disadvantages, such as power output, comparatively longer charging times, and increased vehicle weight.

6.4.2.2 Inductive charging system

Wireless charging systems and inductive charging for electric vehicles can be divided into two groups according to their intended uses:

Static wireless charging
Dynamic wireless charging

6.4.2.2.1 Static wireless charging

In order to give customers a user-friendly atmosphere and prevent any safety concerns with the plug-in chargers, WEVCS opens a second door.

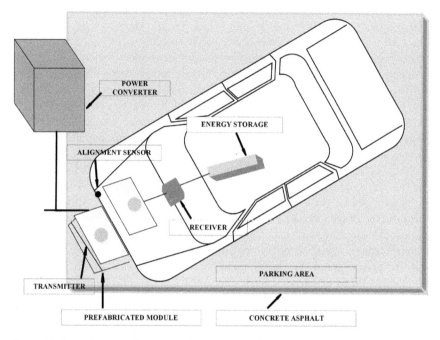

Figure 6.2 Basic diagram of static wireless electric vehicle charging system.

With little assistance from the driver, static WEVCS may quickly replace plug-in chargers and eliminate related safety risks including electric shock and trip hazards. A simple setup of static WEVCS is shown in Figure 6.2. Together with auxiliary power converters and circuits, the primary coil is placed beneath the surface of the ground or the road. Typically, the receiver coil, also known as the secondary coil, is mounted beneath the front, rear, or center of the EV. The power converter transforms the incoming energy from AC to DC before sending it to the battery bank. Power control and battery management systems are equipped with a wireless communication network to receive any feedback from the primary side in order to prevent any safety hazards. The source power level, charging pad size, and air space between the two windings all affect how long a battery takes to charge. Between lightweight duty vehicles, there is an average gap of around 150–300 mm. Park 'n' ride facilities, residential and commercial buildings, parking lots, and car parks can all have static WEVCS installed. Universities have created several prototypes for both commercial and scientific purposes [16, 17]. Their costs range from about USD 2700 to $13,000 for charging capacities between 3.3 and 7.2 kW [18]. Their power levels, encompassing frequency ranges of 81.9–90 kHz, are in compliance with the recently issued worldwide SAE standards (J2954) power class for levels 1 (3.3 kW) and 2 (7.7 kW) [19]. The SAE organization is currently working on rules pertaining to the position of receiver pad installation in the automobile and the amount of misalignment that is permitted. Different mounting positions for the receiver pads on the underside of the automobile, including the front, rear, and center, have been shown on a number of prototypes. Oak Ridge National Laboratory (ORNL) is primarily focused on increasing power transfer efficiency through coil design. Overall, laboratory studies or prototypes of stationary WCS for EVs have been created with efficiency ranging from 71 to 95% with power ranges of 1–20 kW and air-gap distances of 100–300 mm.

6.4.2.2.2 Dynamic wireless charging system (DWCS)

ORNL is largely focused on improving power transfer efficiency through coil design, even though the University of Auckland has proposed specific hardware and software (including the installation of charging pads) to boost plug-in efficiency. Overall, stationary WCS for EVs has been developed through laboratory research or prototypes, with efficiency varying from 71 to 95% throughout power ranges of 1–20 kW and air-gap lengths of 100–300 mm. As seen in Figures 6.3(a) and (b), the high voltage, high frequency AC source and compensation circuits to the micro grid and/or RES are included into the road concrete at a certain distance from the primary coils. The secondary coil is installed beneath the cars, much like static-WEVCS. Using the power converter and BMS, the transmitter uses the magnetic field that the EVs travel over to convert it to DC so that the battery bank can be charged. Compared to existing EVs, frequent charging facilities for EVs lower the overall battery demand by around 20%. [20, 21].

Transmitter pads and power supply segments must be built on specified sites and pre-planned routes in order to use dynamic-WEVCS [22, 23]. As seen in Figure 6.3(a) and (b), the power supply segments are primarily separated into individual and centralized power frequency schemes. Under the centralized power supply concept, many small charging pads are employed in a big coil (about 5–10 m) that is mounted on the road surface. The centralized plan is less efficient than the segmented scheme, with greater installation and maintenance costs as well as larger losses [24]. All things considered, the first infrastructure installation for this technology would be expensive. In the future, a self-driving automobile will make it easier to position the transmitter and receiver coils precisely, which can greatly increase the efficiency of power transmission overall. Numerous EV transportation applications, including light-duty cars, buses, trains, and rapid transit, may readily integrate dynamic-WEVCS. A development overview of dynamic WEVCS is shown in Table 6.2 [24,25,26, 27].

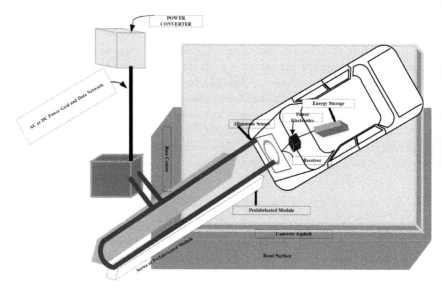

Figure 6.3a Schematic of dynamic wireless electric vehicle charging system.

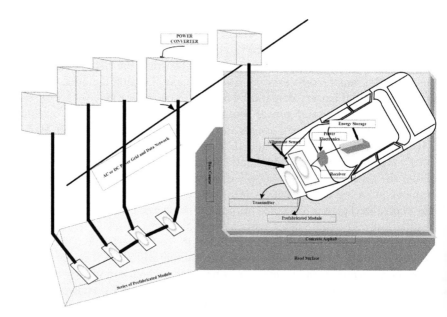

Figure 6.3b Schematic of dynamic wireless electric vehicle charging system.

Challenges faced by WEVCS

Since the present setup is unsuitable for the installations, new infrastructure development is needed in order to place static and dynamic wireless charging stations on the highways.

For the sake of human health and safety, EMC, EMI, and frequency requirements must be upheld.

6.4.2.3 BSS (battery swap station)

An electric vehicle (EV) battery swap station (BSS) is a location where fully charged EV batteries may be rapidly and easily replaced. BSSs are made to make it unnecessary for drivers to wait around for an EV battery to fully charge; instead, they enable them to quickly replace their empty battery with a fully charged one. These stations usually have several charging bays, each with automated mechanisms that take out the EV's exhausted battery and swap it out with a fully charged one. EV owners who need to quickly recharge their vehicles after lengthy journeys or hectic commutes may readily utilize BSSs because they are frequently positioned strategically along major roads or in urban areas. Since drivers can easily change out their depleted battery for a fully charged one instead of having to wait for hours at standard charging stations, BSSs can help drivers overcome the range anxiety that is frequently associated with driving electric vehicles. Subscription-based services are provided by certain BSS providers, enabling EV owners to pay a monthly charge for unrestricted access to the swapping service at several sites. Although BSSs provide faster and more convenient ways to recharge, in order to guarantee compatibility and easy battery switching, they need standardized batteries that are compatible with a variety of car types. By solving issues with limited range and lengthy charging periods, battery swap stations are seen as an alternate infrastructure solution to regular charging stations, with the goal of accelerating the adoption of electric vehicles.

Among the advantages of BSS are the following:

There's no reason to hold off on charging your battery: you may avoid having to wait hours for your battery to charge by just swapping out your empty battery for a fully charged one with a battery swap station.

Extended driving range: by swapping out their used, exhausted batteries with new, fully charged ones, battery swap stations enable owners of electric vehicles (EVs) to considerably increase the range of their vehicles. For long-distance trips or locations with inadequate charging infrastructure, this is quite helpful.

Because battery switch stations offer a quick fix when your battery is low, they help to reduce this concern.

Fit for all kinds of electric vehicles: no matter what kind of EV you drive, battery swap stations are convenient and accessible since they are made to fit a wide range of makes and models.

Improved longevity and upkeep: it guarantees that every user obtains optimally performing, well-maintained batteries at a designated BSS, hence increasing the total lifetime and efficiency of their electric car.

Accessibility in remote places: battery swap stations are more accessible in rural or underdeveloped areas since they may be set up in isolated locations without requiring a significant power supply infrastructure, unlike charging stations that need electrical infrastructure.

Places with limited power supply infrastructure, which makes them easier to reach in rural or underdeveloped areas.

Eco-friendly substitute fuel source: by enabling users to replace empty batteries with fully charged ones instead of depending on fossil fuels or conventional grid electricity sources, battery swapping encourages the use of sustainable energy.

Challenges

Infrastructure: a substantial investment in infrastructure is needed to set up a network of battery swap stations. Every station must be equipped with the tools required, including battery storage facilities and units for switching and charging.

Battery standardization: one of the challenges in deploying battery swap stations is ensuring compatibility between various kinds of electric vehicles. To facilitate seamless battery switching between different car models, EV manufacturers must come to an agreement on a standardised battery design and size.

Battery ownership and liability: in a swap station arrangement, figuring out who owns what batteries and who is liable for them may be tricky. When many cars utilize the same battery at various times, disagreements over ownership rights and issues surrounding liability for damaged or defective batteries may occur.

User adoption: it might be difficult to persuade EV owners to use battery swap stations rather than only their homes or public charging facilities. Convenience, affordability, and the availability of stations that are compatible will all be important in promoting user adoption.

Regulatory framework: the successful deployment of battery swap stations depends on the establishment of precise norms and standards. This contains recommendations for the safe disposal or recycling of spent batteries, as well as information on quality assurance, data privacy, and safety precautions.

Scalability: as the number of EVs rises worldwide, scalability becomes a crucial factor to take into account while implementing BSS. Thorough planning and thoughtful placement of these facilities are necessary to guarantee that there are sufficient switch stations available to fulfil demand while ensuring efficient operations.

Maintenance and upkeep: to guarantee the best possible performance from the switched batteries as well as the charging infrastructure, battery swap stations need to be maintained on a regular basis. This include keeping an eye on the condition of the batteries, repairing damaged devices right once, updating the software, and keeping each station clean.

Integration with current infrastructure: battery swap stations must be easily included into the current system for charging electric vehicles. In order to provide a consistent supply of electricity and prevent overburdening the nearby power infrastructure, coordination with other charging stations, grid operators, and energy providers is essential. It will be crucial to inform customers about the advantages of this technology, such as shorter charging times and more mobility for long-distance trips, in order to influence public opinion and encourage the use of BSS.

6.4.3 Connector types (AC and DC charging)

Based on the kind of electrical current they are intended to manage, connections for charging electric vehicles may be divided into two primary categories: AC connectors and DC connectors. Here are some popular AC and DC charging connectors: Table 6.3 shows a schematic of charging ports and connectors according to its standards

6.4.3.1 AC charging connectors

SAE J1772: In North America, the SAE J1772 connection is frequently used for level 1 and level 2 AC charging [12,13]. In the US and Canada, the majority of EVs and plug-in hybrid electric cars use this standard connection.

Type 1 (IEC 62196): in areas like North America and some parts of Asia, type 1 connections are frequently used for AC charging. Though they are designed differently and have a slightly different pin arrangement, they are comparable to the SAE J1772 connection.

Type 2 (IEC 62196): in Europe and many other regions of the world, type 2 connections are often used for AC charging. These adaptable connections are appropriate for both home and public charging, handling a range of power levels.

Tesla connector (type 2, Tesla-specific): when it comes to AC charging, Tesla automobiles are equipped with their own unique connectors that work with both type 2 charging stations and Tesla's own charging infrastructure [14].

Table 6.3 Schematic of the connections and charging ports in accordance with its specifications

	CHAdeMO	GB/T 20234 DC	CCS combo 1	CCS combo 2
	SAE J1722 Type 1	IEC 62196-2 Type 2	GB/T 20234 AC	Tesla Supercharger
CHARGING TYPE	DC Charging	DC Charging	DC Fast Charging	DC Fast Charging
NO OF PINS	7	5	7	9
CAPACITY	50 kW to 400 kW	Up to 187.5Kw	50–100 kW	200 kW
VOLTAGE	200–500 V	750 to 1000 V	600 V	1000V
CURRENT RATING	125 A and 400 A	250 A	Up to 200 A	Up to 350 A

CHARGING TYPE	AC Charging	AC Charging	AC Charging	DC Fast Charging
NO OF PINS	5	7	7	6
CAPACITY	7.68 kW	12.8 kW	12.6 Kw	140 kW
VOLTAGE	120V to 240V	400V	380V	480V
CURRENT RATING	Up to 80 A	Up to 63 A	10 A	250 A

6.4.3.2 DC charging connectors

The CCS connector is a multipurpose connector that combines two extra DC pins for high-speed DC rapid charging with the regular SAE J1772 AC connector. CCS connections are intended for DC rapid charging and are widely used in North America and Europe.

CHAdeMO: DC rapid charging is the exclusive purpose of CHAdeMO connections. They are used worldwide, mostly by Japanese manufacturers, such as Nissan and Mitsubishi, and have a unique spherical shape [14].

Tesla supercharger connection: exclusive to Tesla automobiles and supercharger stations, the Tesla supercharger network use a unique DC rapid charging connection.

GB/T connector (China): in China, charging electric vehicles with a GB/T connector is the norm. It is made to accommodate both DC and AC charging.

Another DC fast charging connector that is utilized in China is the CCF connector (Chinese charging forum). It is utilized for particular DC rapid charging applications and is different from the GB/T connection.

6.4.4 Electric vehicle charging control architecture

Three primary kinds of electric car charging control architectures exist: distributed control, decentralized control, and centralized control. Every one of these methods has unique qualities, benefits, and applications. Let us discuss each of these control schemes in more detail:

Demand response management, load balancing, and smart grid integration are features of centralized control.

Centralized management: this design has a central system or organization in charge of managing EV charging. All charging stations are coordinated and adjusted for effective charging thanks to this central control [27].

EV penetration into the grid has been aided by favorable government regulations and the socio-environmental benefits of growing EV adoption rates. Dumb charging is the process of refueling an electric car by utilizing standard household outlets and ordinary charging procedures to recharge the battery. It is an unregulated charging method that makes plug-and-charge easier. The grid is badly impacted by significant EV integration that uses dumb charging. Plug-and-charge devices that are not regulated can lead to high peak loading problems. Maintaining generation-demand balance at peak loading period becomes more difficult as a result of this high peak loading issue. It demands that costly generators be scheduled and that new power units be installed.

Due to its high cost and the fact that traditional generating sources can already provide the extra power needed, this approach to the high peak loading problem is neither ecologically or economically feasible. The installation of conventional generators will result in a straightforward change in the amount of non-renewable fuel used and the emissions released into the atmosphere. Uncertain loading is also linked to high demand and plug-and-charge mechanisms, necessitating additional backup storage. When EVs are charged without oversight, a significant quantity of electricity is drawn out, overwhelming the network. Equipment overloading, accelerated device aging that causes errors to occur more frequently, and, in the worst case scenario, system instability are all examples of network overloading conditions.

Stress on equipment and accelerated aging lead to the need for significant upgrades and reconfigurations. Power-line congestion is caused by simultaneous EV charging and increased supply power extraction from EV-centric locations. Blackouts and instability may result from it. Smart charging offers a solution to all of the aforementioned problems associated with uncontrolled electric vehicle charging. The disadvantages and restrictions of dumb charging are lessened by smart charging, which also offers the added benefits of supporting auxiliary services, optimizing the use of renewable energy sources, and offering backup storage. When charging an EV smartly, all of the system's decision-making characteristics as well as the needs of the EV owner are taken into account. An outside party or individual manages charging and determines a charging schedule that complies with EV owners' interests. Put differently, smart charging refers to the process of externally regulating EV charging in order to meet predetermined goals and limitations. Because smart charging is externally regulated, communication and observability between the entities are necessary. The two main parties involved in smart charging are EV owners and system operators. The goals that each stakeholder has for performing and engaging in smart charging are varied. System operators promote smart charging in order to preserve grid stability, whereas EV owners are more concerned with lowering the cost of EV charging. The system operator is a central organization, and it is highly challenging to handle the relationship between a system operator and a specific EV owner in the real-world use of smart charging shown in Figure 6.4. An aggregator, the third smart charging stakeholder, is added to the system to address this. The aggregator serves as a middleman between the system operator and the EV owner, working with both parties to create an indirect link. It gathers data from the system operator and the owner of the EV, and it makes an appropriate choice about EV charging after taking into account the requests and limitations of both parties. Aggregator's goal is to maximize profits as well. Smart charging is dependent on the goal and constraints that must be met at each time slot. The goal of smart charging differs based on the needs and parties involved. The main goals of a system operator are to minimize overall system costs, maximize RE utilization, load level and fill valleys, and provide grid support services. From the standpoint of an electric vehicle owner, the common goals are load leveling, maximizing

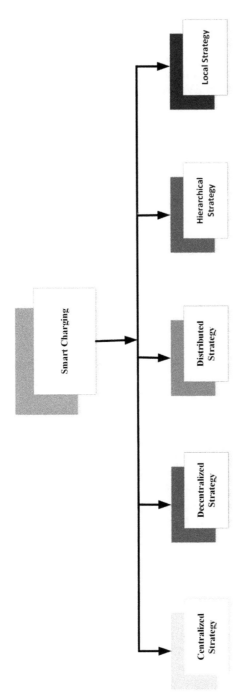

Figure 6.4 Smart charging strategies based on control architecture.

of happiness factor, and minimization of charging cost. Different methodologies are used for smart charging, which combine the aggregator's and the EV owner's abilities to make decisions with information flow. Figure 6.5 illustrates how several solutions for smart charging are classified based on the flow of information and decision-making.

Power requests from EVs are sent to an aggregator in centralized strategy information signal, viz., and the aggregator determines scheduling while taking system limits into account. In this case, the aggregator makes the decision and informs the EV. On the other hand, EV owners decide when to charge, and aggregators attempt to sway EV owners' decisions by manipulating power costs. Furthermore, a decentralized technique involves a collection of aggregators interacting with one another to determine the best possible price [28]. Each of the aforementioned tactics primarily aims to achieve a specific stakeholder goal. Every stakeholder in the real EV charging ecosystem wants to accomplish their goal.

Accordingly, a hierarchical approach enables all stakeholders at all levels to accomplish their goals. The approach is further divided into groups according to different combinations of decentralized and centralized methods for making decisions at different levels. In addition to the aggregator-dependent tactics mentioned above, there is also one aggregator-independent strategy. To accomplish the intended goal, the EV owner makes a smart charging decision while taking local factors into account. Time-of-use tariff structure refers to an intelligent pricing technique that is based on the cost of power. Using this strategy, the load and generating availability in the system determine the appropriate power pricing. The grid operator tries to persuade EV owners to move their EV charging to an off-peak time so that the load is balanced by using time-of-use tariffs.

Customers are drawn to time-of-use rates because they may be able to lower their expenses by billing during off-peak hours. The goal and technique of implementation have an impact on the output of smart charging. Smart charging employs a variety of implementation techniques, including deterministic, heuristic, artificial intelligence, and GAME theory-based techniques. A suitable approach can be chosen based on the charging problem's optimization type. The most popular techniques for implementing smart charging are linear optimization, convex optimization, mixed integer linear programming (MILP), and no cooperative GAME theory. The charging schedule in a smart charging system is influenced by the objective function of an optimization problem. The two most important prerequisites for integrating smart charging into the EV ecosystem are communication and processing capacity. The usability of smart charging is affected by the varying communication and computing needs of the smart charging schemes shown in Figure 6.5. In order to prevent delays in the charging process, a centralized method needs higher bandwidth communication, whereas a decentralized and dispersed strategy needs medium

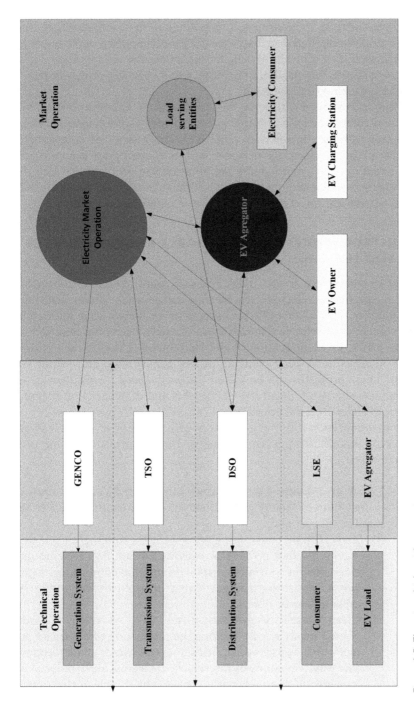

Figure 6.5 Electric vehicle grid conversion system.

bandwidth communication. The necessity for high bandwidth communication is minimal for local strategies. According to the computational aspect, a decentralized method distributes the need for computing to the lower level of EVs, whereas a centralized plan demands the most computational power because of central managing. In real use, smart charging primarily relies on the charger's kind of connection.

The market is filled with a variety of connections. Connectors are divided into two categories based on the smart charging requirement: connectors with and without control pilot pins. While both types of connectors are capable of smart charging, the ones with a control pilot pin can pass a modulated charging signal due to an optimization problem and have finer adjustments to the charging power, while the ones without one can use ToU tariffs to perform smart charging with basic on/off functionality.

6.5 INTEGRATION WITH RENEWABLE ENERGY SOURCES AND THE GRID

Power providers face several difficulties as a result of electric automobiles. Over-integration of electric vehicles into the network affects distribution grid stability. This adverse effect is brought on by variations in the load profile, voltage and frequency imbalances, excessive harmonic injection, and power losses. Over-integration of electric vehicles (EVs) into the grid may result in issues with peak demand, power quality loss, and power regulation. These problems can be solved using advanced power management techniques. Figure 6.6 illustrates the benefits and drawbacks of integrating electric vehicles with the power grid.

Combining renewable energy sources with EVs has several advantages, both economically and environmentally. The following are some of the main benefits:

(a) **Lower greenhouse gas emissions:** combining EVs with renewable energy sources lowers greenhouse gas emissions dramatically for a number of reasons.
   (i) **Zero tailpipe emissions:** electric vehicles running on renewable energy produce no tailpipe emissions at all. EVs have no direct emissions, in contrast to cars with internal combustion engines, which release particulate matter, nitrogen oxides (NO_x), and carbon dioxide (CO_2).
   (ii) **Clean electricity generation:** no CO_2 or other hazardous pollutants are released during the production of electricity using renewable energy sources including sun, wind, and hydropower. The total emissions of the vehicle are significantly reduced over its whole lifespan when it is powered by this clean electricity.

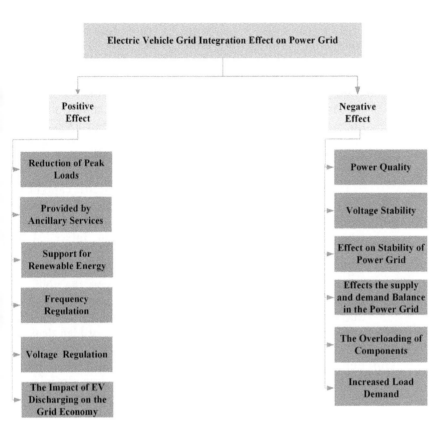

Figure 6.6 Grid integration of electric vehicles' impact on the power system.

(iii) **Decrease in dependency on fossil fuels:** plug-in hybrid EVs that integrate renewable energy sources lessen emissions related to the extraction, transportation, and burning of fossil fuels. This reduces the demand for fossil fuels.

(b) **Grid stabilization:** EV integration with renewable energy sources can aid in grid stabilization.

(i) **Technology for vehicles to grid (V2G).**
Thanks to a technology called vehicle-to-grid (V2G), electric cars (EVs) may now exchange energy with the electrical grid in both ways. Consequently, EVs may now function as portable energy storage devices by consuming energy and releasing it back into the grid. This capability strategically contributes to system stability by reducing the probability of power outages by strategically delivering extra electricity during periods of high demand.

Conversely, EVs equipped with V2G can take advantage of lower power prices by recharging during off-peak hours. V2G technology improves grid resiliency and makes it easier to integrate renewable energy sources. Nevertheless, the effectiveness of this interaction depends on the charging mechanism that is employed. Many EVs today operate in uncoordinated charging modes regardless of grid conditions, which might have an impact on overall quality and dependability. Coordinated V2G modes are being developed to optimize control within the existing infrastructure [29]. Developing adaptable EV charging and discharging techniques is part of this.

The two-way power flow between plug-in electric cars (PEVs) and the grid in both the uncoordinated charging and V2G modes is shown graphically in Figure 6.5. In both modes, power flows from the grid to the PEVs and then back again. Tables 6.4 and 6.5 provide a description of the three power flow orientations, highlighting the similarities and differences between them.

(ii) **Load shifting:** intelligent charging systems have the ability to move EV charging to periods of strong renewable energy production. By reducing the requirement to utilize fossil fuels or other non-renewable resources during periods of high demand, this enhances grid stability.

(iii) **Enhanced system resilience:** EVs may act as backup power sources for residences and vital infrastructure during emergencies or power outages, enhancing the resilience and dependability of the system.

(c) **Lower energy costs:**
Cost reductions are possible when EVs and renewable energy sources are combined:

(i) **Lower fuel costs:** compared to gasoline-powered cars, operational costs for EVs can be reduced by using renewable energy for charging. In many cases, renewable energy is less expensive than fossil fuels.

Table 6.4 Indicating three modes of power flow

Direction of power flow	Modes of function	Features of the modes
Power flow can be either from grid to EV or EV to grid	Bidirectional V2G	Coordinated, controlled and intelligent charging and discharging
Power flow from grid to EV	Unidirectional V2G	Coordinated, controlled and intelligent charging
Power flow from grid to EV	Uncontrolled charging	Unregulated, dumb and regular charging

Table 6.5 The distinctions between bidirectional and unidirectional V2G power flows

V2G power flow	Bidirectional	Unidirectional
The Level of Power	Level I and Level 2 are expected	Level I, Level 2, and Level 3
Facilities	• supports both reactive and active power. • Improve the grid's dependability by doing the power factor correction. • The filter for harmonics. • Controlling the occurrence. • Manage backup.	A power grid's regulatory spinning reserve
Economy	Good	Poor
A Hardware Based Infrastructure	The bi-directional battery charger used in communication networks	A correspondence system
Various Utilities	• Reducing power grid losses is necessary. • It is important to prevent overloading power grids. • Increased charging profile. • Verify that the voltage is kept constant. • Variable renewable energy source. • Minimizing emissions while optimizing advantages • How to recover from failures.	The Power Grids must not be overloaded in order to reduce pollution

(ii) **Time-of-use rates:** these rates, which offer cheaper power during off-peak hours, are provided by many utilities. EV owners are encouraged to charge their cars during these hours, which lowers their energy expenses.

(d) **Sustainable transportation:** there are several ways in which combining EVs with renewable energy sources encourages sustainable mobility.

(i) **Lessening of environmental impact:** EVs running on renewable energy have a lower carbon footprint, which helps to mitigate climate change and reduce air pollution.

(ii) **Energy efficiency:** EVs have a lower environmental effect than internal combustion engine vehicles since they are typically more energy-efficient.

(iii) **Less noise pollution:** EVs emit less noise than conventional cars, making cities a more tranquil and pleasant place to live.

(e) **Global energy security**
Integrating EVs with renewable energy sources improves global energy security:
(i) **Diversification of energy sources:** using indigenous renewable resources to lessen dependency on imported fossil fuels improves a nation's energy security. It reduces the dangers brought on by supply outages and geopolitical unrest.
(ii) **Price fluctuation resistant:** compared to fossil fuels, renewable energy generation is frequently less vulnerable to price changes. In addition to lowering economic susceptibility to energy price shocks, this can help stabilize energy costs.

Durational sustainability
Long-term energy security is provided by renewable energy resources, which are essentially limitless and sustainable and lessen reliance on finite fossil fuel supplies.

Challenges: one of the biggest issues facing owners of electric vehicles is cost. Electric vehicles must have enormous quantities of charge storage. One of the biggest issues facing owners of electric vehicles is cost. Batteries for electric automobiles must be able to retain a significant amount of charge. This requires expensive materials, some of which are difficult to find, therefore producing them requires expensive technologies. Electric automobiles are more expensive to purchase than equivalent gasoline vehicles since they are more expensive to build. As a result, customers are less inclined to accept them [30]. The issue with organic eggs and free-range chicken is that they contain pesticides. Increasing manufacturing numbers and taking use of economies of scale might drastically lower the price of electric vehicles. A large price reduction will be necessary to purchase electric cars, which might not occur until costs are reduced. Persuading customers that electric cars are worth the cost is the largest obstacle facing producers of these vehicles. Some folks do not think they are a good fit for electric vehicles. This situation presents a variety of anxiety issues. Manufacturers of electric vehicles are worried that consumers would run out of batteries before traveling far in their vehicles. In around five minutes, a gasoline-powered automobile may be filled up; all you have to do is pull into the gas station, fill up, and drive away. It is not as simple as it seems to charge an electric car [31]. An electric car's range is only about 100 miles (160.9 kilometers) when it initially hits the market. For example, you will need to allow around eight hours for your battery to fully charge if you do not have access to a dedicated charging station—which are currently hard to come by. Even with the fact that most people can leave their cars overnight and drive less than 40 miles (64.4 kilometers) a day, electric cars are still not the best option for lengthy road trips. Wouldn't it be odd if you drove 80 miles (128.7 kilometers) in one day, arrived home, and then realized you had to go 30 more miles (483 kilometers) because of an emergency? It is difficult for electric cars to get beyond a barrier when buyers think about situations like those [32]. Another problem is that charging stations may alleviate a lot of consumer concerns about electric cars. The emergence of electric vehicles has led to a significant alteration in the country's infrastructure. While some charging stations are available for trial, such as those at Best Buy that allow users to recharge while they shop, most individuals charge at home in their garages.

The people who live in shared housing or park on the street will thus have the biggest environmental problems. It goes without saying that more people would buy electric vehicles if infrastructure and charging stations were improved. There will always be a need for a sizable number of electric vehicles to convince infrastructure to change [33].

6.6 POLICY ANALYSIS

This section addresses some of the initiatives the Indian government has taken to encourage the use of electric vehicles. MoP states that an EV charging station's operation does not need a license [34]. To promote the quicker adoption of EVs, the MoP published a policy on charging infrastructure. Private charging is allowed at homes and places of business, provided that the cost of providing energy to the EV charging station does not exceed the average cost of supply + 15%. For both self-operated and commercial battery-operated cars, green boards are now available, according to the Ministry of Road Transport & Highways (MoRTH). Additionally, it said that it will waive the requirement for homologation in order to enable the importation of 2,500 electric cars that adhere to international standards. The Bureau of Indian Standards (BIS) publishes the general CCS and CHAdeMO charging standards. A request for quote (RFQ) document was released by the Indian Space Research Organization (ISRO) with the intention of commercializing lithium-ion battery technology that was created in the country [35]. The Ministry of Housing & Urban Affairs (MoHUA) updated the local planning and construction codes to allow the installation of EV charging stations in both residential and commercial buildings. In an additional attempt to support "Made in India" and the use of electric cars, the metal-organic frameworks (MoF) lowered the customs tariff for all kinds of electric vehicles, battery packs, and cells (notification no. 03/2019-Customs) [36]. As part of the EV adoption program, after August 1, 2019, an EV's GST will drop from 12% to 5%, and there will not be a registration cost [37]. Given that transportation is primarily a state issue, every state will have its own regulations. There are robust state policies in place in Delhi and Gujarat to promote the use of EVs. States would experience competitive federalism if they kept modifying their EV laws. Local inventions would be improved under competitive federalism.

6.7 CONCLUSION

The next ten years should see a major increase in the popularity of electric cars as a result of grid integration, charging infrastructure development, and technology advancements. To maximize the advantages, EVs with distributed generators also require other technological advancements like intelligent charging infrastructure, dependable communication systems, and coordinated charging systems. With the help of cutting-edge energy management technologies, the electrical grid might one day be totally automated thanks to grid technology based on the Energy Internet. This chapter presents a study of grid integration infrastructure and EV charging.

Modern stationary and dynamic WEVCS have been investigated. Additionally, the benefits and drawbacks of several components of the current grid integration and charging infrastructure, including as power, communication, control, and coordination, are carefully considered.

Researchers and engineers will have a thorough understanding of the state of EV charging and grid integration research after reading this chapter.

6.8 FUTURE SCOPE OF WORK

SiC and GaN are examples of wide band-gap technologies that have made it feasible to create high-power bidirectional converters and facilitate incredibly rapid charging or draining of EV batteries. This has opened up new avenues for study and development. These devices can enable higher power density for the Si-based EV charger, which may have favorable implications for future applications. Furthermore, a smart-grid infrastructure based on renewable energy may be built based on ongoing research on different smart EV charging and discharging methodologies. Future study and technology studies on EV charging stations would center on the following topics:

- Using electric vehicles to replace fleets of conventional automobiles in the transportation sector to achieve high efficiency and a low carbon impact.
- Wireless charging stations for EVs are being used as a solution to the limitations of conventional converters. Additionally, high efficiency, high power density AC/DC and DC/DC power converters based on WBG devices are being developed to address power quality concerns with grid-connected EV quick charging stations.

REFERENCES

[1] Ghosh, A., 2020. Possibilities and challenges for the inclusion of the electric vehicle (EV) to reduce the carbon footprint in the transport sector: A review. *Energies* 13(10), 2602.

[2] Habib, S., Kamran, M., Rashid, U., 2015. Impact analysis of vehicle-to-grid tech- nology and charging strategies of electric vehicles on distribution networks–A review. *J. Power Sources* 277, 205–214.

[3] Praveen Kumar et al., 2013. *Potential Need for Electric Vehicles, Charging Station Infrastructure and its Challenges for the Indian Market.* Research India Publications.

[4] Sanguesa, J.A., Torres-Sanz, V., Garrido, P., et al., 2021. A review on electric vehicles: Technologies and challenges. *Smart Cities* 4(1), 372–404.

[5] Miele, A., Axsen, J., Wolinetz, M., et al., 2020. The role of charging and refuelling infrastructure in supporting zero-emission vehicle sales. *Transp. Res. Part D* 81, 102275.

[6] Tan, K.M., Ramachandaramurthy, V.K., Yong, J.Y., 2016. Integration of electric vehicles in smart grid: A review on vehicle to grid technologies and optimization techniques. *Renew. Sustain. Energy Rev.* 53, 720–732.

[7] Springel, K., 2021. Network externality and subsidy structure in two-sided markets: Evidence from electric vehicle incentives. *Amer. Econ. J. Econ. Policy* 13(4), 393–432.

[8] Li, L., Dababneh, F., Zhao, J., 2018a. Cost-effective supply chain for electric vehicle battery remanufacturing. *Appl. Energy* 226, 277–286.

[9] Li, R., Wu, Q., Oren, S.S., 2013. Distribution locational marginal pricing for optimal electric vehicle charging management. *IEEE Trans. Power Syst.* 29 (1), 203–211.

[10] Miele, A., Axsen, J., Wolinetz, M., et al., 2020. The role of charging and refuelling infrastructure in supporting zero-emission vehicle sales. *Transp. Res. Part D* 81, 102275.

[11] Thompson, S.T., James, B.D., Huya-Kouadio, J.M., et al., 2018. Direct hydrogen fuel cell electric vehicle cost analysis: System and high-volume manufacturing description, validation, and outlook. *J. Power Sources* 399, 304–313.

[12] Schroeder, A., Traber, T., 2012. The economics of fast charging infrastruc- ture for electric vehicles. *Energy Policy* 43, 136–144.

[13] Tan, K.M., Ramachandaramurthy, V.K., Yong, J.Y., 2016. Integration of electric vehicles in smart grid: A review on vehicle to grid technologies and optimization techniques. *Renew. Sustain. Energy Rev.* 53, 720–732.

[14] Mayfield, D., Ohio, C.F., 2012. *Siting Electric Vehicle Charging Stations.* Editor Carlotta Collette.

[15] Illmann, U., Kluge, J., 2020. Public charging infrastructure and the market diffusion of electric vehicles. *Transp. Res. Part D* 86, 102413.

[16] K.A. Kalwar, M. Aamir, S. Mekhilef, 2015. Inductively coupled power transfer (ICPT) for electric vehicle charging—A review, *Renew. Sustain. Energy Rev.* 47, 462–475.

[17] D. Leskarac, C. Panchal, S. Stegen, J. Lu, 2015, PEV charging technologies and V2G on distributed systems and utility interfaces, In: J. Lu, J. Hossain (Eds.), *Vehicle-to-Grid: Linking Electric Vehicles to the Smart Grid*, The Institution of Engineering and Technology (IET), London, United Kingdom, pp. 157–209.

[18] 2017, 27 February. Plugless Power. Available: https://pluglesspower.com/.

[19] Wireless Power Transfer for Light-Duty Plug-In EVs and Alignment methodology, ed. Warrendale, Pennsylvania, United States: SAE International, 2017, p. 150. Available: https://saemobilus.sae.org/content/j2954_202010

[20] C.C. Mi, G. Buja, S.Y. Choi, C.T. Rim, 2016. Modern advances in wireless power transfer systems for roadway powered electric vehicles, *IEEE Trans. Ind. Electron.* 63, 6533–6545.

[21] O.C. Onar, J.M. Miller, S.L. Campbell, C. Coomer, C.P. White, L.E. Seiber, 2013. A novel wireless power transfer for in-motion EV/PHEV charging, In: *2013 Twenty-Eighth Annual IEEE Applied Power Electronics Conference and Exposition (APEC)*. IEEE, pp. 3073–3080.

[22] F. Musavi, M. Edington, W. Eberle, 2012. Wireless power transfer: A survey of EV battery charging technologies, In: *2012 IEEE Energy Conversion Congress and Exposition (ECCE)*. IEEE, pp. 1804–1810.

[23] J. Young Jae, K. Young Dae, J. Seungmin, 2012. Optimal design of the wireless charging electric vehicle, In: *Electric Vehicle Conference (IEVC)*. 2012 IEEE International, pp. 1–5.

[24] E. Coca, 2016. *Wireless Power Transfer—Fundamentals and Technologies*. InTech.

[25] R. Walli, 2016, 27 February. ORNL surges forward with 20-kilowatt wireless charging for vehicles. Available: www.ornl.gov/news/ornl-surges-forward-20-kilowatt-wireless-charging-vehicles

[26] Throngnumchai, A . Hanamura, Y . Naruse, K. Takeda, 2013. Design and evaluation of a wireless power transfer system with road embedded transmitter coils for dynamic charging of electric vehicles, *World Electr. Veh. J.* 6(4), 848–857.

[27] Esmaili, M., Goldoust, A., 2015. Multi-objective optimal charging of plug-in electric vehicles in unbalanced distribution networks. *Int. J. Electr. Power Energy Syst.* 73, 644–652.

[28] Moeini-Aghtaie, M., Abbaspour, A., Fotuhi-Firuzabad, M., et al., 2013. PHEVs centralized/decentralized charging control mechanisms: Requirements and impacts. In: *2013 North American Power Symposium (NAPS)*. IEEE, pp. 1–6.

[29] G. Fabbri and G. Tarquini, 2014. Impact of V2G/G2V technologies on distributed generation systems, In: *IEEE International Symposium on Industrial Electronics*, pp. 1677–1682.

[30] Liu, H., Qi, J., Wang, J., et al., 2016. EV dispatch control for supplementary frequency regulation considering the expectation of EV owners. *IEEE Trans. Smart Grid* 9 (4), 3763–3772.

[31] Arias, N.B., Hashemi, S., Andersen, P.B., et al., 2020. Assessment of economic benefits for EV owners participating in the primary frequency regulation markets. *Int. J. Electr. Power Energy Syst.* 120, 105985.

[32] King, C., Datta, B., 2018. EV charging tariffs that work for EV owners, utilities and society. *Electr. J.* 31 (9), 24–27.

[33] Pevec, D., Babic, J., Carvalho, A., et al., 2020. A survey-based assessment of how existing and potential electric vehicle owners perceive range anxiety. *J. Clean. Prod.* 276, 122779.

[34] S.P. Sathiyan, C.B. Pratap, A.A. Stonier, G. Peter, A. Sherine, K. Praghash, V. Ganji, 2022. Comprehensive assessment of electric vehicle development,

deployment, and policy initiatives to reduce GHG emissions: Opportunities and challenges, *IEEE Access* 10, 53614–53639.

[35] M.K. Metwaly, J. Teh, 2020. Probabilistic peak demand matching by battery energy storage alongside dynamic thermal ratings and demand response for enhanced network reliability, *IEEE Access* 8, 181547–181559.

[36] Advance Ruling (January 2019–December 2019), The institute of cost accountants of India, 2019. Source: https://icmai.in/upload/Taxation/Adv ance_Ruling.pdf.

[37] Source: https://okcredit.in/blog/gst-on-electric-vehicles/.

Chapter 7

Modeling of electronic-waste recycling intentions among Generation Z

Chand Prakash,[1] Ritu Yadav,[2] and Sarita Rathee[3]
[1]School of Management and Liberal Studies, The North Cap University, Gurugram, India
[2]Department of Management, Gurugram University, Gurugram, India
[3]Electrical and Electronics Department, School of Engineering and Technology, JECRC University, Jaipur, India

7.1 INTRODUCTION

The tremendous growth of industries and information technology has acted as a boon for the economy and benefited human life in terms of health, transport, security, education, etc. However, irresponsible and unwise use of technological resources raised several environmental issues. This irresponsible usage has created a challenge of balancing sustainability and technological advancement for the current and future generations [1]. The disposal of electrical and electronic equipment (EEE) waste or e-waste is a byproduct of this technical advancement that requires serious attention [2, 3]. The adoption of electric and electronic equipment has risen during the last decade. The life span of most electric and electronic equipment is short, and their repair is difficult and costly [4]. Once the equipment becomes outdated, it is converted into electronic-waste. Compared to solid waste, e-waste is rising faster, about 5% per annum [5, 6]. As per a study, 57.4 million metric tons of e-waste were generated during 2021, out of which only 17.4% of e-waste is collected for recycling and reuse. China, the US, and India were the top producers of e-waste [4].

Electronic-waste can be explained as the waste generated from damaged and unwanted electronic and electric devices, including batteries, mobile phones, video cameras, monitors, laptops, motherboards, etc. [7]. E-waste is generated when electric and electronic equipment are discarded as waste or rubbish without recycling or reusing it [8, 9]. Numerous global problems in terms of environmental, health, and food chain pollution occurred due to e-waste generation [10, 11]. Environmental pollutants generated due to e-waste disturb the ability of microbial metabolism, slow down the diversity of microbial communities, restrain the activity of microbial enzymes, etc. [12, 13]. Adverse impacts on human life can be witnessed in the form of accumulation of metals and metalloids, liver damage due to copper, behavior and learning ability interference due to lead, etc. [7, 14, 15].

DOI: 10.1201/9781003495574-7

The government is targeting to have e-vehicle (EV) sales accounting for 5% of private cars and 70% of commercial vehicles by the end of 2030 [16]. The growing popularity of EVs is also becoming a severe challenge for e-waste handling. EVs rely on lithium-ion batteries (LIBs) that become a significant potential source of e-waste. These batteries require charging after every 250 kms and have a life span of 5–10 years [17]. It creates a threat to the environment and ecosystem if not disposed of wisely. Global annual quantity and weight of waste of LIBs generating trouble for e-waste handling [18]. So, a proper strategy should be framed for reuse, recycling, and final disposal of any e-waste.

E-waste can be proved beneficial if appropriately managed. E-waste comprises various functional and valuable parts that can be used as secondary components if e-waste is processed and appropriately recycled [19, 20]. Unwise handling of e-waste can lead to several environmental and human problems. Unmanaged e-waste can significantly cause global warming. China produces 10129-kilo tonnes of e-waste and recycles only 16%, while India produces 3230-kilo tonnes of e-waste in the year 2021 with a recycling rate of 1 % [4]. The researcher showed concern towards the e-waste handling problem through this research. Further research aimed to identify the influential factors of e-waste recycling intention.

7.2 REVIEW OF THE LITERATURE

One of the major negative results of technological advancement is the generation of e-waste that seeks serious attention [21]. E-waste contains various hazardous materials that need sustainable treatment to minimize its adverse impact [19, 22]. Many developing countries face challenges in the disposal of e-waste and the threat of illegal import of e-waste or scrap [23, 24]. Weak policy framing and implementation, infrastructure, scarcity of collection centers, and lack of awareness among producers and users created hurdles for e-waste management [25]. An integrated e-waste management system with the involvement of the general public is required for e-waste handling rather than depending only on the legal framework [11]. Considering the role of the general public in e-waste management, this study extensively reviewed the literature related to the selected motivators for e-waste recycling intention.

7.2.1 Received information

Information received from various sources about the hazardous nature of e-waste and its disposal mechanism draws the attention of individuals. Accessibility of information about the e-waste recycling drop boxes and government schemes encourages e-waste recycling intention [11]. Limited availability of information with users of electric and electronic equipment

(EEE) results in the transfer of e-waste to scrap dealers [26]. Scrap dealers show limited interest in the safe and eco-friendly disposal of e-waste [27]. Thus, the following hypothesis can be proposed:

H1: Information received significantly impacts Generation Z's intention to recycle e-waste.

7.2.2 Knowledge

Knowledge about the toxicity of e-waste [28] controls the behavior of individuals towards the environment [29]. Knowing the severity of e-waste generates hedonic motivation for recycling intention [30]. Knowledge positively correlates to attitude towards recycling and intention [11]. This research argued that knowledge of the containment of hazardous substances in e-waste and usable secondary components positively influences the residents' intention to recycle e-waste. Previous research [27, 31] clarified that knowledge about the hazards of e-waste is not only a component of e-waste disposal intention but also impacts recycling intention because the previous recycling experience and the drop-off facility also impact recycling intention. Thus, it can be hypothesized

H2: Knowledge significantly impacts Generation Z's intention to recycle e-waste.

7.2.3 Convenience

Convenience to recycle waste has its significance in recycling intention. More convenience for recycling results in more intention among the general public [29]. Traveling long distances, paying for e-waste disposal, and sparing time for e-waste disposal showed its linkage with e-waste recycling intention [11]. E-waste recycling cost was found to correlate with the e-waste recycling intention. Due to less cost and convenience, residents prefer curbside disposal of e-waste. Incentives for e-waste recycling lead to residents' participation in e-waste recycling [32]. Some researchers showed contradictory results that e-waste recycling behavior is independent of incentives [33].

Based on the above discussion, it can be hypothesized that

H3: Convenience significantly impacts Generation Z's intention to recycle e-waste.

7.2.4 Government regulation

A well-established legal framework is also required to manage e-waste in a country effectively. Along with framing policies, implementing policies is also a concern for e-waste handling [34]. The government should provide e-waste drop boxes at offices and public places. Also, hotline service benefits should be provided to citizens who request extensive e-waste collection, such as refrigerators and washing machines, from their homes. Such frameworks and regulations encourage residents to dispose of e-waste [11] effectively. In India, the nodal administrative agency for e-waste rules is the Ministry of Environment, Forest and Climate Change. A previous study [11, 35] about e-waste management and awareness in India highlighted the unawareness of citizens about e-waste management and accepted the role of the government in developing strategies and regulatory frameworks for integrating all stakeholders in e-waste management practices. Thus, it can be hypothesized that

H4: Government regulations significantly impact Generation Z's intention to recycle e-waste.

7.2.5 Environment concern

Without formal recycling or disposal centers, e-waste can harm the environment adversely and create health hazards [36]. The chemical pollutants in e-waste can transfer to the human body through direct and indirect exposure [29]. In such a situation, an individual's environmental attitude decides their intention towards recycling e-waste [29, 37]. Attitude towards e-waste recycling results from knowledge, information and convenience [11]. Environmental concern motivates individuals to handle e-waste wisely. Thus, the following hypothesis can be framed:

H5: Environmental concerns significantly impact Generation Z's intention to recycle e-waste.

7.3 MATERIALS AND METHODS

An empirical study was conducted to study the intention to recycle e-waste among Generation Z (Figure 7.1). This study was conducted in India's National Capital Region (NCR). Delhi is facing a challenging situation with e-waste handling. More than 2 lakh tonnes of e-waste are produced in Delhi annually, about 9.5 per cent of the total e-waste produced in India [38, 39], which justified the selection of the NCR area (Delhi, Gurgaon, Faridabad, Noida) for research.

The sample was selected based on purposive sampling design because users of selected products, computer devices and electric vehicles were taken in the study. Computer devices, telecom products, and electric vehicles were well-known for high e-waste generators. A semi-structured questionnaire with 24 items on a five-point Likert scale ranging from strongly disagree to agree strongly was used to gather primary data. Twenty statements grouped

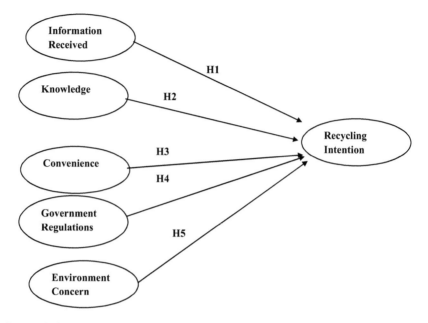

Figure 7.1 Conceptual framework.

Source: Framed by authors on the basis of an extensive literature review.

under five headings were related to the drivers of e-waste recycling intention. Four statements were used to measure recycling intention. Further demographic information was also covered in the questionnaire.

Initially, pilot testing was conducted over a sample of 25 respondents to measure the reliability and face validity of the constructs. Based on the pilot testing results, changes have been made to the questionnaire. The instrument showed its reliability using Cronbach's alpha (0.907) and face validity, measured through expert opinion.

Data were entered and coded by using SPSS 21. The responses of 14 participants were eliminated during the data-cleaning stage. Structure equation modeling (SEM) using AMOS 19 was used to establish the relation between drivers for e-waste recycling and recycling intention. The two-step model the researchers used was the measurement model and the structure model for structural equation modeling, as recommended by Anderson and Gerbing [6].

7.3.1 Data description

A total of 386 respondents of 18–30 years were considered final for the analysis. Of these, 185 (47.93%) were female, and 201 (52.07%) were male.

Most of the respondents were postgraduates (150, 38.86%), followed by graduates (126, 32.64%) and doctorates (110, 28.50%). 190 (49.22%) respondents were unmarried, and the remaining 196 (50.78%) were married. The majority of the respondents were from Delhi (120, 31.09%), followed by Gurgaon (98, 25.39%), Noida (86, 22.28%) and Faridabad (82, 21.24%). 55% of respondents were aware of e-waste generated through computer devices, and 35% were aware of EV waste generation. 10% of respondents were aware of e-waste generation for computer devices and EVs.

7.4 DATA ANALYSIS AND INTERPRETATION

Structure equation modeling is a useful technique for examining the relationship between dependent and independent variables [40]. The study has chosen five independent variables, namely information, knowledge, convenience, government regulation, and environmental concern, based on an extensive literature survey, and their linkage with e-waste recycling intention has been studied. A six-factor measurement model with 24 indicators has been framed to assess the reliability and validity of the constructs. Initially, the measurement model was assessed on the ground of fit indicators. CMIN/df, comparative fit indicator (CFI), root mean square error of approximation (RMSEA), Incremental Fit Index (IFI) and Tucker-Lewis Index (TLI) fit the researchers used indicators to check the fitness of the model to data. These model fit indicators were widely accepted and used by various previous researchers [41, 42, 43, 44, 45, 46, 47]. The recommended fitness criteria for the fit indicators are CMIN/Df: 2-5 [48]. CFI: ≥ 0.90 [49]; RMSEA: <0.08 Good fit [50]; TLI: ≥ 0.80 [49]; IFI: ≥ 0.90 [51].

The initial measurement model needed to show its appropriateness to the data. Hence, it was refined based on modification indices and standardized regression weight. Two indicators with weak loadings have been deleted from the model. The refined model was found appropriate and proved its fitness to data (CMIN = 511.817, Df = 192, P = 0.000, CMIN/Df = 2.666; CFI = 0.948; TLI = 0.937; IFI = 0.948; RMSEA = 0.066). Standardized indicator loadings with indicator descriptions have been shown in Table 7.1.

Additionally, the model's validity and reliability were assessed (Table 7.2). Cronbach's alpha value for the constructs, mottled from 0.823 to 0.921, falls under the recommended criteria [52]. Thus, the measurement model proved its internal consistency. Obtained average variance explained (AVE) and composite reliability (CR) scores lying in the recommended threshold value, AVE> 0.5; CR> 0.7 [53], proving the convergent validity of the construct. Also, Forenell and Lacker criteria for discriminant validity assessment were obtained in the model and proved the discriminant validity of the constructs [54]. Thus, the model was considered reliable and valid for further analysis.

Table 7.1 Standardized indicator loadings

Construct	Code	Indicator description	Standardized loadings
Information received	INF1	I receive information from local bodies about the collection program for e-waste.	0.68
	INF2	I received information about the nearest e-waste drop box.	0.73
	INF3	The social campaign keeps me updated about e-waste disposal.	0.89
	INF4	Government initiatives for e-waste disposal awareness keep me updated towards the e-waste disposal mechanism.	0.88
Knowledge	KNOW1	I know the fact that e-waste contains various hazardous substances.	0.94
	KNOW2	I am aware that useful secondary components can be found in e-waste.	0.93
	KNOW3	I know the importance of e-waste recycling.	0.71
	KNOW4	I know the long-term benefits of e-waste recycling.	0.78
Convenience	CON1	The approachability of e-waste recycling sites is a matter of concern.	0.61
	CON2	Incentives for e-waste recycling matter to me.	0.69
	CON3	I dispose of e-waste at a safe place if it demands limited time only.	0.87
	CON4	For me, affordability is a matter of concern for e-waste recycling.	Removed
Government regulation	GR1	There is a requirement for well-regulated e-waste disposal policies.	0.90
	GR2	The government should make arrangements for collecting e-waste from homes.	0.88
	GR3	The government should make laws stronger for effective e-waste disposal.	0.86
	GR4	In case of careless disposal of e-waste, a fine should be imposed.	0.81
Environment concern	EC1	I want to protect the environment from the negative effects of e-waste.	0.88
	EC2	I wish for a clean environment free from any e-waste.	0.83
	EC3	I make efforts to keep the environment free from e-waste.	0.75
	EC4	Everybody should try to keep the environment free from e-waste.	0.81
Recycling intention	REI1	I show a keen interest in formal e-waste collection.	0.77
	REI2	I urge others in my immediate vicinity to properly dispose of their electronic debris.	0.79
	REI3	I am always ready to search out innovative ways for e-waste recycling.	Removed
	REI4	I prefer to drop e-waste only at formal collection centres.	0.78

Source: Primary data (Amos Output).

Table 7.2 Reliability and validity assessment

	Cronbach's alpha	CR	AVE	MSV	MaxR(H)	EC	INF	KNOW	Conv	GR	REI
EC	0.876	0.876	0.640	0.537	0.879	**0.800**					
INF	0.880	0.877	0.645	0.461	0.904	0.486	**0.803**				
KNOW	0.903	0.908	0.715	0.566	0.944	0.565	0.479	**0.845**			
Conv	0.823	0.771	0.534	0.528	0.823	0.481	0.559	0.720	**0.831**		
GR	0.921	0.921	0.745	0.516	0.926	0.473	0.428	0.678	0.663	**0.863**	
REI	0.826	0.826	0.613	0.578	0.826	0.733	0.679	0.752	0.760	0.718	**0.783**

Source: Primary data (Amos Output).

Note: AVE – Average Variance Explained; CR – Composite Reliability; EC – Environment Concern; KNOW – Knowledge; Conv – Convenience; GR – Government Regulations; REI – Recycling Intention.

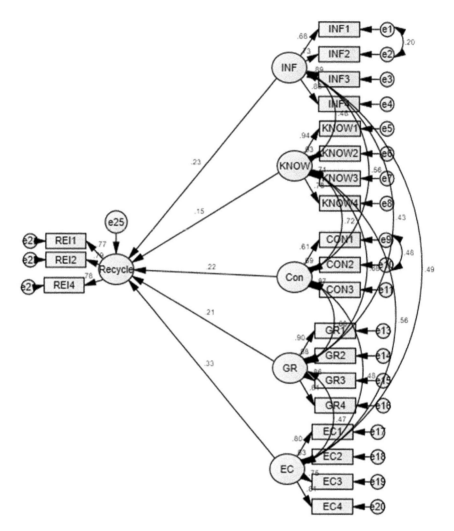

Figure 7.2 Structure model.

Source: Amos Output.

A structure model (Figure 7.2) has been drawn to study the significance of hypothesized relationships among variables. The desired model also found fitted to the data (CMIN = 511.817; Df = 192; P = 0.000; CMIN/Df = 2.666; CFI = 0.948; TLI = 0.937; IFI = 0.948; RMSEA = 0.066). Independent variables explained 83% of the variance of the dependent variable. Results of the study further proved that recycling intention among Generation Z was found to be significantly impacted by information (β = .231; P = 0.000); knowledge (β = 0.149; P = 0.016); Cconvenience (β = 0.224; P = 0.002); government regulation (β = 0.215; P = 0.000), and environment concern (β = 0.327; P = 0.000). Thus the hypothesis H1, H2, H3, H4, H5, and H6 were accepted hereby. The results further interpreted that environmental concern was the main reason for recycling intention among Generation Z, followed by information, convenience, government regulations, and knowledge.

7.5 DISCUSSION AND CONCLUSION

The result of the study was in alignment with previous research. This study highlighted that environmental concerns significantly impacted intentions to recycle. This study result was supported by previous studies [36]. Information received was the second most vital driver for recycling intention; that result was in line with the previous research [11]. Convenience for recycling e-waste was also a significant determinant of recycling intention among Generation Z. Previous studies [11] supported the study's results. Government regulations had a significant impact on e-waste recycling intention. Studies by [34, 35] favored the results. The last significant contributor to recycling intention was knowledge about waste. This study result was supported by previous research [11, 30].

Awareness towards e-waste handling or recycling is growing by the time among Generation Z. E-waste has a negative effect on both the environment and public health. Researchers request that people be concerned about the environment and be wise when using and disposing of e-waste. To do this, the government should launch awareness-raising programs and impose stringent regulations on how e-waste is disposed of. Recycling or disposal of e-waste should be convenient for users. The authorities should develop reachable eco-parks for e-waste recycling. Self-awareness towards the harmful effects of e-waste is required among Generation Z; only then can e-waste be managed effectively, as e-waste contains many usable and secondary valuable products. Thus, recycling habits should be developed among people that can only help to manage the harmful effects of e-waste.

7.6 FUTURE RESEARCH DIRECTIONS

This study made a significant contribution in suggesting ways for e-waste management, but it still needs to be made free of limitations that create scope for future research. Further research can be done to measure the challenges faced during e-waste handling. More research can be conducted over a sample of Pan India as this research targeted only the NCR area. A comparative analysis can be done among Generation Z and aged persons about their e-waste recycling habits. The impact of social influencers like social media, family, and peer pressure can be studied further to measure Gen Z's intention for recycling. The role of technology like recycling apps, online platforms, or gamification for encouraging people to recycle their e-waste can be studied further. However, the role of other influencers, like economic incentives, cross-disciplinary approaches, educational interventions, etc., can be researched in the future.

REFERENCES

1. Maphosa, Vusumuzi. "Students' awareness and attitudinal dispositions to e-waste management practices at a Zimbabwean University." *Journal of Information Policy*, 11 (2021): 562–581.
2. Hoerning, L., S. Watry, T. Burgett, and S. Matthias. "Advances in recycling & waste management." *Advances in Recycling & Waste Management*, 2 (2017), 128. Doi:10.4172/2475-7675.1000128
3. Perkins, Devin N., Marie-Noel Brune Drisse, Tapiwa Nxele, and Peter D. Sly. "E-waste: A global hazard." *Annals of Global Health*, 80, no. 4 (2014): 286–295.
4. Ruiz, Arabella (2022). Latest global E- waste statistics and what they tell us. Retrieved from https://theroundup.org/global-e-waste-statistics/ on Jan 30, 2023
5. Amankwah-Amoah, Joseph. "Global business and emerging economies: Towards a new perspective on the effects of e-waste." *Technological Forecasting and Social Change*, 105 (2016): 20–26. DOI: 10.1016/j.techfore.2016.01.026
6. Anderson, James C., and David W. Gerbing. "Structural equation modeling in practice: A review and recommended two-step approach." *Psychological Bulletin*, 103, no. 3 (1988): 411.
7. Parande, Anand Kuber Babu, Balakrishnan Ramesh, and Chiya Ahmed Basha. "Electrical and electronic waste: A global environmental problem." *Waste Management & Research*, 25, no. 4 (2007): 307–318.
8. Sajid, Muhammad, Jabir Hussain Syed, Mehreen Iqbal, Zaigham Abbas, Imran Hussain, and Muhammad Anwar Baig. "Assessing the generation, recycling and disposal practices of electronic/electrical-waste (E-Waste) from major cities in Pakistan." *Waste Management*, 84 (2019): 394–401.
9. Wath, Sushant B., P.S. Dutt, and Tapan Chakrabarti. "E-waste scenario in India, its management and implications." *Environmental Monitoring and Assessment*, 172 (2011): 249–262. DOI:10.1007/s10661-010-1331
10. Frazzoli, Chiara, Orish Ebere Orisakwe, Roberto Dragone, and Alberto Mantovani. "Diagnostic health risk assessment of electronic waste on the general population in developing countries' scenarios." *Environmental Impact Assessment Review*, 30, no. 6 (2010): 388–399.
11. Siringo, R., H. Herdiansyah, and R.D. Kusumastuti. "Underlying factors behind the low participation rate in electronic waste recycling." *Global Journal of Environmental Science and Management*, 6, no. 2 (2020): 203–214.

12. Johnston, Gloria P., and Laura G. Leff. "Bacterial community composition and biogeochemical heterogeneity in PAH-contaminated riverbank sediments." *Journal of Soils and Sediments*, 15 (2015): 225–239.
13. Petrić, I., D. Bru, N. Udiković-Kolić, D. Hršak, L. Philippot, and F. Martin-Laurent. "Evidence for shifts in the structure and abundance of the microbial community in a long-term PCB-contaminated soil under bioremediation." *Journal of Hazardous Materials*, 195 (2011): 254–260.
14. Chan, Janet Kit Yan, and Ming H. Wong. "A review of environmental fate, body burdens, and human health risk assessment of PCDD/Fs at two typical electronic waste recycling sites in China." *Science of the Total Environment* 463 (2013): 1111–1123.
15. Song, Qingbin, and Jinhui Li. "A review on human health consequences of metals exposure to e-waste in China." *Environmental Pollution*, 196 (2015): 450–461. DOI:10.1016/j.envpol.2014.11.004
16. Majumder, B. (June 13, 2022). Amidst EV boom, managing e-waste including battery disposal is a major challenge. Retrieved from www.news18.com/news/auto/amidst-ev-boom-managing-e-waste-including-battery-disposal-is-a-major-challenge-5360971.html on September 7, 2023
17. Dinger, Andreas, Ripley Martin, Xavier Mosquet, Maximilian Rabl, Dimitrios Rizoulis, Massimo Russo, and Georg Sticher. "Batteries for electric cars: Challenges, opportunities, and the outlook to 2020." *The Boston Consulting Group*, 7 (2010): 1–18.
18. Zeng, Xianlai, Jinhui Li, and Yusen Ren. "Prediction of various discarded lithium batteries in China." In *2012 IEEE International Symposium on Sustainable Systems and Technology (ISSST)*, pp. 1–4. IEEE, 2012. DOI:10.1109/ISSST.2012.6228021
19. Dai, Yifeng, Xia Huo, Yu Zhang, Tian Yang, Minghui Li, and Xijin Xu. "Elevated lead levels and changes in blood morphology and erythrocyte CR1 in preschool children from an e-waste area." *Science of the Total Environment*, 592 (2017): 51–59.
20. Das, Avimanyu, A. Vidyadhar, and Surya P. Mehrotra. "A novel flowsheet for the recovery of metal values from waste printed circuit boards." *Resources, Conservation and Recycling* 53, no. 8 (2009): 464–469.
21. Garlapati, Vijay Kumar. "E-waste in India and developed countries: Management, recycling, business and biotechnological initiatives." *Renewable and Sustainable Energy Reviews*, 54 (2016): 874–881.
22. Du, Yanan, Yan Wang, Liqing Du, Chang Xu, Kaihua Ji, Jinhan Wang, and Qiang Liu. "Cytogenetics data in adult men involved in the recycling of electronic wastes." *Data in Brief*, 17 (2018): 1405–1416.
23. Olowu, Dejo. "Menance of e-wastes in developing countries: An agenda for legal and policy responses." *Law Environment and Development Journal*, 8 (2012): 59.
24. Tansel, Berrin. "From electronic consumer products to e-wastes: Global outlook, waste quantities, recycling challenges." *Environment International* 98 (2017): 35–45.
25. Osibanjo, Oladele, and I. C. Nnorom. "The challenge of electronic waste (e-waste) management in developing countries." *Waste Management & Research*, 25, no. 6 (2007): 489–501.

26. Skinner, Alexandra, Yvonne Dinter, Alex Lloyd, and Philip Strothmann. "The Challenges of E-waste management in India: Can India draw lessons from the EU and the USA." *Asien*, 117, no. 7 (2010): 26.

27. Sinha, S., P. Mahesh, E. Donders, and V. Breusegem. (2011). Waste electrical and electronic equipment the EU and India: Sharing best practices. Retrieved from www.eeas.europa.eu/delegations/india/eu-india-partners-circular-econ omy-and-resource-efficiency_en

28. Akhtar, Rulia, Muhammad Mehedi Masud, and Rafia Afroz. "Household perception and recycling behaviour on electronic waste management: A case study of Kuala-Lumpur, Malaysia." *Malaysian Journal of Science*, 33, no. 1 (2014): 32–41. DOI: 10.22452/mjs.vol33no1.5

29. Otto, Siegmar, Alexandra Kibbe, Laura Henn, Liane Hentschke, and Florian G. Kaiser. "The economy of E-waste collection at the individual level: A practice oriented approach of categorizing determinants of E-waste collection into behavioral costs and motivation." *Journal of Cleaner Production*, 204 (2018): 33–40.

30. Wang, Zhaohua, Bin Zhang, Jianhua Yin, and Xiang Zhang. "Willingness and behavior towards e-waste recycling for residents in Beijing city, China." *Journal of Cleaner Production*, 19, no. 9–10 (2011): 977–984. DOI:10.1016/j.jclepro.2010.09.016

31. Saphores, Jean-Daniel M., Oladele A. Ogunseitan, and Andrew A. Shapiro. "Willingness to engage in a pro-environmental behavior: An analysis of e-waste recycling based on a national survey of US households." *Resources, Conservation and Recycling*, 60 (2012): 49–63.

32. Jafari, Amin, Jafar Heydari, and Abbas Keramati. "Factors affecting incentive dependency of residents to participate in e-waste recycling: A case study on adoption of e-waste reverse supply chain in Iran." *Environment, Development and Sustainability*, 19 (2017): 325–338.

33. Nduneseokwu, Chibuike Kingsley, Ying Qu, and Andrea Appolloni. "Factors influencing consumers' intentions to participate in a formal e-waste collection system: A case study of Onitsha, Nigeria." *Sustainability*, 9, no. 6 (2017): 881.

34. Sulami, Antonius Priyo Nugroho, Takehiko Murayama, and Shigeo Nishikizawa. "Current issues and situation of producer responsibility in waste management in Indonesia." *Environment and Natural Resources Journal*, 16, no. 1 (2018): 70–81.

35. Srimathi, H., A. Krishnamoorthy, and S. Dharshini. " E-waste management and awareness." *International Journal of Scientific & Technology Research*, 8, no. 11 (2019), 2627–2631.

36. Needhidasan, Santhanam, Melvin Samuel, and Ramalingam Chidambaram. "Electronic waste–an emerging threat to the environment of urban India." *Journal of Environmental Health Science and Engineering*, 12 (2014): 1–9.

37. Wäger, P.A., Roland Hischier, and Martin Eugster. "Environmental impacts of the Swiss collection and recovery systems for Waste Electrical and Electronic Equipment (WEEE): A follow-up." *Science of the Total Environment*, 409, no. 10 (2011): 1746–1756.

38. ASSOCHAM Report (2018). Rerieved from https://timesofindia.indiati mes.com/ city/delhi/dispose-of-e-waste-properly-depts-told/articleshow/84956085.cms

39. Et. Government. Com (July 9, 2022). India's first e-waste eco park to be established in Holambi Kalan in Delhi: Env. Retrieved from https://governm ent.economictimes.indiatimes.com/news/governance/indias-first-e-waste-eco-park-to-be-established-in-holambi-kalan-in-delhi-environment-minister-gopal-rai/92765791

40. Zhang, Zhongheng. "Structural equation modeling in the context of clinical research." *Annals of Translational Medicine*, 5, no. 5 (2017). DOI: 10.21037/atm.2016.09.25

41. Hair, Joseph F. Jr., Rolph E. Anderson, Ronald L. Tatham, and W. C. Black. "Multivariate data analysis" (3rd edition) (1995). New York: Macmillan.

42. Hooper, Daire, Coughlan, Joseph, and Mullen, Michael R. Structural equation modelling: Guidelines for determining model fit. *The Electronic Journal of Business Research Methods*, 6, no. 1 (2008): 53–60.

43. Hult, G., M. Tomas, Joseph F. Hair Jr , Dorian Proksch, Marko Sarstedt, Andreas Pinkwart, and Christian M. Ringle. "Addressing endogeneity in international marketing applications of partial least squares structural equation modeling." *Journal of International Marketing*, 26, no. 3 (2018): 1–21.

44. Hu, Li-tze, and Peter M. Bentler. "Cutoff criteria for fit indexes in covariance structure analysis: Conventional criteria versus new alternatives." *Structural Equation Modeling*, 6, no. 1 (1999): 1–55.

45. Prakash, Chand, Ritu Yadav, Amardeep Singh, and Aarti. "An empirical investigation of the higher educational institutions' attractiveness as an employer." *South Asian Journal of Human Resources Management*, 9, no. 1 (2022): 130–148.

46. Prakash, C., R. Yadav, A. Singh, and K. Yadav. (2021). Modeling the entrepreneurial intention among business students. *Pacific Business Review International*, 14(3): 1–14.

47. Yadav, Kanchan, Anshul Arora, Ritu Yadav, and Chand Prakash Saini. "Gamified apps and customer engagement: Modeling in online shopping environment." *Transnational Marketing Journal*, 10, no. 3 (2022): 593–605. DOI:10.33182/tmj.v10i3.2199

48. Wheaton, Blair, Bengt Muthen, Duane F. Alwin, and Gene F. Summers. "Assessing reliability and stability in panel models." *Sociological Methodology*, 8 (1977): 84–136. DOI:10.2307/270754

49. Byrne, Barbara M. *Structural Equation Modeling with LISREL, PRELIS, and SIMPLIS: Basic Concepts, Applications, and Programming.* Psychology press, 1998.

50. MacCallum, Robert C., Michael W. Browne, and Hazuki M. Sugawara. "Power analysis and determination of sample size for covariance structure modeling." *Psychological Methods*, 1, no. 2 (1996): 130.

51. Bentler, Peter M. "Comparative fit indexes in structural models." *Psychological Bulletin*, 107, no. 2 (1990): 238.

52. Nunnally, Jum C. *Psychometric Theory: 2d Ed.* McGraw-Hill, 1978.

53. Malhotra, Naresh K. *Marketing Research: An Applied Orientation.* Pearson, 2020.

54. Cha, Jaesung. "Partial least squares." *Advanced Methods of Marketing Research*, 407 (1994): 52–78.

Chapter 8

Vision-based target tracking for UAVs using YOLOv2 deep algorithms

Raja Munusamy[1] and S. Rankesh Laxman[2]
[1]Hindustan Institute of Echnology and Sciences, Chennai, India
[2]Department of Aeronautical Engineering, Hindustan Institute of Technology and Sciences, Chennai, India

8.1 INTRODUCTION

One of the basic issues in the fields of image processing, computer vision, and recognition of patterns is object detection, that serves as the conceptual theory for a number of effortless image evaluation and comprehension techniques like target identification and behavior analysis. Categorizing particular objects as members of a given class when they exist and localizing each one using a bounding box are the two basic activities involved in identifying an object [1]. The convolutional neural network (CNN), with excellent results in image processing, has improved object recognition precision to a level equivalent in an individual because of its strong capacity of extracting features from images in the past few decades with the explosive growth of deep learning (DL) and associated techniques. This has drawn a lot of scholars who are starting to examine using the superior image characteristics that CNN has retrieved in its object recognition [2].

The primary goal of detecting objects, a typical problem in the field of computer vision, is to identify and find a particular item in an image. The satellite images include many, multi-scale items that were photographed by multiple cameras on multiple devices, and as a result, they offer potential and a wealth of information for object recognition. Object identification has been done on space borne, aerial, and terrestrial satellite images utilizing a variety of remote detecting systems [3]. In general, the term remote sensing relates to a satellite tracking system using tall structures, automobiles that move, and floating levels[4]. These databases are used to provide many optically labeled datasets but only a small number of infrared heat records exist for various surface objects. The disadvantages of monitoring satellites, such as the lack of great-resolution thermal images because of the limits of space sensors, are compensated for by the capacity of UAV systems to gather high spatially and temporal quality images shown in Figure 8.1. Additionally, the requirement for extremely accurate and smart identification techniques has increased as a result of the fast growth of UAVs.

DOI: 10.1201/9781003495574-8

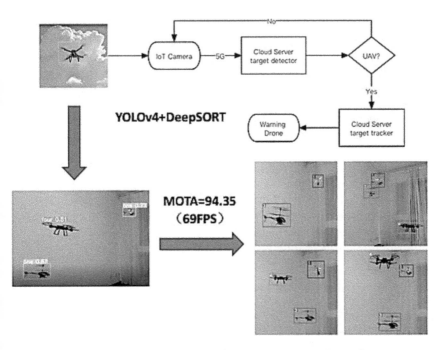

Figure 8.1 Deep learning algorithm using Yolo2 (remote sensing application).

A kind of planes known as UAV is piloted by an automated pilot, as opposed to a human pilot. A sizable element of the armed force's conflict equipment in today's world consists of UAV. Furthermore, they are used in public settings for things like emergency situation awareness and security surveillance [4]. UAV, or drones, are used more often for both local monitoring and remote information collection. New UAVs have exciting applications in a variety of industries since they may either be actively guided by a computerized automation system or remotely supervised by an individual. These scenarios include those for relief efforts, highway security, the transportation and transportation of pharmaceuticals, agriculture, recreation, and various other purposes. These initiatives have generated a variety of new needs and many innovative ideas for using UAV [5]. Devices utilized for aerial privacy, general safety for everyone, and military defense are all at danger from UAV uses. UAV enhanced management as a consequence; nonetheless, cooperation, storage of information, and quick, logical choices are still necessary. Systems mostly rely on the internet system to evaluate information using complex DL techniques.

The area recommendation-based object detection model has improved greatly in terms of object detection accuracy; however, the extraction of potential areas requires a longer period, which slows down the entire detection model. Figure 8.1 shows the development of the YOLOv2 object recognition model, which addressed that issue of computing difficulty by recasting the object identification issue as a single regression issue and simultaneously predicting the bounding box dimensions and category possibilities. The input image is divided into an S×S grid by the YOLO.

When an item's center drops into a grid cell, that cell assumes authority over that object and forecasts the B bounding boxes and confidence ratings associated with those boxes [6]. The confidence score provides two types of data: the model's level of certainty assuming an object is inside the box and the accuracy of its predictions. End-to-end training and actual time velocity object detection models are made possible by the YOLO approach, which minimizes the level of detail of model training and significantly increases the operation effectiveness of the whole detection model, enabling an improvement in duration for the object detection model built on CNN. The key contribution of the chapter is given below.

8.1.1 Organization of research work

- The three primary processes of the suggested system are data collection, model training, and identification and monitoring of the target item.
- To train the YOLOv2 model, a dataset of videos and images of the target objects is first gathered and pre-processed.
- After that, the YOLOv2 model is developed based on the data that has been gathered, allowing it to recognize and pinpoint the target objects in the real-time video streams that the UAV has taken.
- The YOLOv2 model detects and tracks the target objects from the data set after training.
- To monitor a target's location and motion, the YOLOv2 model produces the bounding box coordinates of the intended objects in every frame of the video.
- The final step is to utilize the monitored target items to steer along with the UAV.

The remaining portions of the essay are arranged as follows. The literature on object motion detection using a video series is illustrated in Section 8.2. The problem statement is presented in Section 8.3. The suggested method for detecting object motion is covered in Section 8.4. The results are summarized in Section 8.5. The conclusion is outlined in Section 8.6.

8.2 RELATED WORKS

The electricity industry has given a lot of thought to the use of UAV in disaster mitigation and assistance with the goal to increase the effectiveness of following a disaster rehabilitation for the electrical supply system[9]. The research suggests a novel method of pole recognition and identification in distribution channels based on UAV inspection line video in order to address the loss evaluation requirements of above power lines. The CNN is used to identify the pole position in images in combination with the traits of YOLO's quick identification. Additionally, when identifying the evaluation line video, the pole information and associated images are also acquired. In order to deal with the tragedy, the electrical division can immediately quantify the damages. YOLOv3 modifies the connection value prior to image training and defines the matching ROI for the UAV inspection line standards. The article suggests an estimation method that uses the ongoing coordinate shift in the bounding box of a single pole in each side frame of video to rapidly collect the loss evaluation for post-disaster pole accommodation. The technique ensures that the categorized calculating of pole is precise and the accuracy of detection is above 0.9. The outcomes of the video testing demonstrate the extent to which this approach works for determining and identifying the status of the elevated line for transmission pole in the distributing system [7, 8].

Hossain [5] discussed detecting and tracking objects using camera vision with utilization of machine learning algorithms.

AI has made significant strides recently, opening the door to the development of independent computers, robots, and gadgets that are notably typified by their capacity for independent decision-making and job completion. UAV, sometimes known as drones, are a few of these tools and are frequently employed to carry out duties including monitoring, rescue efforts, object recognition and monitoring targets, among many others. Effective actual time recognition of objects in aerial recordings is urgently needed, particularly with the expansion of UAV use across a variety of industries. Drones have to be trustworthy and productive since the duties at hand are sensitive. The CNN YOLO-v2 built around the video footage of a drone are used in the study to demonstrate the study advancements in the creation of software for recognizing and monitoring the presence of people. DL-based machine vision is used to detect a person's location and condition. The findings of the individual's identification indicate the high degree of object recognition and classification precision provided by YOLO-v2. The system for tracking reacts more quickly for continuous monitoring than commonly used methods, effectively monitoring the identified individual while removing it from view [9].

Jiang et al. [10] discussed how thermal cameras are used to detect thermal image during night vision with the help of yolo models.

Among the biggest and most important problems in visual computing and satellite imagery is the identification of objects, which identifies specific groups of diverse things in images [11]. Two crucial sources of information for security purposes are the infrared thermal sensor data and the images and videos produced by UAVs. Due to the complex scene details, low resolution relative to the viewable films, and dearth of publicly available datasets with labels for developing models, their item recognition procedure is still difficult. A UAV TIR object identification structure for images as well as videos was suggested in the current investigation. The FLIR lenses used to gather surface-based TIR images and videos were to use YOLO designs, whose are centered on the design of CNN. In conclusion, evaluation techniques were employed to ascertain which approach would be the most effective in finding objects in TIR videos captured by UAVs. The findings showed that humans and automobile occurrences in the validating task had the highest mAP, which was 88.69%. YOLOv5-s had the smallest model size and 50 FPS was the quickest rate of recognition. The program assessed the intersect-detection effectiveness on persons and cars in UAV TIR videos under a YOLOv5-s model independent of the different UAVs' viewing views, demonstrating the utility of the YOLO structure. The study provides favorable support for the subjective and statistical evaluation of object recognition from TIR images and film using models [10].

Juewen et al. [12] discussed the detection of a stationary target and a target in motion. The collected UAV videos/images were compared with the pre-determined position using Yolo algorithms.

To estimate yield and increase output, the tomato plant's productive systems must expand and grow. A quick and computerized solution is needed because the labor-intensive hand measuring techniques are unreliable and expensive in a difficult setting, involving leaves and stem blockage and duplicated tomato numbers. In order to create autonomous gathering, which increases farmers' productivity and reduces the necessary manpower, this research presents an image recognition and AI-based drone technology to recognize and count tomato blossoms and fruits [13]. The suggested approach uses the aerial images of a greenhouse tomato sample set, which is divided into three different groups, to train and test an estimation model using state-of-the-art DL techniques YOLO V5 and Deep Sort. With a precision of 0.628 at mAP 0.15, epoch 96 yields the most accurate model for every class. At 0.913 and 0 levels of trust, the precision and recall values are calculated to be 1 and 0.85, correspondingly. The F1 scores for the tomato classes – red, green, and flower – are calculated to be 0.73, 0.46, and 0.62, correspondingly. The average overall F1 score is similarly calculated to be 0.63. The tomato's fruits and blossoms are gathered regularly from the greenhouse's surroundings using the derived recognition and enumeration model. Red tomato, flowers, and green tomato had accordingly, 86%, 98%, and 50% accuracy when counted manually and by AI-Drone [12].

MOD in UAV footage is now gaining significant traction in a variety of industries[13]. Nevertheless, the reliability of identification varies widely depending on the items and methods used. The SSD version and YOLO version 5 are two common detection models, and for improving accuracy of detection, their ability to detect objects is constantly assessed and contrasted with other better methods. To increase the precision of detection even more, a modified YOLO_v5 detecting technique was put out in the study. To increase the accuracy of detecting objects that move, it implemented a transmitted integrate-frame confirmation procedure that depends on neural networks, leverages spatial data, and incorporates object velocity and orientation as well. The methods were tested using available UAV footage from the University of Stanford, and three different sorts of objects that move were examined to gauge their effectiveness. The testing of the experiment shows that the suggested MOD approach may increase accuracy in the identification of tiny objects that move, which has tremendous practical value and can serve as a starting point for further research in the field.

8.2.1 Problem statement

Convolutional neural network (CNN) technique has been hailed as an especially effective tool for the classification and recognition of objects. CNNs are biologically inspired systems of hierarchy that might be trained to do a variety of finding, identifying, and segmenting tasks. These designs primarily concentrate on improving the ability to identify and computation difficulties of their approaches in order to achieve real-time effectiveness for wirelessly and computerized systems. Additionally, CNN-based object detectors need a lot of computation, and achieving high efficiency in devices that integrate is difficult [14]. So here in this chapter YOLOv2 is introduced for object detection.

8.3 METHODOLOGY

The YOLO-v2 object detector is used in this research to demonstrate how a UAV can identify and track an object, regardless of whether it moves or is stationary [15]. Additionally, a YOLO-v2 network-based method for target recognition using vision is provided in this research. The method is based on the idea of DL. The suggested method has two parts: tracking objects and recognizing the object. ParrotAR.Drone 2 is used for carrying out the object recognition and monitoring. A personal computer (PC) and the ParrotAR. Drone 2 are connected through Wi-Fi. In Figure 8.2, the workflow diagram is displayed.

8.3.1 Data collection

The dataset utilized in this study is the UAV DRONE dataset. The dataset contains the total of 936 images among which 704 images are used as training images and the remaining 232 images are taken as testing images. The data collection is given in Table 8.1

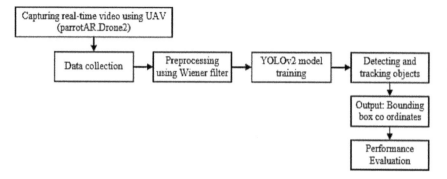

Figure 8.2 YOLOv2 machine learning block diagram.

Table 8.1 UAV drone data collection

Training images	704
Testing images	232
Total images	936

8.3.2 Pre-processing

Following the collection of the images, a pre-processing phase utilizing the Wiener filter is carried out. To lessen the noise that is created during the image capture, a Wiener filter was used. In many situations, the Wiener filter is used to repair signals that have been corrupted by noise. The mathematical basis of the filter is based on the assumption that the noise and signal are static linear stochastic processes with spectrum properties. This method works better because it balances the bias-variance trade-off the best. In other words, the Wiener filter is a flexible filter that determines the variance and mean of a neighborhood before smoothing data to a range of intensities depending on the degree of variability in the area [16]. The filter's basic theory pre-supposes conjugated, convoluted integers that produced a complex dataset with a square magnitude. The Wiener filter equation is shown in equation (8.1).

$$H(x,y) = \left[\frac{1}{G(x,y)} \frac{|G(x,y)|^2}{|G(x,y)|^2 + S_a(x,y)/S_b(x,y)} \right] W(x,y) \qquad (8.1)$$

Here, the noise power spectrum is denoted by $S_b(x,y) = |R(x,y)|^2$. The equation $S_a(x,y)/S_b(x,y)$ is replaced by a constant K since the power spectral density of the unmodified image is not well recognized. The Wiener filter is capable of helping remove noise that can be present continually in images during digital analysis. The size of the neighborhood and the sounds consequently constitute the Wiener filter's characteristics.

8.3.3 Training the model

By utilizing a single neural network structure, YOLO-v2 automatically forecasts the bounding box and categorization probabilities. The image is partitioned into $R \times S$ grid of cells, where every cell is able to forecast one item. A grid cell's function is to find objects whose centers lie within it. Each grid cell may forecast the B bounding boxes, their confidence rating, and the classification possibilities. There are five components that make up the bounding box: (u, v, w, z, confidence C). In relation to the position of a grid cell, the (u, v) measurements refer to the box's center. The parameters are between 0 and 1. (w, z) box measurements, that are similarly constructed on a scale of 0 to 1, are used to describe the bounding box's breadth and length in relation to the image size. The anticipated confidence ratings have a double significance: they indicate the model's level of confidence in the thing the box contains, and the degree to which it thinks the box can foresee the object [17, 18]. The fact because the confidence ratings are 0 indicates that there are no items in the current cell. Otherwise, it is anticipated that the confidence level will be the intersection over union (IOU) of the anticipated box and the actual data. In rare circumstances, many items can fit inside an individual grid cell.

8.3.4 Detection and tracking of targeted object

The visual serving technique is utilized wherein the objective is to keep the aerial vehicle at an approximate range of 1 m from the object being shot and to keep the object centered in the image. The YOLO-v2 CNN provides the image and a boundary box on the identified item after the thing has been found in the image. The data regarding the location of an object on the image is contained in this boundary box. The YOLO-v2 method's detecting flow diagram is shown in Figure 8.3. It is discovered that the variables of pixels determine the object's location (u_{min}, v_{min}), (u_{max}, v_{min}), (u_{min}, v_{max}), (u_{max}, v_{max}). Based on these positional data, the object's core is determined [19].

$$(u_0, v_0) = \left(\frac{u_{min} + u_{max}}{2}, \frac{v_{min} + v_{max}}{2} \right) \tag{8.2}$$

Figure 8.3 UAV images.

In order to follow the item, the image's centroid must also be determined, which is done as follows [20]:

$$(u_i, v_i) = \left(\frac{\text{image}_{\text{width}} - \text{image}_{\text{width}}}{2}, \frac{\text{image}_{\text{height}} - \text{image}_{\text{height}}}{2} \right) \tag{8.3}$$

$$(u_i, v_i) = (0,0) \tag{8.4}$$

For the sake of clarity, the image's centroid is assumed to be (0, 0). The following is the description of the error that occurs between the object's core and the image's core:

$$e_u(t) = u_0 - u_i = u_0 \qquad (8.5)$$

$$e_v(t) = v_0 - v_i = v_0 \qquad (8.6)$$

Figure 8.4 shows UAV images of the following; the image includes (a) cars; (b) bus; (c) light; (d) people; (e) remote sensing; (f) landing; (g) ground navigation [21].

Figure 8.4 shows the YOLOv2 detection flowchart with conditional possibility of C classifications is predicted.

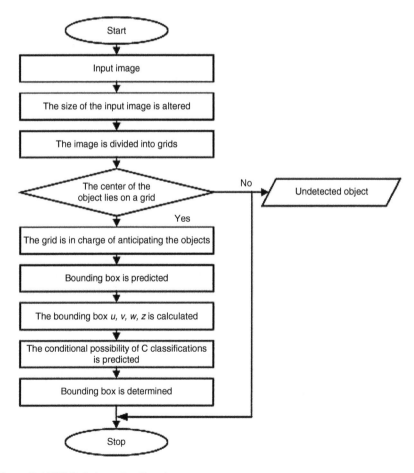

Figure 8.4 YOLOv2 detection flowchart.

Table 8.2 Performance metrics of the proposed YOLOv2 model

Accuracy	0.95
Precision	0.78
Recall	0.88

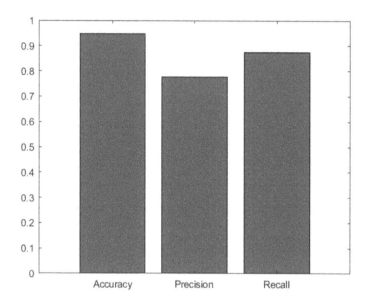

Figure 8.5 Performance of evaluation metrics of YOLOv2.

8.4 RESULTS AND DISCUSSION

The performance metrics of the proposed YOLOv2 model is evaluated and the values are given in Table 8.2. And the graphical representation of the performance metrics is given in Figure 8.5.

8.4.1 Accuracy

Accuracy is used to gauge the prediction algorithm's effectiveness as a whole. In essence, it is the idea that every interaction can be correctly foreseen [22]. Accuracy is provided in equation (8.7),

$$\text{Accuracy} = \frac{T_{Pos} + T_{Neg}}{T_{Pos} + T_{Neg} + F_{Pos} + F_{Neg}} \tag{8.7}$$

8.4.2 Precision

Precision is the measure of how closely or accurately multiple calculations match each other. How well a result can be replicated is revealed by the link among precision and accuracy. Equation (8.8) allows for the computation of precision.

$$P = \frac{T_{Pos}}{T_{Pos} + F_{Pos}} \tag{8.8}$$

8.4.3 Recall

Out of every one of the positive data, the recall counts indicate how numerous true positives were really correctly identified as positives. It is given the percentage of equation (8.9) forecasts, which were accurate [23]

$$R = \frac{T_{Pos}}{T_{Pos} + F_{Neg}} \tag{8.9}$$

8.5 CONCLUSION

UAV vision-based target tracking and following is a significant area of study with multiple uses in industry. For identifying objects and tracking in real-time video streams, deep learning methods like YOLOv2 have recently demonstrated considerable potential. This study describes a YOLOv2-based target monitoring and surveillance device for unmanned aerial vehicles. The three primary phases of the suggested system are data gathering, model training, and target object recognition and monitoring. A database consisting of videos and images of the desired products or objects is gathered in the data acquisition stage in order to further develop the YOLOv2 model. After being trained with the gathered database, the YOLOv2 model is then able to recognize and identify the target item in real-time video streams recorded by the UAV's camera. The YOLOv2 model may be used to find and follow the target object in real-time video streams once it has been trained. In each frame of the video, the YOLOv2 model provides the coordinates of the bounding box of the target item, allowing you to follow its location and motion. An improved algorithm for moving object detection in YOLO UAV to control the UAV's flight and follow the target, the tracked target object is utilized last. Numerous real-world uses for this strategy exist, such as aerial photography, monitoring, and rescue operations. Vision-based object surveillance and tracking might, with more work, becomes a crucial tool for UAVs in a variety area.

REFERENCES

1. Opromolla R, Inchingolo G, Fasano G. Airborne visual detection and tracking of cooperative UAVs exploiting deep learning. *Sensors* 2019; 19: 4332.
2. Hossain S, Lee D. Deep learning-based real-time multiple-object detection and tracking from aerial imagery via a flying robot with GPU-based embedded devices. *Sensors* 2019; 19: 3371.
3. Truong NQ, Nguyen PH. Deep learning-based super-resolution reconstruction and marker detection for drone landing | *IEEE Journals & Magazine* | IEEE Xplore. https://ieeexplore.ieee.org/abstract/document/8710329 (accessed 24 April 2023)
4. Shinde C. Multi-view geometry and deep learning based drone detection and localization | IEEE Conference Publication | IEEE Xplore. https://ieeexplore. ieee.org/abstract/document/8715593 (accessed 24 April 2023)
5. Hossain S. Deep learning-based real-time multiple-object detection and tracking from aerial imagery via a flying robot with GPU-based embedded devices. www.mdpi.com/1424-8220/19/15/3371 (accessed 24 April 2023)
6. Giray SM. Anatomy of unmanned aerial vehicle hijacking with signal spoofing. In: *2013 6th International Conference on Recent Advances in Space Technologies (RAST)*. Istanbul, Turkey: IEEE, pp. 795–800.
7. Renault A. A model for assessing UAV system architectures. *Procedia Computer Science* 2015; 61: 160–167.
8. Arola S, Akhloufi MA. UAV Pursuit-evasion using deep learning and search area proposal, Unmanned system technology. DOI 10.1117/12.2520310 May 2019
9. Chen B, Miao X. Distribution line pole detection and counting based on YOLO using UAV inspection line video. *Journal of Electrical Engineering & Technology* 2020; 15: 441–448.
10. Jiang C, Ren H, Ye X, et al. Object detection from UAV thermal infrared images and videos using YOLO models. *International Journal of Applied Earth Observation and Geoinformation* 2022; 112: 102912.
11. Boudjit K, Ramzan N. Human detection based on deep learning YOLO-v2 for real-time UAV applications. *Journal of Experimental & Theoretical Artificial Intelligence* 2022; 34: 527–544.
12. Juewen Hu JH, Juewen Hu PW, Pei Wang JY, et al. An improved algorithm for moving object detection in YOLO UAV videos. *Journal of Computers* 2022; 33: 147–158.
13. Egi Y, Hajyzadeh M, Eyceyurt E. Drone-computer communication based tomato generative organ counting model using YOLO V5 and deep-sort. *Agriculture* 2022; 12: 1290.
14. Kvasić I, Mišković N, Vukić Z. Convolutional neural network architectures for sonar-based diver detection and tracking. In: *OCEANS 2019 – Marseille*. IEEE, 2019, pp. 1–6.
15. Dos Santos JCM, Carrijo GA, de Fátima dos Santos Cardoso C, et al. Fundus image quality enhancement for blood vessel detection via a neural network using CLAHE and Wiener filter. *Research on Biomedical Engineering* 2020; 36: 107–119.

16. Kumar A, Kumar V, Modgil V, Kumar A. "Stochastic Petri nets modelling for performance assessment of a manufacturing unit." *Materials Today: Proceedings* 2022; 56: 215–219.

17. Kumar A, Singh H, Kumar P, AlMangour B, eds. *Handbook of Smart Manufacturing: Forecasting the Future of Industry 4.0.* CRC Press, 2023. https://doi.org/10.1201/9781003333760

18. Rani S, Tripathi K, Kumar A. "Machine learning aided malware detection for secure and smart manufacturing: A comprehensive analysis of the state of the art." *International Journal on Interactive Design and Manufacturing (IJIDeM)* 2023: 1–28.

19. Rani S, Tripathi K, Arora Y, Kumar A. "A machine learning approach to analyze cloud computing attacks." In *2022 5th International Conference on Contemporary Computing and Informatics (IC3I)*, pp. 22–26. IEEE, 2022.

20. Joshi VD, Agarwal P, Kumar A. "Fuzzy transportation planning: A goal programming tactic for navigating uncertainty and multi-objective decision making." *International Journal on Interactive Design and Manufacturing (IJIDeM)* 2023: 1–29.

21. Rani S, Kumar A, Bagchi A, Yadav S, Kumar S. "RPL based routing protocols for load balancing in IoT network." In Journal of Physics: Conference Series, vol. 1950, no. 1, pp. 012073. IOP Publishing, 2021.

22. Rajendra P, Kumari M, Rani S, Dogra N, Boadh R, Kumar A, Dahiya M. "Impact of artificial intelligence on civilization: Future perspectives." *Materials Today: Proceedings* 2022;56: 252–256.

23. Rani S, Tripathi K, Arora Y, Kumar A. "Analysis of anomaly detection of malware using KNN." In *2022 2nd International Conference on Innovative Practices in Technology and Management (ICIPTM)*, vol. 2, pp. 774–779. IEEE, 2022.

Chapter 9

Flight delay prediction
A comprehensive review of models, methods, and trends

Richa Sharma, Rohit Kaushik, Mukkisa Indhu,
Anupam Kumar, and Aman Kumar Upadhyay
Department of Computer Science & Engineering, Chandigarh University, Mohali,
India

9.1 INTRODUCTION

Air transport has been an important part of the economies throughout the world for many years. This makes it easier and cheaper to move wares and passengers to different parts of world. Due to the inter-linkage of many key factors, the air service industry often faces the challenge of allocating resources to avoid air travel and flight delay issues. The aim of this study is to authenticate a model designed to assist both airlines and passengers in scheduling flights effectively while minimizing the risk of delays. Flight delays incur significant costs for business, including fuel costs, crew salaries, and passenger compensation. On the other hand, travelers may experience inconvenience, lack of connectivity, and other downsides of travel planning. The flight delay estimation process is based on historical data and statistical analysis. However, machine learning models have shown the potential to predict flight delays by taking into account more factors, such as whether, air quality, and other external factors. Extensive research has been conducted in the field of estimating flight delays by harnessing machine learning [1] algorithms, including neural networks, decision trees, and support vector machines. These studies examined the significance of various factors on flight delays, including departure time airport location, aircraft, and weather conditions. Using machine learning to estimate delays could improve the accuracy of predictions and help airlines and passengers plan their trips better. Nonetheless, there are persisting challenges in the development of models capable of predicting flight delays, encompassing issues related to data accessibility and quality, model intricacy, and their general applicability across various airports and aircraft. Overall, using machine learning models to predict flight delays in an important and widely researched area that could benefit airlines and passengers by reducing delays and improving travel.

About 20 percent of flights are canceled or delayed every year, which is costing passengers more than 20 billion dollar in time and money. The

DOI: 10.1201/9781003495574-9

population is growing and for many wealthy people timing is everything. Flights became more important here, but they were more costly and had frequent delays, which led to a decline in flight maintenance in the 1960s, therefore, more products were produced for airports that lead to flight control. The aviation industry holds a crucial role within the nation's economy but is also a source of substantial economic losses. Recent studies predominantly employ three methods to estimate flight delays, namely (i) binary classifiers; (ii) multi-class classifiers; and (iii) regression techniques.

9.1.1 Causes of delay

A flight is considered delayed when it lands or takes off from the airport past its originally scheduled arrival or departure time. The realm of research focusing on predicting flight delays through machine learning employs a range of algorithms to accurately anticipate these delays. Figure 9.1 shows various reasons why the flights are being delayed.

9.1.1.1 Adverse weather conditions

Adverse weather conditions can cause flight delays for a variety of reasons. Poor visibility, high winds, thunderstorms, and heavy snow or ice can all impact a plane's ability to take off, fly, and land safely. Airports and airlines have safety protocols in place to ensure that flights do not operate in hazardous conditions, such as during thunderstorms or periods of

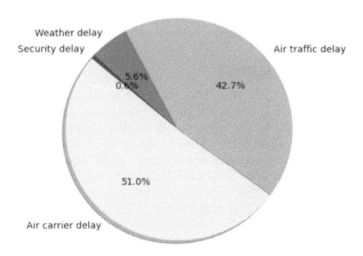

Figure 9.1 Factors affecting flight delay.

heavy snowfall. This can lead to flight cancellations or delays as planes are grounded until the weather improves.

9.1.1.2 Air traffic congestion

Air traffic congestion is another common cause of flight delays. As air travel has become more popular, the number of flights in the air has increased, leading to more crowded airspace and longer wait times for planes to take off and land. Air traffic controllers work to manage the flow of planes in the air and on the ground, but during peak travel times or in areas with limited runway capacity, delays can occur. This is especially true at major hub airports, where many flights may be scheduled to arrive and depart within a short period of time.

9.1.1.3 Security issues

Flight delays can also arise from security concerns, as airlines and airports implement measures to guarantee the safety of both passengers and crew members. In extreme cases, security threats such as terrorist attacks or hijackings can result in the grounding of all flights or the diversion of planes to alternate airports. These incidents can cause significant disruption to air travel and may result in long delays or cancellations.

9.1.1.4 Air carrier delay

This type of delay occurs when an airline carrier is responsible for flight delay where they are no able to operate the flight it scheduled. It can be happened because of various reasons, it can be because of a mechanical problem in the aircraft, unaccepted maintenance need, or crew unavailability.

9.2 LITERATURE SURVEY

In their 2019 study, Yu and colleagues [2] harnessed a combined deep belief network model, which has proven highly successful in addressing the challenges posed by vast datasets and effectively capturing the primary factors influencing flight delays. Their model achieved an impressive coefficient of determination accuracy of 93% and a mean absolute error (MAE) of 8.41 minutes. However, it is noteworthy that the study did not incorporate arrival and global flight data into its analysis.

In their 2023 work, CAI and their team [3] introduced a geographical and operational graph convolution network (GOGCN) designed for the prediction of multiple flight delays across different airports. They introduced an operational aggregator to assimilate global operational data using the graph structure, alongside a geographical aggregator to encompass the shared characteristics of geographically proximate airports. GOGCN variant without geo aggregator provide better results with 28.26% mean absolute percentage error. They do not, however, make it easier for others to understand their projections. In their 2023 study, Mokhtarimousavi and Mehrabi [4] employed a support vector machine (SVM) model enhanced by the artificial bee colony (ABC) algorithm. This approach was devised to investigate the intricate, non-linear connections between flight delay occurrences and the underlying contributing factors. ABC-SVM resulted 11.04% more accuracy than conventional SVM. The combination of SVM and MXL models has enhanced our understanding of flight delays, although it is worth noting that a larger dataset was not utilized in the analysis.

The authors of [5] developed a logistic model. This research involved two random aircraft operations that happen at an airport, departure, and arrival. They resulted in 92% for departure delay and 82% arrival delay. It relies upon calculations of aviation and meteorological parameters

The authors of [6] reviewed naive Bayes, decision tree, and linear regression. The conclusion of our analysis indicates that the decision tree model outperforms the other models, achieving a perfect score of 1 and displaying the lowest error rate of 0 across all aspects. Furthermore, this model effectively reveals which day of the week, departure airport, and vacation destination airport experience the highest frequency of flight delays.

Reference [7] proposed a model called kernel density estimation and its extensions, to predict probability of flight delay. These are data-driven methods, only considering past observations. The estimates received appear to be better than those used by FlightCaster (its long-term estimates are based on the distribution of electronic components). Since the kernel density estimation method is a database method, it can always be used to rebuild probabilistic models.

Reference [8] came up with the flight-to-gate assignment model, which significantly decreases the count of aircraft conflicts by as much as 74% compared to the deterministic flight-to-gate assignment model. Additionally, it is feasible to predict probability distributions for future delays within a CRPS of 11 minutes, even several days in advance, by amalgamating probabilistic flight shift forecasts for various airport operation modes.

The authors of [9] worked on the XGBoost algorithm. Accuracy of 82% is achieved by multi-layer perceptron. Due to the stochastic nature of delays, this study investigates the qualitative prediction of airline delays to put into effect essential changes and provide higher consumer experience.

Reference [10] developed a Levenberg-Marquart algorithm. The Levenberg-Marquardt algorithm yields superior accuracy for the SDA-LM model when dealing with imbalanced datasets, surpassing the tan SAE-LM and SDA models by 8.2% and 11.3%, respectively. The LM algorithm is not only effective for optimizing outcomes but also for balancing datasets.

The authors of [11] employed the gradient boosting decision tree. The accuracy of the arrival delay prediction outcomes using the gradient boosting decision tree (GBDT) algorithm stood at 92.77% for EWR, 81.23% for LGA, and 81.77% for JFK.

Table 9.1 describe the previous work that was done by the different researches for flight delay prediction and it shows the different models that they used to predict the delay and this table also shows the benefits they achieve and limitation.

9.3 PROBLEM STATEMENT

Flight delay can cause serious inconvenience to passengers, airlines, and airports, leading to customer satisfaction/loss and economic losses, while several studies have been performed on flight delay or air delays, the accuracy of those model are still limited. Many of these studies focus on a specific region or airline, making it difficult to discover the result. So, there is a need to perform a review of the existing research papers or literature [22] on flight delay prediction to analyze the common challenges and limitations for the current models. Conducting such a review will aid researchers and stakeholders within the aviation sector in gaining a deeper insight into the latest advancements in flight delay prediction. This, in turn, will enable them to formulate more effective strategies for mitigating the repercussions of these delays.

9.4 GOAL/OBJECTIVES

1. To provide a comprehensive overview of the existing research and literature on flight delay prediction, including common challenges and limitations of current models.
2. To give an idea to future researchers and developers in the field of flight delay prediction.
3. The emphasis is placed on the necessity of precise and dependable flight delay predictions, serving the interests of both air travelers and various stakeholders within the aviation industry.
4. To review and synthesize the relevant literature on flight delay prediction, including research papers, industry reports, and other sources of information.
5. To analyze the weaknesses and strength of different approaches to flight delay prediction, including statistical methods, machine learning algorithms, and hybrid models.

9.5 DESIGN AND FLOW

9.5.1 Analysis of feature and finalization subject to constraints

This chapter studies and analyzes more than 30+ research papers on flight delay prediction and it then concludes by identifying the best models from

Table 9.1 Existing work of flight delay prediction using different technology

S no.	Author name	Year of publication	Technology used	Advantages	Limitation
1.	[12]	2020	• Multiple linear regression • Support vector machine (SVM) • Extremely randomized trees (extra RT) • Light gradient boosting machine (light GBM)	• It was allowed by four types of airport-related comprehensive characteristics.	• The model's performance is less impressive when using weather-related attributes in comparison to its performance with meteorological or climate data.
2.	[13]	2018	• A priori algorithm was used. • Regression tree • Rep tree	• The maximum significance standards of accuracy is F1 score and ROC location.	• Try to use a data set with a huge number of instances. • It can lead us to manage big data mining technologies.
3.	[14]	2014	• Random forest • Classification • Regression model	• This paper offered new network-primarily based air visitors put off prediction fashions that included both temporal and community postpone states as explanatory variables.	• It cannot predict individual flight delays.
4.	[15]	2020	• Naïve Bayes model • Logical tree	• Naïve Bayes is smart while giving real time prediction. • The algorithmic rule for computation may be superimposed along with the system scalability as another independent property.	• Significant events, whether they are natural disasters or human-made incidents, have the potential to cause substantial flight delays. • Establish a strong connection between the challenges, scope, and methodology to attain the most precise results.

(continued)

Table 9.1 (Cont.)

S no.	Author name	Year of publication	Technology used	Advantages	Limitation
5.	[16]	2022	• Synthetic minority over-sampling technique (SMOTE) • Cat-boost, XG-Boost, Light GBM	• In order to avoid being impacted by the dataset's instability, the SMOTE approach was applied.	• It may not be feasible to predict the delays caused in connecting flights.
6.	[17]	2020	• LSTM-based method (long short-term memory) • Random forest-based mode	• The LSTM-based architecture is achieving notably superior accuracy in comparison. • LSTM proves to be an efficient model for time-related tasks.	• Overfitting problem occurs on using this LSTM model.
7.	[18]	2020	• Probabilistic neural network • Decision tree • Random forest • Gradient boosted trees	• Gradient boosted trees are well-suited for detecting temporal anomalies in departure flight data with a high degree of accuracy. • The implemented supervised machine learning model confirmed that the first-class set of rules to locate time deviation short and with excessive accuracy.	• In scenarios where the flight time distribution varies, it is advisable to steer clear of MLP and SVM algorithms.
8.	[19]	2021	• Logistic Regression • K-nearest neighbor • Gaussian naïve Bayes • Decision tree • Random forest • Gradient boosted tree	• Weighted evaluation metrics are applied when dealing with imbalanced data distributions.	• For improved prediction techniques like SMOTE will be a better option.

No.	Ref.	Year	Methods	Description	Remarks
9.	[20]	2017	• Hybrid method (decision tree combined with cluster classification) • Random forest • Decision tree • Bayesian modeling	• Statics were tested on the basis of real dataset.	• Combing the hybrid method with strong light scheduling indicates capability as an exciting research course.
10.	[21]	2018	• K-means clustering algorithm • CHAID decision algorithm	• It analyzes the topology traits of the aviation community after which it combines node attributes with okay-approach clustering set of rules to divide the busy level of all airports.	• The problem of over fitting has not been resolved.

all of the previous models used. Here the least accurate to the most accurate models are included and the various models discussed and reviewed are outlined in the following.

9.5.2 Various models used

Decision tree: this is most powerful and famous tool for classification and prediction. It has a tree-like structure where internal node, branch, leaf node will be there.

> Internal node – it denotes a test on attribute.
> Branch – it gives outcome of the test.
> Leaf node – it holds a class node.

DTCC (decision tree combined with cluster classification): in machine learning and data analysis, techniques like decision trees and clustering are frequently used. A set of binary decisions are used to classify data or make predictions using decision trees. Data points are grouped using clustering according to how similar they are. These two methods are sometimes combined to provide a more potent categorization model.

Random forest: the random forest machine learning technique amalgamates diverse decision trees to deliver a more robust and accurate model. Employing ensemble learning, it integrates the forecasts from multiple models to yield more precise predictions.

Light gradient boosting machine (light GBM): Microsoft created the well-known open-source gradient boosting system known as light gradient boosting machine (light GBM). It is particularly suited for large-scale machine learning challenges since it is made to be extremely efficient in terms of memory utilization and training speed. Multiple decision trees are sequentially trained using the ensemble learning technique known as gradient boosting, and each new tree learns from the mistakes of the previous trees. Using a gradient boosting framework called light GBM, decision trees are constructed in a depth-first fashion.

NBM (naïve Bayes model): this machine learning algorithm is occupied for categorization jobs. It is founded on Bayes' theorem, a statistical principle that enables one to determine the likelihood of a hypothesis based on the likelihood of the evidence that has been observed. The naïve Bayes method selects the class that has the highest probability after enumerating the probability of each class given the observed characteristics.

LSTM (long short-term memory): RNN architectures featuring long short-term memory (LSTM) were specifically developed to combat the vanishing and exploding gradient issues encountered by traditional RNNs. They find wide application in tasks such as time series forecasting, natural language processing, and speech recognition. The LSTM architecture incorporates three distinct gates responsible for governing the inflow and outflow of data into a memory cell that retains information over time. These gates, namely the input gate, output gate, and forget gate, are controlled by sigmoid and hyperbolic tangent (tanh) activation functions to manage their operations.

XG-Boost (extreme gradient boosting): a machine learning technique called XG-Boost (extreme gradient boosting) is utilized for supervised learning issues including classification, regression, and ranking. It is built with efficiency, scalability, and accuracy at its core and is based on the gradient boosting architecture. A group of decision trees is assembled by XGBoost, and each tree is trained using the residual mistakes of the one before it. The objective function of the method, which is often a loss function measuring the discrepancy between the predicted and actual values, is optimized using a regularized gradient boosting framework. It also offers enhanced precision and generalization performance.

REP tree: 'REP tree' stands for 'reduced error pruning tree,' referring to the algorithm's usage of a pruning approach that decreases the possibility of excessive fitting. The algorithm constructs a decision tree using the training data, prunes the tree by deleting branches that don't increase the model's overall accuracy, and then repeats the process.

GAT (gradient augmented tree): the algorithm builds decision trees sequentially, with each tree's purpose being to rectify the shortcomings of the one that precedes it. Using the training data, the method first constructs a single decision tree before computing the errors or residuals of the predictions generated by the tree. Once these faults have been fixed, it constructs a second tree and repeats the process until the required number of trees has been accomplished.

Binary classification: binary classification, commonly denoted as 'positive' or 'negative' classes, represents a form of supervised learning in machine learning, where the primary aim is to classify incoming data into one of two possible categories. In other words, based on the values of input characteristics or variables, the model is trained to differentiate between two categories of data [23].

1. Comparative analysis

Table 9.2 shows the various models used in research for the prediction of flight delay. To find accuracy the researchers used various techniques and algorithms that they perform. This helps to find the best out of many algorithms that can be used in future works.

Figure 9.2 gives details of the best accuracy and the least accuracy given by different models. In this LSTM (long short-term memory) has given the greater accuracy with 99%, and the least accuracy is given by DTCC with 71.39%.

Table 9.2 Performance comparison for different technique

S no.	Reference	Year of Publication	Technology used	Performance parameter
1.	[11]	2020	• Multiple linear regression (linear R) • Support vector machine (SVM) • Extremely randomized tree (extra RT) • Light gradient boosting machine (light GBM)	GBM will give accuracy of 86.5% with error margin of 6.65 min as best.
2.	[13]	2018	• A priori algorithm was used. • Regression tree • REP tree	This algorithm provides the highest TPR (true positive rate) rules with 82.8% and REP tree provides the highest percentage (79.9%) among all tree classifiers.
3.	[14]	2014	• Random forest • Classification • Regression model	The best result is given by classification algorithm with an average 81% accuracy.
4.	[15]	2020	• Naïve Bayes model • Logical tree	Logical tree results with 93% accuracy.
5.	[16]	2022	• Synthetic minority over-sampling technique (SMOTE) • CatBoost, XGBoost, Light GBM	96.9% accuracy is provided by XGboost.
6.	[17]	2020	• LSTM-based model (Long short-term memory) • Random forest based model	The LSTM-based network achieves 99% accuracy.
7.	[18]	2020	• Probabilistic neural network • Decision tree • Random forest • Gradient boosted trees	The highest accuracy is obtained by using gradient augmented trees with 96.02%

No.	Ref.	Year	Methods	Results
8.	[19]	2021	• Logistic regression • K-nearest neighbor • Gaussian naïve Bayes • Decision tree • Random forest • Gradient boosted tree	The best results are given by binary class choice tree algorithm with 97.77 % of accuracy.
9.	[20]	2017	• Hybrid method (decision tree combined with cluster classification) • Random forest • Decision tree • Bayesian modeling	Accuracy degree of 71.39% is exhibited by hybrid method.
10.	[21]	2018	• K-means clustering algorithm • CHAID decision algorithm	The best results are provided by forecast (cause) with 79.54%.

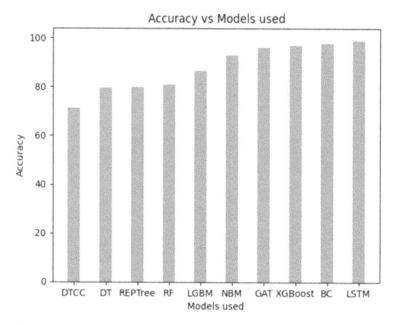

Figure 9.2 Accuracy of various models.

The primary parameter for comparing existing models is accuracy, which is a fundamental measure of how often a machine learning classification algorithm correctly classifies data points.

- Accuracy: accuracy represents the ratio of correctly predicted data points to all data points and is formally calculated as the sum of true positives and true negatives divided by the sum of true positives, true negatives, false positives, and false negatives.
- True positives and true negatives are data points correctly classified as true or false, respectively, while false positives and false negatives are data points incorrectly classified.
- These metrics collectively provide a comprehensive means of evaluating the performance and reliability of machine learning models.

9.6 CONCLUSION

The prediction of flight delays holds a significant place in the literature, given its economic [24] and environmental repercussions. Cause of this there may be increase costs of customer and operation cost of airlines. This is directly related to the passenger. Flight delay prediction is an essential component of decision-making for all stakeholders within the transportation system [25].

Table 9.3 Comparison parameters

Comparison parameters
Accuracy
True positive rate
Error margin

So, relevant to this researcher developed flight delay prediction model over the last year, this work contributes to the analysis of these models and to let you know which model is best for flight delay prediction.

DTCC is giving less accuracy according to our research because it is highly unstable, meaning on adding one data or deleting one data from the dataset it shows major fluctuation in accuracy, which is not practical to use but in LSTM it does not show major fluctuation and is much more stable as compared to DTCC. Also, DTCC works on tabular data, which is easily understandable to human beings but for machine learning models it is not easy to traverse but LSTM works on sequential data, which is much easier to work on. This is the reason why DTCC is giving much less accuracy as compare to LSTM. Future investigations could concentrate on tailoring LSTM models to the specific needs of individual airlines or airports, incorporating real-time data to heighten prediction accuracy, and designing user-friendly applications that offer passengers up-to-the-minute flight delay forecasts. As deep learning continues to make inroads into the aviation industry, we aspire for our work to be a catalyst for driving further innovations in this field

9.7 FUTURE SCOPE

The future scope of the work is that the researchers need to study more advanced methods or techniques to analyze the performance of the system in order to minimize the flight delay. In order to predict the flight delay prediction in a better way, future research is aimed to develop a model that will provide better accuracy.

REFERENCES

[1] K. A, Rani, and Sangeeta, Khushboo Tripathi, "Machine learning aided malware detection for secure and smart manufacturing: A comprehensive analysis of the state of the art," *Int. J. Interact. Des. Manuf.*, vol. 17, pp. 1–28, 2023.

[2] B. Yu, Z. Guo, S. Asian, H. Wang, and G. Chen, "Flight delay prediction for commercial air transport: A deep learning approach," *Transp. Res. Part E Logist. Transp. Rev.*, vol. 125, no. March, pp. 203–221, 2019. doi: 10.1016/j.tre.2019.03.013

[3] K. Cai, Y. Li, Y. Zhu, Q. Fang, Y. Yang, and W. DU, "A geographical and operational deep graph convolutional approach for flight delay prediction," *Chinese J. Aeronaut.*, vol. 36, no. 3, pp. 357–367, 2023. doi: 10.1016/j.cja.2022.10.004

[4] S. Mokhtarimousavi, and A. Mehrabi, "Flight delay causality: Machine learning technique in conjunction with random parameter statistical analysis," *Int. J. Transp. Sci. Technol.*, vol. 12, no. 1, pp. 230–244, 2023. doi: 10.1016/j.ijtst.2022.01.007

[5] R. Wesonga, F. Nabugoomu, and P. Jehopio, "Parameterized framework for the analysis of probabilities of aircraft delay at an airport," *J. Air Transp. Manag.*, vol. 23, pp. 1–4, 2012. doi: 10.1016/j.jairtraman.2012.02.001

[6] T. Nibareke, and J. Laassiri, "Using Big Data-machine learning models for diabetes prediction and flight delays analytics," *J. Big Data*, vol. 7, no. 1, 2020. doi: 10.1186/s40537-020-00355-0

[7] H. Malkar, "Flight_Delay_Prediction | Kaggle," 2021. [Online]. Available: www.kaggle.com/code/hrishikeshmalkar/flight-delay-prediction

[8] M. Zoutendijk, and M. Mitici, "Probabilistic flight delay predictions using machine learning and applications to the flight-to-gate assignment problem," *Aerospace*, vol. 8, no. 6, 2021. doi: 10.3390/aerospace8060152

[9] R. T. Reddy, P. B. Pati, K. Deepa, and S. T. Sangeetha, "Flight delay prediction using machine learning," *2023 IEEE 8th Int. Conf. Convergence Technol. (I2CT)*, pp. 1–5. IEEE, 2023.

[10] M. F. Yazdi, S. R. Kamel, S. J. M. Chabok, and M. Kheirabadi, "Flight delay prediction based on deep learning and Levenberg-Marquart algorithm," *J. Big Data*, vol. 7, no. 1, 2020. doi: 10.1186/s40537-020-00380-z

[11] Y. Wu, G. Mei, and K. Shao, "Revealing influence of meteorological conditions and flight factors on delays Using XGBoost," *J. Comput. Math. Data Sci.*, vol. 3, no. December 2021, pp. 100030, 2022. doi: 10.1016/j.jcmds.2022.100030

[12] B. Ye, B. Liu, Y. Tian, and L. Wan, "A methodology for predicting aggregate flight departure delays in airports based on supervised learning," *Sustain.*, vol. 12, no. 7, 2020. doi: 10.3390/su12072749

[13] S. M. Al-Tabbakh, H. M. Mohamed, and Z. H. El, "Machine learning techniques for analysis of egyptian flight delay," *Int. J. Data Min. Knowl. Manag. Process*, vol. 8, no. 3, pp. 01–14, 2018. doi: 10.5121/ijdkp.2018.8301

[14] J. J. Rebollo, and H. Balakrishnan, "Characterization and prediction of air traffic delays," *Transp. Res. Part C Emerg. Technol.*, vol. 44, pp. 231–241, 2014. doi: 10.1016/j.trc.2014.04.007

[15] Yogita Borse, Dhruvin Jain, Shreyash Sharma, and Viral Vora, Aakash Zaveri, "Flight delay prediction system," *Int. J. Eng. Res.*, vol. V9, no. 03, pp. 88–92, 2020. doi: 10.17577/ijertv9is030148

[16] I. Hatıpoğlu, Ö. Tosun, and N. Tosun, "Flight delay prediction based with machine learning," *Logforum*, vol. 18, no. 1, pp. 97–107, 2022. doi: 10.17270/J.LOG.2022.655

[17] G. Gui, F. Liu, J. Sun, J. Yang, Z. Zhou, and D. Zhao, "Flight delay prediction based on aviation big data and machine learning," *IEEE Trans. Veh. Technol.*, vol. 69, no. 1, pp. 140–150, 2020. doi: 10.1109/TVT.2019.2954094

[18] P. Stefanovič, R. Štrimaitis, and O. Kurasova, "Prediction of flight time deviation for lithuanian airports using supervised machine learning model," *Comput. Intell. Neurosci.*, vol. 2020, 2020. doi: 10.1155/2020/8878681

[19] Y. Tang, "Airline flight delay prediction using machine learning models," *ACM Int. Conf. Proceeding Ser.*, pp. 151–154, 2021. doi: 10.1145/3497701.3497725

[20] H. Khaksar, and A. Sheikholeslami, "Airline delay prediction by machine learning algorithms," *Sci. Iran.*, vol. 26, no. 5 A, pp. 2689–2702, 2019. doi: 10.24200/sci.2017.20020

[21] T. Zhou, Q. Gao, X. Chen, and Z. Xun, "Flight delay prediction based on characteristics of aviation network," *MATEC Web Conf.*, vol. 259, pp. 02006, 2019. doi: 10.1051/matecconf/201925902006

[22] M. D. Rajendra, P., Mina Kumari, Sangeeta Rani, Namrata Dogra, Rahul Boadh, Ajay Kumar, "Impact of artificial intelligence on civilization: Future perspectives.," *Mater. Today Proc.*, vol. 56, pp. 252–256, 2022.

[23] Kumar A,. Rani, Sangeeta, Khushboo Tripathi, Yojna Arora, "A machine learning approach to analyze cloud computing attacks," *2022 5th Int. Conf. Contemp. Comput. Informatics (IC3I)*, pp. 22–26. IEEE, 2022.

[24] Kumar Ajay, Hari Singh, Parveen Kumar, and Bandar AlMangour, "Handbook of smart manufacturing: Forecasting the future of industry 4.0," *CRC Press.* 2023.

[25] Ajay Kumar Joshi, Vishwas Deep, and Priya Agarwal, "Fuzzy transportation planning: A goal programming tactic for navigating uncertainty and multi-objective decision making," *Int. J. Interact. Des. Manuf.* doi:10.1007/s12008-023-01634-9

Selection of electric car using multi-attribute decision-making methods

A.S. Sanap and A.G. Kamble

School of Mechanical Engineering, MIT Academy of Engineering, Alandi, Pune, India

10.1 INTRODUCTION

When an automobile of the same size is charged with electricity rather than petrol, it may go the same distance for around 40% less money. Electric cars do not emit any pollution. Renewable energy such as having a solar PV system can further lower your greenhouse gas emissions by switching to an electric car and charging it throughout the day. An alternate choice is to buy Green Power from an electrical supplier. When harmful exhaust emissions are minimized, our health benefits. Better air quality will lead to fewer health problems and financial expenditures caused by air pollution. Furthermore, electric cars are less expensive than automobiles powered by petrol or diesel and contribute less to noise pollution. Effective management of electric car charging, particularly outside of peak electricity demand hours, will enable us to develop a lower 24-hour demand profile for the electrical network. Introduction and comparison of AHP methodology in a choice problem involving public transportation development attributes are as follows: accessibility, directness, timing, availability, swiftness, dependability, physical comfort, mental comfort, and travel safety [1]. This will improve our ability to use the electricity grid, enable electric car users to avoid more expensive charging times, increase the efficiency of the entire electricity system, and encourage the addition of more small- and large-scale renewable energy sources to the grid.

Multi-attribute decision-making MADM strategies are used to select the best possibilities from a variety of alternatives because choosing an acceptable electric automobile can be difficult for decision-makers. The different methods employed by the MADM, such as the analytical hierarchy process AHP and multi-objective optimization based on ratio analysis MOORA. The MADM approach, is designed to overcome difficulties with selecting a decision from limited options to assess the process economics in the attributes of multi-variate loss functions, such as the breaking point, softening point, heat resistance point, peeling resistance, and shear resistance, analytical

 DOI: 10.1201/9781003495574-10

hierarchy method is used [2]. These methods require both between and within attribute comparisons as well as the appropriate explicit concessions. The best optimal solutions to a variety of situations have been the focus of research on the analytic hierarchy method attribute selection for enterprise resource planning software, financial, and supplier-related [3]. The use of AHP in buildings should be analyzed [4]. The goal of the current work is to identify the ideal ranking using the techniques that have been suggested along with electric car attributes and alternatives.

10.2 LITERATURE REVIEW

Several researchers work on various selection problems. The use of MADM techniques for choosing among different alternatives and attributes has been extensively studied. This section gives the works that use different decision-making strategies in the selection of different problem statements.

Kaya et al. [5] used ELECTRE-I and Fuzzy AHP for site selection for electric vehicle-sharing stations with an eye toward sustainability. A multi-criterion GIS-based approach to decision-making methodology was applied to Istanbul, a metropolitan city in Turkey. Więckowski et al. [6] explained the MCDM approach as an application of multi-criteria decision analysis to complex sensitivity analysis in the choice of an electric vehicle. Komnos et al. [7] examined the use of gasoline and energy conventional in electric cars in Europe. Dwivedi et al. [8] explained the entropy method and topics method to evaluate and ranking of electric vehicles, having criteria like quick charge time, maximum power, electric range, battery capacity, top speed, and base price. Lai et al. [9] explained the car-sharing service for electric vehicles with multi-temporal and multi-task operation-optimized scheduling. Lee et al. [10] used AHP for assessing adult learning preferences research in assessing preferences. The four activities suggested for adult learning are (a) lectures; (b) in-class discussion and reflections; (c) group-based projects; and (d) individual projects. Bahmani et al. [11] explained the AHP method for a consumer choice problem. This approach is illustrated in an application to the prediction of consumer choice behavior attributes as follows: cost, on-time performance, reputation, and service. Trivedi et al. [12] features an analytical hierarchy process for road collision severity rating using a multi-criteria decision-making tool and Boroumandi et al. [13] utilized an analytic hierarchical method for landslide danger zonation in the Iranian Province of Zanjan and factor Laduse drainage volume seismicity separation from flaws in the weight of precipitation relative.

Ramkumar et al. [14] described the MOORA technique ratio analysis used to select the biopolymer for the injection molding process utilizing multi-objective optimization.

Agrawal et al. [15] proposed the MOORA technique for critical evaluation of the rank method for sustainable material selection in additive manufacturing. Gupta et al. [16] discuss the MOORA approach, using prestigious multi-criteria decision-making methodologies, material selection for rotational molding attributes in coir, banana, coconut, bamboo, cotton, and hemp. Erdoğan et al. [17] consider the optimal fuel choice for a CI engine using hybrid multiple-criteria decision-making techniques while using their blends and pure biodiesels manufactured from various sources. Gurumurthy et al. [18] use the MOORA method and MOORA technique optimization of a bio-based iquid transformer insulator.

Prasad et al. [19] described the MOORA approach for using WASPAS and MOORA, experimental research and parametric optimization were conducted during abrasive jet machining on nickel 233 alloy. Wankhede et al. [20] input parameter selection for a solar-powered absorption refrigeration system using MOORA and TOPSIS. Sarkar et al. [21] used MOORA and MOOSRA to create an effective decision-support system for choosing unconventional machinery attributes. The following attributes have absolute numerical values: TSF (m), PR, C, and MRR. Kamble et al. [22] describe COPRAS, OCRA, and PSI methods for the selection of raw material suppliers for cold-rolled mild steel manufacturing. Kamble et al. [23] explained the AHP, TOPSIS, and VIKOR methods to the application of multi-attribute decision-making methods for the selection of conveyors with attributes of six attributes, i.e., fixed cost (FC) per hour, variable cost (VC) per hour, conveyor speed (CS), product width (PW), product weight (W), and flexibility (F). Kumar et al. [24] explained the results of the analysis can be used to pinpoint the subsystems that have the greatest impact on the availability of the system. By creating individual maintenance plans for each subsystem, production loss caused by a subsystem's inability to function as planned can be minimized. Rajendra et al. [25] describe the changes in society and the economy brought about by artificial intelligence use since the invention of smartphones. Pundir et al. [26] discuss the QoS measure using the WSN's layered architecture. Classic-layered architecture and cross-layered architecture are the two categories of layered architecture. QoS in a traditional layered architecture is determined by each layer independently. Arya et al. [27] explained that by identifying the most effective replenishment plan, this study helps to lower overall inventory expenses. The model's methodology is illustrated through a numerical example and a sensitivity analysis on a small number of parameters. Kumar et al. [28] explain the application of the stochastic Petri Nets modeling method to the performance assessment of the paint production (PM) unit. The modeling approach based on Petri Nets yields more accurate availability results for evaluating the operation of intricate industrial systems. Mittal et al. [29] explained technologies for incremental sheet forming: overview, advantages and disadvantages, and uses. Kumar et al. [30] explained about modeling, characterization, and processing of smart materials. Kumar et al. [31] discuss waste management and recovery as a pathway to sustainable development goals. Kumar et al.

[32] examined artificial intelligence modeling of additive manufacturing processes, examining how designs, methods, and material fabrication can be optimized, as well as how additive manufacturing uses simulation. The summary of the literature survey is given in Table 10.1.

The study presents a novel and extremely practical approach to the selection of electric vehicles by using decision-making approaches. The methods used in

Table 10.1 Summary of literature survey

Author's name & publication year	Title of chapter	Methods used
Kaya et al. (2020)	Site selection for EVCS in Istanbul by GIS and multi-criteria decision-making	AHP
Więckowski et al. (2023)	Complex sensitivity analysis in Multi-Criteria Decision Analysis: An application to the selection of an electric car	TOPSIS
Komnos et al. (2022)	Analyzing the real-world fuel and energy consumption of conventional and electric cars in Europe	-
Dwivedi et al. (2022)	Evaluation and ranking of battery electric vehicles by Shannon's entropy and TOPSIS methods	TOPSIS and ENTROPY
Lai et al. (2020)	Optimal scheduling of electric vehicles car-sharing service with multi-temporal and multi-task operation	_
Savage et al. (2015)	Assessing adult learning and learning styles	AHP
Bahmani et al. (2014)	An Application of the Analytical Hierarchy Process for a Consumer Choice Problem	AHP
Trivedi et al. (2020)	Identification of Road Crash Severity Ranking by Integrating the Multi-Criteria Decision-Making Approach	AHP
Boroumandi et al. (2015)	Using of Analytic Hierarchy Process for Landslide Hazard Zonation in Zanjan Province, Iran	AHP
Ramkumar et al. (2021)	Bio-polymer selection for injection molding process using Multi-Objective Optimization by Ratio Analysis method	MOORA
Rohit Agrawal (2021)	Sustainable material selection for additive manufacturing technologies: A critical analysis of rank reversal approach	MOORA
Gupta et al. (2021)	Material selection for rotational molding process utilizing distinguished multi-criteria decision-making techniques	MOORA
Erdoğan et al. (2019)	The best fuel selection with hybrid multiple-criteria decision making approaches in a CI engine fueled with blends and pure biodiesels produced from different sources	MOORA
Gurumurthy et al. (2020)	MOORA Method MOORA Technique Optimization of Bio-based Liquid Transformer Insulator	MOORA

(continued)

Table 10.1 (Cont.)

Author's name & publication year	Title of chapter	Methods used
Prasad et al. (2018)	Experimental investigation and parametric optimization in abrasive jet machining on nickel 233 alloy using WASPAS and MOORA	WASPAS and MOORA
Wankhede et al. (2022)	Input parameter selection for a solar-powered absorption refrigeration system using MOORA and TOPSIS.	MOORA and TOPSIS.
Sarkar et al. (2015)	Developing an efficient decision support system for non-traditional machine selection: an application of MOORA and MOOSRA	MOORA and MOOSRA
Kamble et al. (2022)	Selection of raw material supplier for cold-rolled mild steel manufacturing industry	AHP and COPRAS
Fulzele et al. (2021)	Application of Multi-Attribute Decision-Making Methods for the Selection of Conveyor	AHP
Kumar et al. (2021)	Performance analysis of complex manufacturing system using Petri nets modeling method	–
Rajendra et al. (2022)	Impact of artificial intelligence on civilization: Future perspectives.	–
Pundir et al. (2021)	Quality-of-service prediction techniques for wireless sensor networks.	–
Aarya et al. (2022)	Selling price, time-dependent demand, and variable holding cost inventory model with two storage facilities.	–
Kumar et al. (2022)	Stochastic Petri nets modeling for performance assessment of a manufacturing unit.	–
Mittal et al. (2020)	Incremental sheet forming technologies: principles, merits, limitations, and applications. CRC Press.	–
Kumar et al. (2023)	Modeling, Characterization, and Processing of Smart Materials.	–
Kumar et al. (2023)	Waste Recovery and Management: An Approach Toward Sustainable Development Goals. CRC Press.	–
Kumar et al. (2022)	Advances in Additive Manufacturing: Artificial Intelligence, Nature-Inspired, and Biomanufacturing.	–

previous research on electric car selection have limitations in providing a full assessment of electric car possibilities. In contrast, the present research provides novel standards and methodologies that not only prevent these constraints but also result in substantial advances in the field. The present work not only promotes the long-term shift to electric vehicles but also gives customers and decision-makers a better decision-making platform and intends to provide more educated and efficient tools for electric cars, ultimately promoting the broad adoption of cleaner and more environmentally friendly transportation alternatives. This is accomplished by employing decision-making methods such as AHP and MOORA in the ranking of electric cars.

The literature survey shows the use of decision-making strategies to address diverse selection challenges. However, no researchers have tried selection of an electric car using AHP and MOORA approaches considering five attributes, such as car speed, battery capacity, battery charging time, mileage, and price. The Kia EV 6, Hyundai Kona, Mahindra XUV400, Tata Nexon, and Tata Tigor are the five cars under assessment in this present work.

10.2.1 AHP method

In 1980, Thomas L. Saaty and Ernest Foreman jointly developed this technique. By arranging and analyzing the situation, this strategy aids in solving complicated decision-making problems. It is one of the MADM approaches that can deliver the finest outcomes. The decision-maker must assess the appropriate course of action for each factor separately to get results that are more precise and provide superior rankings for the posited options. This methodology is referred from [33].

Step 1. Creation of a hierarchical structure with goals at the top, qualities at the bottom, and options at the top.
Step 2. Find out the relative importance of every attribute concerning the goals.

To determine criteria weight, we must create a pair-by-pair comparison matrix used with the scale of relative relevance. The number of attributes determines how large a pair-wise comparison matrix should be. To provide values for the remaining matrix, the decision-maker must select one characteristic over another based on their judgment. Take the geometric mean of the qualities to calculate their relative normalized weight matrix. Consequently, weight calculations

$$Wn = \frac{GM}{\Sigma GM_n} \tag{10.1}$$

Step 3. Checking the consistency.

Suppose, S_1 = pairwise matrix S_2 = weights of given attributes
Hence, $S_3 = S_1 \times S_2$ and $S_4 = S_3/S_2$
Then lambda max is calculated by taking an average of the given M_4 and M = size of the matrix

$$\lambda_{\max} (\text{eigen value}) = \frac{A4}{M} \tag{10.2}$$

$$CI = \frac{(\lambda_{\max} - M)}{(M-1)} CR = \frac{CI}{RI} \tag{10.3}$$

A consistency ratio must be less than or equal to 0.1 in order to be considered acceptable. Change the decision matrix and return to step if the CR is not less than or equal to 0.1.

Step 4: Use each attribute you gathered to create a normalized matrix.

Step 5: Multiply the relative weight matrix of each feature from Step 2 by its corresponding value for each of the options from Step 4 to determine rank, which measures the overall efficacy of the alternatives. Then find out how you rank. Using the MADM solutions and option ratings in practice.

10.2.2 MOORA method

This method is common because it requires fewer mathematical computations than other ways and has a quick processing time. Brauers introduced the technique in 2004 as an impartial technique. It is a corrective technique. The technique is exclusively used for quantitative qualities. These are the steps in this method: this methodology is referred from [34].

Step 1. Creating a decision matrix is the first step. In a decision matrix, preference is expressed for 'm' choices that are graded according to 'n' attributes. The value Y_{ij} is used to show how well the ith alternative performs about the jth criteria.

$$Y_{ij} = \begin{bmatrix} y_{11} & y_{12} & \cdots & y_{1n} \\ y_{21} & y_{22} & \cdots & y_{2n} \\ \cdots & \cdots & \cdots & \cdots \\ y_{m1} & y_{m2} & \cdots & y_{mn} \end{bmatrix}$$

where $i = 1, 2, 3, \ldots, m$
$j = 1, 2, 3, \ldots, n$
m is used for a number of alternatives
n is used for a number of attributes.

Step 2. The values of every attribute in the decision-making matrix are normalized in the second stage. The qualities may or may not be advantageous. Y_{ij}^* is a convenient way to express a normalized matrix. The formulas must be used to normalize the matrix.

$$Y_{ij}^* = \frac{Y_{ij}}{\sqrt{\sum Y_{ij}^2}} \tag{10.4}$$

Step 3. Evaluation value estimation next, the weight criterion for all the choices must be multiplied by the normalized data. These normalized functions are added to the advantageous criteria for MOORA and subtracted from the non-beneficial criteria. Here, the AHP procedure can be used to calculate the weight criterion.

$$X_i = \sum_{j=1}^{g} w_{ij} \times Y_{ij} - \sum_{j=g+1}^{n} W_{ij} \times Y_{ij} \qquad (10.5)$$

g number of criteria must be maximized.

Step 4. The appropriate option in the rank with the highest X_i value receives the top rank, while the appropriate alternative with the lowest X_i value receives the lowest rank or the worst rank.

10.3 PROBLEM STATEMENT FOR SELECTION OF AN ELECTRIC CAR

In recent times the sales of electric cars are increased very rapidly and there are many electric cars present in the market hence it is a difficult task for decision-makers to select the best electric cars from many options. In the current work, the five electric cars considered are Kia EV 6, Hyundai Kona, Mahindra XUV400, Tata Nexon, and Tata Tigor along with the five attributes for comparing electric car batteries, i.e., top speed, cost, mileage, battery charging capacity, and battery charging time, respectively. Table 10.2 represents the data for electric car selection.

10.4 MADM METHOD SOLUTIONS

10.4.1 Solution by AHP

Calculate the weightage using a pairwise comparison matrix and relative importance scale using step 2. Table 10.3 shows the pairwise comparison matrix.

Table 10.2 Data for electric car selection

Electric cars	Speed (Km/h)	Battery charging time (Hrs)	Battery capacity (kWh)	Mileage (Km)	Price (Rs)
Kia EV 6	192	6	11	425	6000000
Hyundai Kona	167	6.8	39.2	452	2400000
MahindraXUV400	150	6.5	39.4	375	1900000
Tata Nexon	120	8.5	35	437	1700000
Tata Tigor	120	11.2	26	306	1300000

Table 10.3 Pair-wise comparison matrix for the AHP method

	Pairwise comparison matrix				
	Speed (Km/h)	Battery charging time (Hrs)	Battery capacity (kWh)	Mileage (Km)	Price (Rs)
Speed (Km/h)	1	2	5	4	3
Battery charging time (Hrs)	1/2	1	2	3	3
Battery capacity (kWh)	1/5	½	1	3	3
Mileage (Km)	1/4	1/3	1/3	1	3
Price (Rs)	1/3	1/3	1/3	1/3	1

$$W_1 = 0.4229, \ W_2 = 0.2519, \ W_3 = 0.1590, \ W_4 = 0.0988, \ W_5 = 0.0674$$

Step 3 Checking the consistency

$$S_2 = \begin{bmatrix} 0.4229 \\ 0.2519 \\ 0.1590 \\ 0.0988 \\ 0.0674 \end{bmatrix} \quad S_3 = S_1 \times S_2 = \begin{bmatrix} 2.3189 \\ 1.2798 \\ 0.8680 \\ 0.5437 \\ 0.3783 \end{bmatrix}$$

$$S_4 = S_3 / S_2 = \begin{bmatrix} 5.4829 \\ 5.0801 \\ 5.4608 \\ 5.5050 \\ 5.6114 \end{bmatrix}$$

Taking the average of S_4 will now be used to calculate lambda max, or eigen value.

lambda max = 5.4280, consistency index (CL) is 0.1070, and consistency ratio (CR) is 0.09.

Equation (10.3) is used for CI and CR (10.4)

As the CR value in this case is less than 0.1, the weights that were calculated are accurate and will be accepted.

Using steps 3 and 4, create the normalized weighted matrix with overall performance index and rankings as in Table 10.4. The final is determined by ordering the alternative values.

Table 10.4 Normalized weighted matrix for AHP method and ranking

Electric cars	Speed (Km/h)	Battery charging time (h)	Battery capacity (kWh)	Mileage (Km)	Price (Rs)	Performance score	Rank
Kia EV 6	0.4229	0.2519	0.1590	0.0988	0.0146	0.9472	5
Hyundai Kona	0.3679	0.2855	0.5665	0.1050	0.0365	1.3614	1
Mahindra XUV400	0.3304	0.2729	0.5694	0.0871	0.0461	1.3060	2
Tata Nexon	0.2643	0.3569	0.5058	0.1016	0.0516	1.2801	3
Tata Tigor	0.2643	0.4703	0.3757	0.0711	0.0674	1.2488	4

Table 10.5 Decision matrix with maximum and minimum values of attributes

Electric cars	Speed (Km/h)	Battery charging time (h)	Battery capacity (kWh)	Mileage (Km)	Price (Rs)
Kia EV 6	192	6	11	425	6000000
Hyundai Kona	167	6.8	39.2	452	2400000
Mahindra XUV400	150	6.5	39.4	375	1900000
Tata Nexon	120	8.5	35	437	1700000
Tata Tigor	120	11.2	26	306	1300000
Maximum	192	11.2	39.4	452	6000000
Minimum	120	6	11	306	1300000

10.4.2 Solution by MOORA method

Step 1. The creation of a decision matrix is the first step. Weights must be taken from the AHP procedure and copied into the spreadsheet along with the attributes. Table 10.5 displays the attribute's maximum and minimum values.

Step 2. The values of all attributes in the decision-making matrix are in the second phase, as shown in Table 10.6. Take the square of each choice matrix value to obtain the value of Y_{ij}. The value of Y_{ij}^* is then obtained by taking the square root of the sum of the squared values.

Step 3. Estimate the assessment values using the equation in the third stage (16). First, multiply Y_{ij}^* by the weighted criterion, or W_{ij}, to determine the value of X_i. Finally, as indicated in Table 10.7 add up all of the beneficial and non-beneficial criteria, and remove the value of the non-beneficial criteria from the beneficial criteria.

Step 4. Give each choice a rank in this step based on its value. The appropriate option in the rank with the highest X_i value receives the top rank, while the appropriate alternative with the lowest X_i value receives the lowest rank or the worst rank.

Table 10.6 Normalized matrix for MOORA method

Electric cars	Normalized matrix				
Kia EV 6	0.564	0.334	0.154	0.472	0.849
Hyundai Kona	0.490	0.379	0.548	0.502	0.340
Mahindra XUV400	0.440	0.362	0.551	0.417	0.269
Tata Nexon	0.352	0.474	0.490	0.486	0.241
Tata Tigor	0.352	0.624	0.364	0.340	0.184

Table 10.7 Rank table for MOORA method

Electric cars	xi	Rank
Kia EV 6	0.336	5
Hyundai Kona	0.417	1
Mahindra XUV400	0.388	2
Tata Nexon	0.378	4
Tata Tigor	0.385	3

10.5 RESULTS AND DISCUSSION

The consumers in the automotive industry still find selection of electric car confusing because of the numerous options available in the market. Presenting the advantages of electric cars to consumers is now crucial. The appeal of EVs is influenced by a variety of factors, both technological and customer-related. The present work suggests a methodology to guide customers in selecting the best EV by evaluating cars based on a variety of attributes. Extra effort is given during the judging process to include elements defining the perspective of the average customer purchasing the EV. For selecting the best electric car, two MADM methods are used in the presented work: AHP and MOORA. It includes an analysis of all five alternatives in terms of all five attributes of an electric vehicle. After a thorough analysis of several factors such as price, mileage, environmental effect, charging infrastructure, and more, the Hyundai Kona continuously performed better. This study not only confirms the Hyundai Kona's worth and is given first place in the EV industry, but also highlights how useful the multi-attributes decision-making method is for helping people make well-informed decisions. The Kia EV 6 comes in fifth place and is the worst choice of electric car in every category.

10.6 CONCLUSION

Choosing the best EV car using a MADM method helps the decision-maker to choose the best and worst EV cars from numerous options available in the market. The present work has significantly advanced science in the area of electric car selection. An organized structure that can help stakeholders in the industry, and consumers to choose electric cars with knowledge. In addition to providing a thorough analysis of the different factors influencing the choice of electrics, the research presents a useful decision-making model that effectively integrates these factors. This scientific contribution is especially noteworthy in light of the rapidly changing electric car market and the growing significance of environmentally friendly transportation options. The study addresses a significant need for decision support tools that take into account many criteria, such as cost, battery charging capacity, battery charging time, and mileage by providing an organized approach to the selection of electric cars. Among different criteria, the current work provides a clear and rational scientific way for making an informed decision regarding the choice of an electric car. By choosing an appropriate alternative that takes into consideration both competing quantities and qualitative selection criteria, the current methodology supports scientific decision-making. The technique employed in this work aids decision-makers in arriving at high-quality decisions. The presented problem is resolved using the two chosen decision-making methods, specifically the similarity-based AHP and MOORA procedures to fix the issue and increase the reliability of other techniques might be applied. Also, the approaches selected can be used in different engineering and management issues to determine the best course of action. The work determined that the Hyundai Kona car is the finest electric car using the aforementioned techniques.

REFERENCES

[1] Sarbast M., & Szabolcs D. (2018). Application of AHP for evaluating passenger demand for public transport improvements in Mersin, Turkey. *Pollack Periodica*, Vol 13, pp. 67–76. DOI: 10.1556/606.2018.13.2.7

[2] Özler C., Deveci I., Kocako Ç., Kemal A., & Şehirlio G. (2008). Using analytic hierarchy process to determine process economics in multivariate loss functions. *International Journal of Production Research*, Vol 46:4, pp. 1121–1135. DOI: 10.1080/00207540600919357

[3] Czekster R.M., Webber T., Jandrey A.H., Augusto C., & Marcon M. (2019). Selection of enterprise resource planning software using analytic hierarchy process. *Enterprise Information Systems*, Vol 13:6, pp. 895–915. DOI: 10.1080/17517575.2019.1606285

[4] Wong J.K.W., & Heng Li. (2008). Application of the analytic hierarchy process (AHP) in multi-criteria analysis of the selection of intelligent building systems, *Building and Environment*, Vol 43:1, pp. 108–125. ISSN 0360-1323, DOI: 10.1016/j.buildenv.2006.11.019

[5] Ömer A., Ahmet T., Kadir A., & Muhammed C. (2020). Site selection for EVCS in Istanbul by GIS and multi-criteria decision-making. *Transportation Research Part D Transport and Environment*. Vol 80. pp. 1–16. DOI: 10.1016/j.trd.2020.102271

[6] Jakub W ., Jarosław W., Bartłomiej K., & Wojciech S. (2023). Complex sensitivity analysis in multi-criteria decision analysis: An application to the selection of an electric car. *Journal of Cleaner Production*, Vol 390. pp. 136051. DOI: 10.1016/j.jclepro.2023.136051

[7] Komnos S., Tsiakmakis, J., Pavlovic L., & Ntziachristos G. (2022). Analysing the real-world fuel and energy consumption of conventional and electric cars in Europe. *Energy Conversion and Management*, Vol. 270:2022, pp. 116161. ISSN 0196-8904, DOI: 10.1016/j.enconman.2022.116161

[8] Dwivedi P., & Sharma D. (2023). Evaluation and ranking of battery electric vehicles by Shannon's entropy and TOPSIS methods. *Mathematics and Computers in Simulation*, Vol 212:2023, pp. 457–474. ISSN 0378-4754, DOI: 10.1016/j.matcom.2023.05.013

[9] Lai K., Tao C., & Balasubramaniam N. (2020). Optimal scheduling of electric vehicles car-sharing service with multi-temporal and multi-task operation. *Energy*, Vol 204. pp. 117929. DOI: 10.1016/j.energy.2020.117929

[10] Paulette SI. (2009). Assessing adult learning and learning styles. DOI:10.4018/978-1-61520-745-9

[11] Bahmani N., Javalgi, R.G., & Blumburg H. (2015). An Application of the Analytical Hierarchy Process for a Consumer Choice Problem. In: Malhotra, N. (eds.) *Proceedings of the 1986 Academy of Marketing Science (AMS) Annual Conference. Developments in Marketing Science: Proceedings of the Academy of Marketing Science*. Springer, Cham. DOI: 10.1007/978-3-319-11101-8_85

[12] Trivedi P., & Shah J. (2022). Identification of road crash severity ranking by integrating the multi-criteria decision-making approach. *Journal of Road Safety*, Vol 33:2, pp. 33–44. DOI: 10.33492/JRS-D-21-00055

[13] Boroumandi M., Khamehchiyan M., & Nikoudel M.R. (2015). Using of Analytic Hierarchy Process for Landslide Hazard Zonation in Zanjan Province, Iran. In: Lollino, G. (ed.) et al. *Engineering Geology for Society and Territory* – Volume 2. Springer, Cham. DOI: 10.1007/978-3-319-09057-3_165

[14] Ramkumar P., Gupta N., Aman S., & Kumar A. (2021). Bio-polymer selection for injection molding process using Multi Objective Optimization by Ratio Analysis method. *Materials Today: Proceedings*. DOI: 45. 10.1016/j.matpr.2020.12.820

[15] Agrawal R. (2021). Sustainable material selection for additive manufacturing technologies: A critical analysis of rank reversal approach. *Journal of Cleaner Production*, Vol 296, pp. 126500. ISSN 0959-6526, DOI: 10.1016/j.jclepro.2021.126500

[16] Gupta N., Ramkumar P., & Kumar A. (2021). Material selection for rotational molding process utilizing distinguished multi-criteria decision-making techniques. *Materials Today: Proceedings*. DOI: 44. 10.1016/j.matpr.2020.11.960

[17] Erdoğan S., Kemal M., Selman B., & Sayin C., (2019). The best fuel selection with hybrid multiple-criteria decision making approaches in a CI engine fueled with their blends and pure biodiesels produced from different sources, *Renewable Energy*, Vol 134, pp. 653–668. ISSN 0960-1481, DOI: 10.1016/j.renene.2018.11.060

[18] Gurumurthy H., Bheemappa S., Bhat P., & Chidananda R. (2020). *Optimization of Bio-based Liquid Transformer Insulator using MOORA Method. Electric Power Components and Systems.* DOI: 10.1080/15325008.2020.1854380

[19] Prasad S., Ravindranath K., & Devakumar M.L.s. (2019). Experimental investigation and parametric optimization in abrasive jet machining on NICKEL 233 alloy using WASPAS. *Journal of Advanced Manufacturing Systems.* DOI: 18.10.1142/S021968671950029X

[20] Wankhede S., & Hole J. (2020). MOORA and TOPSIS based selection of input parameter in solar powered absorption refrigeration system. *International Journal of Ambient Energy*, Vol 43. pp. 1–6. DOI: 10.1080/01430750.2020.1831600

[21] Sarkar A., Panja S., Das D., & Sarkar B. (2015). Developing an efficient decision support system for non-traditional machine selection: An application of MOORA and MOOSRA. *Production & Manufacturing Research*, Vol 3. pp. 324–342. DOI: 10.1080/21693277.2014.895688

[22] Kamble A.G., Kalos P.S., Mahapatra, K., & Bhosale, V.A. (2022). "Selection of raw material supplier for cold-rolled mild steel manufacturing industry", *International Journal for Simulation and Multidisciplinary Design Optimization*, Vol 13. DOI: 10.1051/smdo/2022004

[23] Fulzele S., Khatke S., Kadam S., & Kamble A. (2022). "Application of multi-attribute decision-making methods for the selection of conveyor" *Soft Computing*, Vol 26, pp. 9873–9881. DOI: 10.1007/s00500-022-07338-8

[24] Kumar A., Kumar V., Modgil V., Kumar A., & Sharma, A. (2021, August). Performance analysis of complex manufacturing system using Petri nets modeling method. In *Journal of Physics: Conference Series* (Vol. 1950, No. 1, p. 012061). IOP Publishing. DOI: 10.1088/1742-6596/1950/1/012061

[25] Rajendra P., Kumari M., Rani S., Dogra N., Boadh R., Kumar A., & Dahiya M. (2022). Impact of artificial intelligence on civilization: Future perspectives. *Materials Today: Proceedings*, 56, pp. 252–256. DOI: 10.1016/j.matpr.2022.01.113

[26] Pundir M., Sandhu J.K., & Kumar A. (2021, August). Quality-of-service prediction techniques for wireless sensor networks. In *Journal of Physics: Conference Series* (Vol. 1950, No. 1, p. 012082). IOP Publishing. DOI: 10.1088/1742-6596/1950/1/012082

[27] Aarya D.D., Rajoria Y.K., Gupta N., Raghav Y.S., Rathee R., Boadh R., & Kumar, A. (2022). Selling price, time-dependent demand and variable holding cost inventory model with two storage facilities. *Materials Today: Proceedings*, 56, 245–251. DOI: 10.1016/j.matpr.2022.01.111

[28] Kumar A., Kumar V., Modgil V., & Kumar A. (2022). Stochastic Petri nets modeling for performance assessment of a manufacturing unit. *Materials Today: Proceedings*, 56, 215–219. DOI: 10.1016/j.matpr.2022.01.073

[29] Mittal R.K. (2020). Incremental sheet forming technologies: Principles, merits, limitations, and applications. CRC Press. DOI: 10.1201/9780429298905

[30] Kumar A., Kumar P., Srivastava A.K., & Goyat V. (eds.). (2023). Modeling, characterization, and processing of smart materials. *IGI Global*. DOI: 10.4018/978-1-6684-9224-6

[31] Kumar A., Mittal R.K., & Goel R. (eds.). (2023). *Waste Recovery and Management: An Approach Toward Sustainable Development Goals.* CRC Press. DOI: 10.1201/9781003359784

[32] Kumar A., Mittal R.K., & Haleem A. (eds.). (2022). *Advances in Additive Manufacturing: Artificial Intelligence, Nature-Inspired, and Biomanufacturing.* Elsevier. DOI: 10.1016/C2020-0-03877-6

[33] Kamble A., Gupta S., Trivedi B., & Jangade O. (2012). Optimization of welding mechanisms using analytic hierarchy process, technique for order preference by similarity to ideal solution and graph theory and matrix approach Int. *Journal of Manufacturing Technology and Management,* Vol. 26, No. 1/2/3/4, 2012. DOI: 10.1504/IJMTM.2012.051437

[34] Rajurkar K., Khade S., Sawant O., Dobe M., & Kamble A. (2023). Selection of fighter aircraft by using multi attributes decision-making methods. *International Journal of Process Management and Benchmarking,* Vol 14, pp. 460–477. DOI: 10.1504/IJPMB.2023.132217

Chapter 11

People's perception of electric vehicles in developing countries

A case study of Jaipur city

Mahjabeen Naz, Ankit Singh Beniwal, and Ram Vilas Meena

Department of Civil Engineering, JECRC University, Jaipur, India

11.1 INTRODUCTION

One of the oldest social science theories is E.M. Rogers' diffusion of innovation, which explains how with the passage of time an idea or product gains momentum and diffusion. As a part of any social system, there is continuous adoption of new ideas, behavior, or products when there is a need for it. So in the context to this theory, it is high time now to adopt new innovative technology in personal commute, i.e., electric vehicles. With the increasing fuel prices and pollution from fuel burning in and around cities, it is the best solution to both of these problems.

Technologies used in the upcoming EV should be very mature and uplifting, leading to performance, ease of use, safety, reliability, and energy efficiency of EVs along with being the main contributor towards the increased sale of EVs, which is more distance coverage per charge [1]. Høyer [2] discussed that times has come to bring electric vehicles back into use, as there are more pulling and pushing factors existing. The pulling factors such as innovation in battery technology and electric motors are making electric vehicles a logical and well-grounded competitor for the conventional one. The pushing side is the limited supply of fuel in the market and increased consciousness of public about the environment and keeping it clean with the use of less polluting electric vehicles. Kley et al. [3] discusses that environmental degradation, climate change, and the shortage of natural renewal resources leads to reconsideration for the traditional system of mobility, i.e., integrated combustion engine and to bring in something new, which is eco-friendly. Their research also provided information about a holistic approach for a business model of electric cars and provided decision support to various stakeholders. Contestabile [4] concluded that the success and long-term acceptance of EVs will greatly depend on upgrades in battery technologies, reduction in cost factor, and proper infrastructure (for charging). Krause et al. [5] performed research on 2,302 individuals from the USA who had a driving license and found that the perception of individuals varies from person to person, based on education, age, gender, environmental concern, and experiences they are having. He also explained that the influential factors, which blowback the purchase of EVs when compared to conventional vehicles are the initial cost, recharging time, and less availability of a charging station. His study was based on rational choice theory. Rezvani et al. [6] in this research presented comprehensive overviews of drivers for and against consumer's perceptions as well as an overview of the theoretical perspectives that could be utilized for understanding consumer intentions and adoption behavior towards electric vehicles. Jin and Slowik [7] reviewed consumer awareness about electric vehicles and mainly focused on this point. Based on their study, they selected five case studies for further research and made consumers aware about electric vehicles. Masurali et al. [8] and Ghasri et al. [9] suggested that acceptance mainly depends on education level. Here the study found that education has a great role in adoption of electric cars as they are aware of the current environment condition and ready to buy but the problems come with low density of charging stations and high charging times taken by batteries for charging. Bhalla et al. [10] and Kumar and Padmanaban [11] recommended that with a combined effort of government and manufacturers, we can promote the electric vehicles in the Indian market as people are well aware of environmental issues. So, the government will have to bring more policies and incentives for social acceptance of electric vehicles and manufactures will have to make more trustworthy models to sell more electric vehicles. de Luca et al. [12] and Krishna [13] mainly focused on people's perception towards electric vehicles on determining the factors influencing in decision-making by people to choose electric vehicles for mobility. Many factors such as psychological factors, attitude, behaviors, etc., defines the user's willingness to buy or not this advanced technology. Ruan and Lv [14] conducted a survey on a wider scale to understand public perception towards electric vehicles in the last decade. They started their study in 2011 and concluded in 2020. Their study used Reddit online social network (OSN) data to capture EV public perception, which included various topics of interest and conspiracies about electric vehicles. Adu-Gyamfi et al. [15] suggested that battery swap technology (BST) is a remedial measure to whatever problems electric vehicles are facing like non-availability of charging stations and more time consumed for charging etc. The research was performed on 405 Chinese consumers and the results reflect that perception of the individual, subjective norm, and knowledge are positive influential factors towards adoption intention of battery swap technology. Transformation of electric vehicles globally has initiated the demand for required minerals. Liu et al. [16] in their paper study the impact of minerals' extraction and suggested to improve governance of electric vehicle minerals from a public point of view, they also found many consumers are not aware of the impact it is going to create but many of them have knowledge about it.

All the existing research suggests that individual perception to any new technology differs and it depends on a lot of factors. This study is aimed at understanding people's perception towards electric vehicles (EVs) in Jaipur city of state Rajasthan, India, and also tries to correlate the underlying factors for a particular perception of EVs and their intention to purchase an EV in the near future. Along with conducting the survey, more awareness can be spread about EVs, its benefits, various government incentives related to EV purchase available to the public currently.

To study buying intention of electric vehicle by Indians (people living in Jaipur city), there is a need to study what are the factors influencing the acceptance of electric vehicles by the consumers. Various factors that influence the purchase intention of EVs are individual thinking on dimensions like cost, environmental issues, not adapting to changes in technology, infrastructure, and social acceptance. There are many factors, which are contributing to purchase intention of individuals, such as its initial cost, range, charging infrastructure, etc.

This study adopts a quantitative approach and represents the results of the survey conducted to investigate people's perception. Based on 1000 offline and online questionnaires from Jaipur city (India) consumers, this study conducts a statistical analysis, i.e., chi-square hypothesis testing and p-value method of testing was used to find the co-relations between consumer's characteristics variables and their perceptions and to know the awareness towards electric vehicles. This research suggest that for the commercial success and purchase intention of electric vehicles there is a need to study the factor influencing the people to buy the EVs, the factor such as individual perception on dimension like environmental concern, cost, technology, etc. Thus to increase the sales of EVs, governments have to support by introducing different policies such as environmental policy, road tax and other taxes, subsidies on buying all types of electric vehicles, lower bank interest loan, etc.

11.2 SAMPLING AND PROCEDURE

A survey with a simple questionnaire was performed in both online and offline mode to collect data for this study. Online survey was taken out through Google forms via the internet and telephonic conversation and offline survey were taken out in the form of printout distribution and collection, and face-to-face conversation. All the questions were kept compulsory so to ensure a complete form and less rejection of data needs to be done. Random sampling techniques were utilized and the sample comprised of general public, owners of conventional fuel vehicles, and the owner of electric vehicles to know the perception and feedback and intention towards buying and adoption of new technology, i.e., electric vehicles. Data was collected from a mixed income group and age group. A total of 1000 respondents filled the survey form with valid data, with different demographics like locations, education level, income, etc. The sample had significantly higher participation of males (64.8%) and the female percentage is a little less (35.2%). Most of the respondents were sampled within the age group of 16–55 years. The study area for sampling was Jaipur city. The questionnaire had 25 questions divided into three sections of which the first section collected data from the individual about their personal factors like age, gender, income, vehicle ownership, etc. The second section of questions was targeted to gauge user awareness on EVs followed by the third section which had choice-based questions concerning people's opinion on EVs and the possible reasons for their choice to buy an EV. Statistical hypothesis testing was used to check any possible relations of factors on the choices made by the respondents. The chi-square test aims to verify the probability of an observed distribution. A chi-square statistic is a test that measures how expectations compare to actual observed data. It is non-parametric test.

11.3 DATA ANALYSIS AND DISCUSSION

The data collected showing the sample population characteristics is shown in Table 11.1 below. About 64.8% of the population surveyed was male, this is also representative of the population as they are the ones making decisions on vehicle purchase most of the times. 63.3% of the respondents were young adults between the ages of 16 to 25 years, they are the ones who would be making vehicle purchasing decisions in the next decade or so as and when they start earning because about 51.6% of this population is dependent on others and has no income of their own. The opinion and perception of EVs on such young people should be studied to understand the future trends and scope of EVs in the market. Other variables like education, household size, vehicle ownership, daily commute distance, and mode are also shown in Table 11.1. Most of the population travels short distances for their daily commute using personal vehicles.

The next section of questionnaire had questions to judge user awareness on EVs. 97.2% of the respondents were aware of the EVs available in the market, 96.2% of the respondents were aware of the possible benefits of owning EVs. It was shocking to know that only 52.6% of the population was aware of the government policies and incentives given to promote EVs. The respondents who are already planning to own an electric vehicle in the near future are 80.4%, some of them have already purchased one. 64.5% of respondents agreed to switch to hybrid vehicles first before completely switching to EVs.

The last section of the questionnaire was focused on user opinion and to find out the factors which are possibly affecting their decision to buy an EV. The probable reasons for switching to EVs were found to be its economical nature, environment friendliness, reduction in noise pollution, and reduced

Table 11.1 Sample population characteristics

Variables	Sample population (%)	Variables	Sample population (%)
Gender		**Monthly Income**	
Female	35.2	10k–30k	23.3
Male	64.8	31k–60k	12.7
		61k–1lakh	1.6
Age groups		Above 1lakh	1.1
16–25	63.3	Below 10k	9.6
26–35	21.6	Dependent	51.6
36–45	6		
46–55	5.4	**Vehicle Ownership**	
Above 55	3.7	No personal vehicle	48
		Two wheeler	42
Education		Four wheeler	9
Below Metric	5.8	Other	1
Metric	4.2		
Intermediate/12th/	13.6	**Daily Commute**	
Diploma		Less than 5 km	35.4
Bachelor's degree/UG	59.5	5 to 10 km	27.3
Master's degree/PG	14.3	11 to 20 km	17.8
Ph. D	1.9	21 to 40 km	12.3
Other	0.7	41 to 60 km	5.2
		Greater than 60 km	2.9
Household size			
2	5.3	**Daily Commute mode**	
3	8.8	Walking/ Cycling	28.1
4	31.8	Two Wheeler	34.3
5	25.6	Four Wheeler	10.3
6	16.4	Public Bus	14.7
greater than 6	12.1	Metro / Rail	0.8
		Cab/ Taxi/ Auto Rickshaw	11.8

dependency on fossil fuels, details of the responses is shown in Figure 11.1. Other reasons, which were selected by some respondents included the latest and better technology of the EV and the fact that it would look cool when they use it. Some respondents also found EVs easy to drive and maintain due to low maintenance costs.

The respondents were also questioned for probable reasons for not switching to EVs, the results of which can be seen in Figure 11.2. The most chosen reasons for not switching to EVs were its high initial cost, longer charging time, and non-availability of charging infrastructure. A few respondents also chose the conventional vehicle because of its driving experience, and due to a greater available choice in conventional vehicle variants, whereas in electric vehicles limited variants are available in the market and that too with limited travel range per charge. Almost 43% respondents would choose

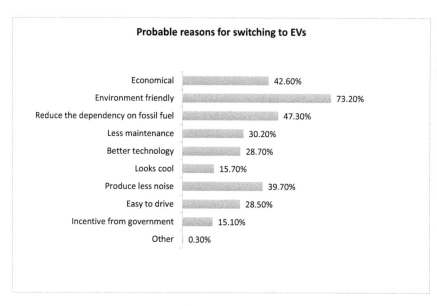

Figure 11.1 Probable reasons for switching to EVs.

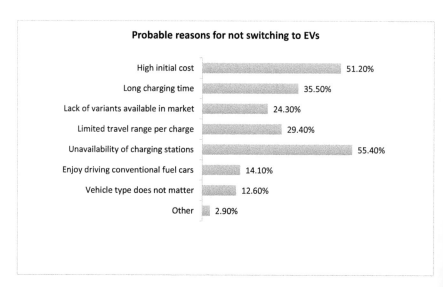

Figure 11.2 Probable reasons for not switching to EVs.

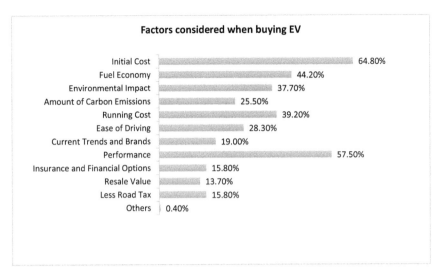

Figure 11.3 Factors considered when buying EVs.

to buy an EV car rather than a two-wheeler if available in their budget, the rest of the others would either go for an e-bike or an e-scooter. When questioned about factors one should consider when buying EVs, the results are depicted in Figure 11.3. People consider the initial cost, performance, fuel economy, and running cost as major factors when choosing any vehicle for purchase. Carbon emissions, environmental impact, vehicle resale value, ease of driving, taxes, insurance, and other financial options are secondary factors when deciding on a vehicle to purchase.

Figure 11.4 depicts the responses of people when asked about the percentage of the amount they are willing to pay extra for a new electric vehicle with similar performance of petrol/diesel vehicle. Around 31.6% and 30.6% respondents agreed to pay an extra 5% and 10%, respectively, for an electric version of the vehicle of their choices. 12.8% respondents do not wish to pay any extra amount for an EV, they expect it to have an initial cost the same as a conventional fuel vehicle. For 11.3% respondents, the EV price is no issue, they are willing to pay any amount extra for the right specifications and technologies. When asked about the ideal charging time for a full battery, 40.2% of the respondents expect their EV to be charged in 1 h or even quicker, which is not possible with current variants available in the market. And the respondents who wanted a 3 h or less charging time for a full battery range of an EV accounted for 46.1% of the population surveyed. Response to the query is shown in Figure 11.5.

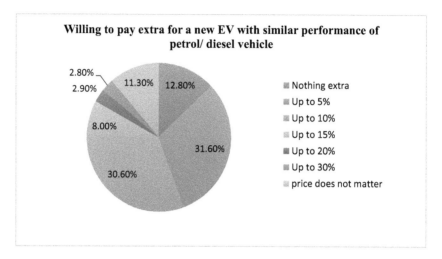

Figure 11.4 Willing to pay extra for a new EV with similar performance of petrol/ diesel vehicle.

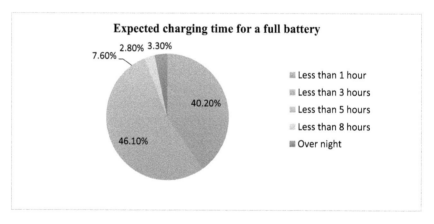

Figure 11.5 Expected charging time for a full battery.

Figure 11.6 depicts the change the consumers would like to see in the market to convince them to buy an EV. Reduction in initial cost and charging time along with availability of charging infrastructure are major expectations of the respondents of the survey.

Even with all these shortcomings of EVs and their lesser market share at present, about 55.2% respondents believed that the EV sales will surpass the conventional fossil fuel vehicle sales in the coming 10 years, and an additional 31.3% believed it to happen in the next 15 years. This shows

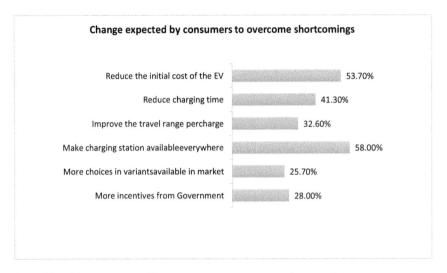

Figure 11.6 Change expected by consumers to overcome shortcomings.

that the way technology is evolving, people believe it will overcome all the shortcomings of the EVs in the coming decade.

11.3.1 Hypothesis conclusions

- There is a relation between gender and the preferable choice of vehicles in electric version. It was observed that whether a person chose an electric car or an electric scooter depended on their gender.
- There is a relation between monthly income of a person and the choice of mode of transport for traveling. The way people commute for daily needs is dependent on their monthly income.
- There is no relation between genders and plan to own an electric vehicle in near future. Gender plays no role in deciding whether a person would plan to buy an EV in the future.
- There is a relation between age group and plan to own electric vehicles in the near future. Age definitely should be a factor, because we all know that the younger generation is more sensitive towards environment and are more conscious of their surroundings.
- There is no relation between education of the respondents and plan to own an electric vehicle in the near future. It was surprising to know that with a little awareness even less educated people are pro EVs.
- There is a relation between monthly incomes of the respondents and plan to own electric vehicles in the near future. Definitely the higher cost of EVs are only attracting people with higher income.

- There is no relation between vehicle ownership and plan to own electric vehicles in the near future. If someone already owns a vehicle or not should never be and is not a factor to the choice of investing in an electric vehicle.

11.4 CONCLUSION

With the exhaustion of fossil fuels and continuous hike in fuel prices, there is a need for an alternate solution for this problem in India. Government of India has taken the initiative to fight against pollution levels by promoting EVs and giving subsidies on purchase and many other policies but while analyzing data of this research survey it is found that 47.4% respondent are unaware of these policies. To boost its production, Govt. has eased the FDI norms. Various emerging brands are launching EVs in India, which is also creating job opportunities in India and boosting skills. As people are well aware of environmental conditions and know the benefits of using electric vehicles and showed positive responses for purchasing EVs but lack of charging infrastructure is one of the main barriers coming across as there are very few charging stations currently available in the Indian market. Higher initial cost of these EVs can be countered by subsidies and incentives but longer charging times can only be overcome by improvements in the technology. In the research, people have shown positive attitude towards EVs and they also expect them to take over conventional vehicles in the coming decade. This study has focused on both primary and secondary data of users perceptions of electric vehicles in Jaipur city (India). Though the research found a potential scope of electric vehicles in India, still there is a scope for in-depth study in more cities with greater number of samples and more factors.

REFERENCES

[1] Lane B, Potter S. The adoption of cleaner vehicles in the UK: exploring the consumer attitude–action gap. *Journal of Cleaner Production*. 2007 Jan 1;15(11–12):1085–92.

[2] Høyer KG. The history of alternative fuels in transportation: The case of electric and hybrid cars. *Utilities Policy*. 2008 Jun 1;16(2):63–7.

[3] Kley F, Lerch C, Dallinger D. New business models for electric cars—A holistic approach. *Energy policy*. 2011 Jun 1;39(6):3392–403.

[4] Contestabile M, Offer G, North R, Akhurst M, Woods JA. *Electric vehicles: A synthesis of the current literature with a focus on economic and environmental viability*. LCA Works, London (Great Britain), June 2012.

[5] Krause RM, Carley SR, Lane BW, Graham JD. Perception and reality: Public knowledge of plug-in electric vehicles in 21 US cities. *Energy Policy*. 2013 Dec 1;63:433–40.

[6] Rezvani Z, Jansson J, Bodin J. Advances in consumer electric vehicle adoption research: A review and research agenda. *Transportation research part D: transport and environment.* 2015 Jan 1;34:122–36.

[7] Lingzhi Jin PS. Literature review of electric vehicle. *International Council on Clean Transportation.* 2017. https://theicct.org/publication/literature-rev iew-of-electric-vehicle-consumer-awareness-and-outreach/

[8] Masurali A, Surya P. Perception and awareness level of potential customers towards electric cars. *International Journal for Research in Applied Science & Engineering Technology.* 2018;6(3):359–62.

[9] Ghasri M, Ardeshiri A, Rashidi T. Perception towards electric vehicles and the impact on consumers' preference. *Transportation Research Part D: Transport and Environment.* 2019 Dec 1;77:271–91.

[10] Bhalla P, Ali IS, Nazneen A. A study of consumer perception and purchase intention of electric vehicles. *European Journal of Scientific Research.* 2018 Jul;149(4):362–8.

[11] Kumar R, Padmanaban S. Electric vehicles for India: Overview and challenges. *IEEE India Informatics.* 2019 Apr;14:139.

[12] de Luca S, Di Pace R, Bruno F. Accounting for attitudes and perceptions influencing users' willingness to purchase Electric Vehicles through a Hybrid Choice Modeling approach based on Analytic Hierarchy Process. *Transportation Research Procedia.* 2020 Jan 1;45:467–74.

[13] Krishna G. Understanding and identifying barriers to electric vehicle adoption through thematic analysis. *Transportation Research Interdisciplinary Perspectives.* 2021 Jun 1;10:100364.

[14] Ruan T, Lv Q. Public perception of electric vehicles on reddit over the past decade. *Communications in Transportation Research.* 2022 Dec 1;2:100070.

[15] Adu-Gyamfi G, Song H, Obuobi B, Nketiah E, Wang H, Cudjoe D. Who will adopt? Investigating the adoption intention for battery swap technology for electric vehicles. *Renewable and Sustainable Energy Reviews.* 2022;156:111979.

[16] Liu W, Agusdinata DB, Eakin H, Romero H. Sustainable minerals extraction for electric vehicles: A pilot study of consumers' perceptions of impacts. *Resources Policy.* 2022 Mar 1;75:102523.

Chapter 12

Significance of AI in automobiles

Sumit Saini,[1] Amit Yadav,[2] Areeb Shazli,[2]
Momin Altaf Itoo,[2] Akhil Ajith,[2] and Divam Vats[2]
[1]Department of Mechanical Engineering, Chandigarh University, Gharuan, India
[2]Department of Automobile Engineering, Chandigarh University, Gharuan, India

12.1 INTRODUCTION

In the modern world of technology, artificial intelligence (AI) has emerged as a powerful source for the transformation of industries especially in the automotive sector. It is now up to the automakers on how to utilize the force of AI and choose how to implement it in the automotive sector. The global pandemic has caused significant disruption to businesses across industries, including the automotive sector. To adapt to these challenges, automotive companies have turned to innovative AI-driven solutions, recognizing artificial intelligence (AI) as a mainstream technology. As the industry undergoes a period of tremendous upheaval, car manufacturers are introducing new features in their vehicles to cater to evolving user needs [1].

The integration of advanced technologies such as artificial intelligence and data science has been a crucial factor in the success of automakers, software developers, automakers, and component suppliers during the pandemic and with the help of artificial intelligence, car designers and development teams have been able to create vehicle models that meet consumers expectations [2].

AI-powered machines have also played a significant role in automotive manufacturing, continuously learning and working alongside humans to improve the production process. Additionally, automotive companies can add or remove innovative features based on consumer preferences, optimizing resources more effectively through the use of artificial intelligence and machine learning. AI is vital for driver assistance technology, which is now commonly offered by different automobile manufacturers. It efficiently determines whether the driver is feeling tired or sleepy by detecting the facial expression of the driver. With the help of AI, the car adapts to the driver's preferred setting to make driving easier, more enjoyable, and less tiring. Automotive companies and software companies are collaborating together for development of user engaging experiences that can adapt according to an individual driver and provide them with the best possible environment

DOI: 10.1201/9781003495574-12

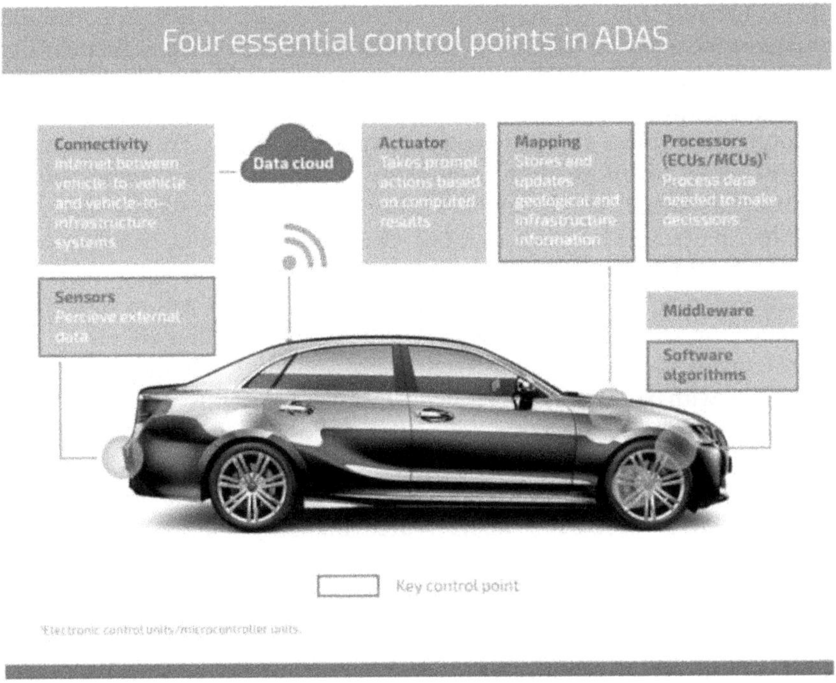

Figure 12.1 Components of autonomous cars.

Source: [2].

while driving. Various essential points of driver assistance and autonomous cars are shown in Figure 12.1.

AI is not only used for improving the driving experiences and production of automobiles, AI also offers a smooth experience for purchasing or selling cars for customers. With AI capabilities, customer interface systems may in the future even suggest the best vehicle to customers based on their driving skills, insurance, medical information, penalties, etc. Additionally, next generation automobiles may receive real-time road congestion alerts and other kinds of emergencies and also by the use of AI it may generate high definition 3D images of real-time roads. This incredible digital revolution will be powered by artificial intelligence for a long time to come. As a result, production, accuracy, and efficiency will be improved in the automotive industry [3].

As time passes by, integration of AI-driven technology in automobiles will surely add value that will be incomparable. By optimizing manufacturing capacity, increasing efficiency, and obtaining unique data, this technology will deliver ever- more-innovative driving experiences. AI will also constantly alter the automotive sector, bringing up new opportunities and assuring a higher return on investment more over there is great rivalry, price pressure, and instabilities in the automotive sector. Automanufacturers of original equipment can expand their market shares by carrying out even small modifications. There are multiple opportunities available in the automotive sector as information technology continues to be a game-changer. AI has been rapidly developing and advancing in the automotive sector [4].

When paired with the capacity of enormous quantities of information and artificial intelligence, it is going to fundamentally alter how we travel. Additionally, traffic will be streamlined and bottlenecks will be monitored, thereby improving driving safety. Furthermore, it will also create new marketing opportunities and entertainment avenues. The world of AI is ever-changing, with ginormous strides being made every day. With time, the technology is being evolved, taking leaps beyond the horizon. Implementation of artificial intelligence is the next biggest step in the automotive industry. This research paper focuses on the core aspect of AI in the automotive industry. Our aim is to provide a thorough research and insight into the fundamental functioning and working of AI, helping others to explore different areas, components, and markets that are related to AI in automobiles [5].

12.2 LITERATURE SURVEY

Khan Muhammad (2020) concluded that the advancements in information and signal processing technology have a ginormous influence on autonomous driving (AD). This ensures driving safety while requiring close to zero human effort thanks to cutting-edge artificial intelligence (AI) technologies. Recently, some challenging real-world problems have been solved using deep learning (DL) approaches. This research paper focuses on different scenarios and provides solutions, techniques, and detailed surveys, which can help with an overview and better understanding of the market and future implementations by predicting a proper timeline as well [5]. The benefits of AD control strategies have not been fully documented and researched. This review presents an overview of revolutionary and safe AD approaches, highlighting their main benefits and limitations, additionally demonstrating the strength of DL structures in terms of dependability and efficient real-time performance. It also covers important manifestations of DL throughout the AD pipeline, including as measurement, analysis, and execution, with an emphasis on road, lane, vehicle, pedestrian, tiredness detection, collision avoidance, and traffic sign. Concentrating on sensor and vision-based DL methods for traffic sign detection, drowsiness identification, vehicle, lane, and road detection. Various formulas and studies on the performance of different tools for AD scenarios have been presented with their outputs [5]. This study report also assesses the advantages and disadvantages of certain solutions that have been studied, as well as their efficacy using different assessment metrics. Furthermore, it provides thorough resources for novices and researchers interested in this emerging field. It does this by outlining the issues with safe DL-based AD as it is now and making recommendations for future study.

Huansheng Ning [6] suggested that the increasing advancement of artificial intelligence (AI) has led to a surge in popularity of autonomous driving. The ability of AI to make decisions for the autonomous driving system opens up new and ever-expanding horizons for study. The limitations of AI make it impossible to comprehend a general intelligence, which also restricts research into autonomous vehicles. A taxonomy and overview of the current autonomous driving architectures are mentioned in this paper. The concept of hybrid human-artificial intelligence (H-AI) is introduced and applied to a driving system that is partially, autonomous. Additionally, this review paper discusses and highlights the benefits of H-AI, offers a novel viewpoint, and proposes a theoretical architecture based on H-AI to better use it. It also examines and classifies possible technologies based on their design. This essay primarily introduces the concept of H-AI while discussing its background, shortcomings, and other difficulties [6].

Arunmozhi Manimuthu et al. [7] found that a smart contract is a self-executing digital agreement that is encoded in computer code and preserved safely on a block-chain. Contract conditions are automatically handled by it, eliminating middlemen and increasing transparency. Although smart contracts are useful for many things, like cost savings and trust-building, there are certain security risks to be aware of. This paper focuses on all the aspects, which include implementations, future scope and solutions to current problems. Thanks to smart sensors and integrated drivers, the automobile industry has progressed significantly in recent years in areas like as AI, ML, and the IoT. In an effort to contend in the field of smart manufacturing, it has also started to create methods for data-driven decision-making. This study proposes a novel design framework for a fully automated smart car manufacturing firm that uses smart contract (SC) rules for process execution and control and federated learning-artificial intelligence (FAI) for decision-making. A state-of-the-art element of the proposed design is the trust threshold limit (TTL), which limits manufacturing process waste by helping to manage the excessive consumption of embedded tools, equipment, energy, and cost functions. The adoption of artificial intelligence (AI) in decentralized block-chains with smart contracts, the company's trading policies, and its advantages for managing market risk assessments during socioeconomic crises are all demonstrated in this study. The model that was developed and supported by actual cases included cost functions, delivery schedules, and energy assessments. The results demonstrate how FAI may qualitatively reduce the threshold level of cost, energy, and other control functions in procurement assembly and production by increasing decision accuracy for the well-established smart contract-based automobile assembly model (AAM). This architecture's flexibility and graphical user interface with cloud connectivity provide obstacles. The research identifies analyses, and categories assembly-related tools, components, and supporting commodities using IoT and vector machine learning. These manufacturing techniques will help in production and distribution processes and offer real-time quantitative assessments of market risk and investor returns, regardless of market investments. TTL limits alternatives for buying, processing, cost, and energy consumption. It assists in building the car from the ground up without having to worry about losses due to sociological, economic, or stock market fluctuations. TTL offers support with energy consumption, procurement of raw materials, delivery, and transportation. In the industrial scenario, the choice of local vendor is tabulated, confirmed, visualized, and modeled in real time [7].

Hofmann et al. [1] suggested that the key technologies shaping the future of the automotive industry involve the use of self-learning and optimization features. These cutting-edge tools encompass data science and machine learning, which are explored in this chapter. It delves into what 'machine learning' and 'data science' mean and how they complement each other. Furthermore, it defines the concept of 'optimizing analytics' and elucidates the pivotal role of automatic optimization in data analysis technology. To illustrate the application of these technologies in the automotive industry, various phases of the automotive value chain are examined, including development, procurement, logistics, production, marketing, sales, and after-sales services. Given that the sector is just scratching the surface, forward-thinking use cases are presented to showcase the groundbreaking potential of these technologies, as the industry is only beginning to explore their vast range of applications. In the concluding section of the essay, the focus shifts to how these technologies can enhance the efficiency and customer-centric approach of the automotive industry across all aspects of its operations, from product development to customer relations. This paper focuses on the basics of AI and machine learning. It introduces an individual to the fundamental concept. It also discusses about the current applications in the automotive sector and the process that goes into it. Vision and scope is also shared, showcasing the advantages and how AIML can help boost the industry—increasing profits and reducing wastage of resources [1]. One of the drawbacks of this research paper is that it does not delve deeper into the core basics and does not cover the topics in great detail. It keeps it brief, which is a plus point for people to get an overview quickly, however, many points and problem identification is missing [1].

According to Liu et al. [2] the mass production of autonomous cars has been made achievable by the swift advancement of autonomous driving technology, especially the most recent developments in deep learning, GPUs, and Li DAR sensors. The introduction of their state-of-the-art autonomous cars onto public roads is a constant push by several companies in the automotive and IT industries, including GM and Waymo. The broad use of AI in ICV is discussed in this research paper, along with a review of current and upcoming trends in autonomous vehicle technology and a list of the main challenges that need to be solved before these cars can be sold. It makes predictions about the conditions and potential paths for the mass production of autonomous cars based on the review and highlights how difficult, time-consuming, and meticulous the process of developing the cars [2].

Through a meticulous analysis of the latest developments and trends in perception, decision, and action technology, this report provides a comprehensive assessment of the advancements made in autonomous vehicle technologies. Along with the main problems and difficulties related to autonomous driving, it also looks at the application of AI in ICV and its future. Careful design considerations are made for things like hardware and software redundancy, fail-safe and fail-operational measures, cybersecurity, geo-fenced operation, remote support, etc. The advancement of autonomous vehicle technology has given firms the confidence to launch self-driving cars. Because inductive learning systems are inherently complex, it can be challenging to test autonomous vehicles—even with enormous training data sets. There is also a plethora of edge scenarios in which data gathering is impractical [2].

Singh and Saini [8] evaluated the foundational subjects surrounding AD vehicles and their future are the main emphasis of this chapter. Internal combustion engine-powered vehicles were developed for use in mass manufacturing. Even now, internal combustion engine technology is still being improved. But gradually, electric cars are becoming more and more integrated into the whole scheme. Evidently, the field of autonomous vehicles is advancing at an exceptional rate. Even though this field has seen amazing advancements, more work still needs to be done. Using autonomous car technology offers several advantages. With the goal of completely commercializing the technology, autonomous car firms have invested a significant amount of money in the development of autonomous vehicle technology. There are several obstacles in the way of achieving this objective. These problems include legal, non-technical, and technological difficulties. The upcoming time for this technology is assuring and ambitious, however, the challenges must be overcome. Despite the fact that fully autonomous car technology has evolved astronomically, it will be many years before the general public can buy one. It may not be feasible to pinpoint a certain year at this time. According to some predictions, fully autonomous cars may become the norm by 2035. Technology is always changing, but we still need to be ready to use it. Overcoming the issues mentioned earlier is also necessary for the technology to advance seamlessly. The goal of this research is to provide a comprehensive knowledge of the field of autonomous vehicle technology. The market is expanding, and as we covered in our research report, artificial intelligence will have a bright future for the automotive industry [8].

According to Sanguesa [3] there are numerous factors why electric cars (EVs) are becoming more and more popular, such as decreased costs and heightened awareness of environmental and climatic issues. This chapter reviews the developments of EVs with regard to trends in battery technology, charging methods, new research challenges, and unexplored opportunities. More specifically, a review of the worldwide EV market's current situation and future prospects is carried out. Since batteries are one of the main parts of electric vehicles (EVs), this page offers a thorough examination of every battery technology now in use, ranging from lead-acid to lithium-ion. This study report also looks at the many EV charging standards that are out now and offers suggestions for battery energy management and power control. Future smart cities will have a significant impact on the EV industry, so it will be especially crucial to have flexible charging techniques that can respond to consumer needs. Future BMS should therefore consider the new scenarios brought about by new batteries and the demands of smart cities. BMS requires sensors and AI that could read the data efficiently, plus EVs are planned to be the next biggest step and AI can be easily integrated in them due to less complex mechanical components. In order to increase mobility and make efficient use of the charging infrastructure, electric vehicles can benefit from the use of communications and artificial intelligence. Artificial intelligence (such as deep learning techniques or optimization strategies) can enable greatly improved charging processes while also significantly lowering expenditures. A variety of AI-based recommendations for various EV systems, such battery temperature control, smarter and more energy-efficient routing, and better charging, utilization of artificial neural networks (ANNs) to lower overall consumption of energy and enhance the thermal management system. This research paper mentions how AI is being utilized in the current EV market and vehicles and how it can be worked upon and improved in the future [3].

Bilal [4] reports India's increasing adoption of electric vehicles demands a higher power supply to keep them charged. Moreover, the transportation sector contributes to greenhouse gas emissions, notably sulfur dioxide (SO_2) and carbon dioxide (CO_2). To accommodate the elevated power requirements of electric vehicle charging, the national grid must consistently deliver substantial power daily. In the northwestern region of Delhi, India, the electric vehicle charging station (EVCS) requires various hybrid energy system configurations to meet its energy demands. These include a combination of solar photovoltaic panels, diesel generators, batteries, and grid power. Three distinct designs are considered. These potential setups are assessed using advanced meta-heuristic methods to determine their feasibility in terms of technology, finances, and the environment. The optimization algorithm's objective is to minimize the overall net present cost while ensuring a reliable power supply. Widely used tools like the HOMER software, the salp swarm algorithm (SSA), and the gray wolf optimization are employed to address this challenge, with their outcomes compared against those achieved with the modified salp swarm method (MSSA). Based on simulation results, MSSA demonstrates superior accuracy and resilience. Furthermore, in terms of computational efficiency, MSSA outperforms SSA and the gray wolf optimization. This highlights the potential of artificial intelligence in advancing these systems and offering more efficient and accessible solutions for their integration [4].

Brown et al. [9] suggest that commercializing autonomous vehicle technology is the automotive industry's primary goal, which is why global research in this field is progressing significantly. Even with this depth of research, there is a lack of literature outlining a simple and reasonably priced process for building an AV research platform. This study paper presents the methods and findings for the AV controls and instrumentation of the 2019 Kia Niro, which were developed for a regional AV pilot project, in order to satisfy this requirement. This platform comprises two GPS receivers for heading information, an in-car computer for environment perception, a stereo camera, a drive-by-wire actuation kit, a MobilEye computer vision system, LiDAR, an inertial measurement unit, and path planning. The system middleware that bridges the instruments and the autonomous application algorithms is called software for the robotic operating system. The data presented in this research report demonstrate the effective utilization of all sensors, the successful drive-by-wire capability, a total increased power* consumption of 242.8 Watts, and an overall cost of $118,189 USD. Compared to other commercially available systems with equivalent capability, this provides a substantial cost savings. This research paper highlights in detail the costs and methods to implement AI in automobiles for researches and emerging players and companies in this sector [9].

Shadrin et al. [10] explored the technological hurdles tied to re-purposing a production vehicle into a testing and development platform for advancements in autonomous driving. It also illustrates the process of reverse engineering the electric power steering (EPS) for external control through a general strategy. The primary aim of this study was to address the challenge of accurately predicting the dynamic trajectory of autonomous vehicles. To tackle this, a fresh equation for calculating lateral tire forces was developed, and some vehicle characteristics were adjusted during real-world road tests. Additionally, the control system for the test autonomous vehicle incorporated an advanced Mivar expert system. The introduction of a more adaptable and robust expert system, achieved by fusing hybrid artificial intelligence with logical reasoning, amplified the system's flexibility and effectiveness for the given application. This new technology offers a solution to the critical issue of liability in cases where autonomous vehicles are involved in accidents. The research paper discusses the derivation and demonstrates its practical implementation to attain the desired outcomes [10].

Koricanac [11] aimed to demonstrate how important it is to integrate artificial intelligence (AI) into the US autoindustry. The paper starts with an overview of artificial intelligence. After an in-depth review of the American automotive industry, the function and expected role of AI in the industry and its supply networks are discussed. The paper will present the case for applying AI to the US autoindustry. The automotive industry is one of the most important in America. It used to contribute three to five percent of the GDP overall; by 2020, that amount has dropped to 2.5 percent ($562.2 billion). The automotive manufacturing process, however, has changed significantly over time, incorporating the newest technological developments, unlike any other industry. Every industry has seen a ginormous shift in the competitive dynamics over the past few years due to the rapid pace of digitization. Businesses now have to work harder to be competitive in the market thanks to innovations. A business's need to create flexible and efficient supply chains makes integrating AI appear like an obvious decision. This paper studies the market in detail, which may help us get an insight on the future of the industry and the share in the market [11].

Ravishankaran, Charan [12] report over the past ten years, the automobile industry has increased its usage of artificial intelligences. The main worry is that the 'safety' about using the artificial intelligences in vehicles. AI might make some bad decisions, which could lead to some danger like accidents etc., to the passengers. When launching a new AI in the industry, creators should test their products so that we can prevent it from causing any accidents. As of now validation of artificial intelligence software and its skills becomes difficult as the usage of AI in vehicles raises. The goal of this study is to recognize and address the current issues related to AI software that are used in cars. The data that are used to train and examine the AI model was reviewed for data-related worries. A method was presented to address these challenges. Data acquired by sensors placed on the vehicle, for instance a camera, RADAR, will be applied to make correct decisions in independent cars [12].

Li et al. [13] investigated the important artificial intelligence algorithms as follows: artificial neural network is one of the most significantly important, AI is specifically a shallow neural network, which is composed of computational units that are closely joined to one another. The number of network ideas might be knowingly more than in traditional network topology. Accordingly, the network may be used to analyze high-dimensional information. Bottomless neural networks are the center of deep learning research, as opposite to an artificial neural network. It learns numerous levels of representations that resemble different levels of idea by using a force of many layers of nonlinear processing units for featuring taking out and manipulation [13].

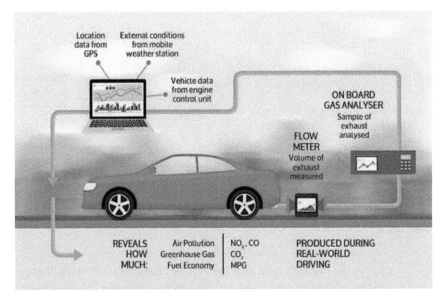

Figure 12.2 Emissions testing and mitigation source.

Source: [14].

12.3 PROBLEM IDENTIFICATION

As the demand for autonomous cars increases in the market, companies are competing to make AI better and moving towards a goal to make AD (autonomous driving) the next big thing, as AI in the automobile has witnessed significant advancements in recent years. However, several challenges and problem areas persist. Some of the problems and challenges are discussed below:

- **Security and privacy:** in today's generation the technologies are evolving and the hope of the driverless cars operating on roads is at hand. Experts believe that the driverless cars will be available in the next five to ten years. However, the most important thing of the AI is the security and the privacy concerns, because it can reveal the owner's data, location etc., as a customer I believe we value our privacy the most, so a customer would not be delighted to get their privacy invaded and make them vulnerable. This should be checked and repaired before these vehicles can be sold in the markets shown in Figure 12.2.
- **Security risks of WI-FI:** WI-FI can be a springboard for hackers/ attackers to launch an attack on vehicles. Through WI-FI hackers can get internal information about the car's network, so attackers

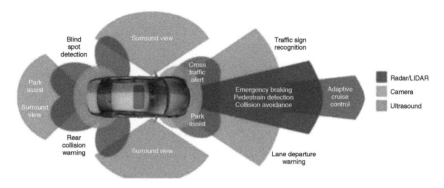

Figure 12.3 Sensors used by AI in automobiles.

Source: [14].

can get the owner's data and the vehicles data also, allowing them to use the vehicle as a weapon and also threatening the safety of people as shown in Figure 12.3.

- **Security risks of satellite comm. (GPS/BEIDOU):**
  It is quite worrying because hackers can use satellite communication to obtain both the owner's position and a replay of the location data.
- **Security risk of cellular mobile communications:**
  facilitates the hacker's ability to bring the data that has been saved by the car devices using microphones may be accessed by hackers using the cellular mobile communication system, who can also disrupt the automotive system by gaining access to the data. A distant WI-FI hotspot is offered by cellular mobile communication systems, which increases the risk of device attacks on cars as shown in Figure 12.2.
- **Privacy issues:** the following are privacy concerns: tracking the owner's whereabouts. Data from both the owner and the passenger is exported. Theft of sensor data from systems like the control system and speech recognition system.
- **Cyber security threats to autonomous cars:** hackers can seize control of the vehicle from a distance at any time.
  Private information access: once the hacker has access, they can steal the information, rendering the product useless.
- **Miscellaneous issues:** There are currently additional problems that modern cars are unable to solve. Although researchers are working around the clock to find solutions, they anticipate that these difficulties will be overcome in the next 5 to 10 years. While we wait for a solution, let us think about a smaller issue that has not been addressed yet: there are no technologies that can automatically

recognize automobiles and inform us which parts need to be modified; fixed. They may feel threatened by a motorist who lacks driving expertise, which might result in a catastrophic accident. There is currently no commercially available technology that can assist these drivers. Nowadays, it is common to see young drivers on the roads, and the only way to capture them is with the help of the police, which has occasionally turned out to be too late in certain circumstances [14].

12.4 OBJECTIVE

The main goal of this chapter is to help individuals, new and existing companies and investors to get a detailed and well researched overview on how AI can be implemented in automobiles and what is its scope in the future. This research chapter aims to cover the following key topics:

- **To discuss the future scope:** this chapter discusses the future scope of AI in the automotive industry, comparing the market caps and stating the future predictions.
- **Identifying constraints in the industry:** there are quite a few constraints that the industry needs to tackle on a large scale before moving forward.
- **Providing viable solutions to them:** the problems that have been identified require quick solutions. This chapter discusses all the viable solutions.
- **Analyzing the features of AI and how the technology is implemented in real-life applications:** this includes the name of the tools that are used by AI in automobiles and how they are implemented in real-world.

12.5 APPLICATION OF AI

- **Adaptive cruise control:** on highways, where drivers may find it difficult to continuously monitor their speed and the cars around them for a lengthy period of time, adaptive cruise control is especially helpful. Based on the motions of nearby objects, advanced cruise control can automatically accelerate, decelerate, and even stop the car as shown in Figure 12.3 [8].
- **Glare-free high beam and pixel light:** systems with glare-free high beams and pixel lights use sensors to adjust to the surrounding environment and the surrounding darkness of the vehicle without disturbing approaching traffic. This cutting-edge lighting system recognizes other cars, illuminates them, and reroutes their beams to shield other road users from momentary blindness.

- **Adaptive light control:** a vehicle's headlights are modified via adaptive light control according to the ambient illumination. According to the darkness and surrounds of the car, it changes the brightness, direction, and movement of the headlights.
- **Automatic parking:** drivers are accountable for human error since they are also people. Drivers can use automatic parking systems to identify blind areas and get steering wheel turn and stop signals. Rearview cameras, as opposed to traditional side mirrors, give drivers a greater perspective of their surroundings when driving. Utilizing information from various sensors, sophisticated systems may even park the car by themselves without the driver's assistance as shown Figure 12.3.
- **Autonomous valet parking:** Innovative technology called automated valet parking controls autonomous automobiles in parking lots using vehicle sensor meshing, 5G network connection, and cloud services. The car's sensors offer vital details on its location, where it is going, and how to safely navigate to the parking place. Up until the car is securely parked, this data is carefully analyzed and used to execute acceleration, braking, and steering as shown in Figure 12.2.
- **Navigation system:** car navigation systems include both voice prompts and on-screen directions to help drivers follow a route while keeping their attention on the road. Some navigation systems may also show detailed traffic information and, if required, plan a different route to avoid gridlock. Even heads-up displays may be offered by more advanced systems to reduce river distraction. These results are considerable results for the common middle-class market in the country. On the analysis of the sales of the already available EVs however, this feedback came to light as shown in Figure 12.3.

12.6 POSSIBLE SOLUTIONS

After analyzing these shortcomings, a few possible solutions that may be applied can be the following:

- **Collaborative effort:** to achieve the greatest standards of caber security for autos, cooperation between automakers and security experts is crucial. Both the integrity of the vehicle data and safeguards for the safety of drivers and passengers should be part of these criteria. This can entail insisting network segmentation, secure authentication mechanisms, and encryption technologies.
- **Continuous monitoring:** automobile manufacturers should use real-time monitoring techniques and systems to make sure that any security vulnerabilities are resolved as soon as feasible. Continuous monitoring of linked cars can assist automakers in spotting any

suspicious activity early on and taking swift action. This will assist in diminishing the effects and harm caused by security assaults. Additionally, manufacturers will be better able to take the required safeguards and stop any similar occurrences if they have a system in place that can identify any possible weaknesses.

- **Improved data privacy measures:** it is crucial to make sure that the data is kept safe and that no authorized individuals or instigation are able to access it. To guarantee that only authored workers are accessing the data, monitoring and tracking of data activities should be implemented. This will make it easier to find any suspicious activities or rules about data access infractions. It is essential to make sure that unauthorized people or organizations do not have access to the data, which is kept safe.

12.7 CONCLUSION

The use of AI in the automobile sector appears to be on the rise. Artificial intelligence has considerable promise in industries including autonomous driving, manufacturing, consumer experience, environment sustainability, reducing emission, carbon footprints, service, and maintenance. However, issues with data security, liability, and legislation need to be resolved in order to fully realize AI's promise in the automobile sector. To guarantee that AI is utilized properly and ethically, the automobile sector has to collaborate closely with regulators, technology suppliers, and other stakeholders. This will enable the industry to fully utilize AI in the automotive sector and pave the way for the integration of this technology with electric and hybrid cars to build a safer and more sustainable future.

12.8 FUTURE SCOPE

The automotive industry has always been at the forefront of adopting innovative technologies, and artificial intelligence (AI) is no exception. AI is poised to revolutionize the way cars are manufactured, serviced, and driven. The market for AI in the automotive industry is growing rapidly, it is currently $6 billion as of 2022 and it is expected to hit $9.3 billion this year, 2023. The market is blooming unstoppable with a projected value of $10.73 billion by 2027 and by 2030 it is expected to hit a market gap of $19.1 billion. This research chapter aims to explore the potential applications of AI in the automotive industry, the impact it will have on the market, and the challenges that need to be addressed to fully leverage its potential.

The potential future applications of AI in the industry are discussed below:

- **Autonomous driving:** the next revolutionary phase in the automotive industry is autonomous driving and it looks promising. AI-powered sensors, cameras, and other advanced technologies are being used to develop self-driving cars that can travel without assistance from humans. This technology may help to lower the number of accidents, improve traffic flow, and reduce the time and effort required for driving. In the future, autonomous driving could also lead to reduced carbon emissions, as cars can be programmed to drive in the most efficient manner possible.

- **Manufacturing:** AI is also being used to optimize the manufacturing process in the automotive industry. Machine learning algorithms are being used to analyze sensor and other data source optimization. This includes everything from predictive maintenance to supply chain management. With AI, it is possible to reduce waste, increase efficiency, and minimize downtime.

- **Service and maintenance:** AI can also play a significant role in service and maintenance. AI- powered diagnostics can identify potential issues with vehicles before they become major problems. This can help reduce maintenance costs and downtime. In addition, AI-powered chatbots can help customers troubleshoot problems and schedule appointments. This can potentially improve the customer experience and will increase customer loyalty.

REFERENCES

1. Hofmann M, Neukart F, Bäck T. Artificial Intelligence and Data Science in the Automotive Industry. *ABC* 2017; 1. http://arxiv.org/abs/1709.01989
2. Liu Z, Jiang H, Tan H, et al. An Overview of the Latest Progress and Core Challenge of Autonomous Vehicle Technologies. *MATEC Web Conf* 2020; 308: 06002. https://doi.org/10.1051/matecconf/202030806002
3. Sanguesa JA, Torres-Sanz V, Garrido P, et al. A Review on Electric Vehicles: Technologies and Challenges. *Smart Cities* 2021; 4: 372–404. https://doi.org/10.3390/smartcities4010022
4. Bilal M, Alsaidan I, Alaraj M, et al. Techno-Economic and Environmental Analysis of Grid-Connected Electric Vehicle Charging Station Using AI-Based Algorithm. *Mathematics*; 10. Epub ahead of print 2022. DOI: 10.3390/math10060924
5. Muhammad K, Ullah A, Lloret J, et al. Deep Learning for Safe Autonomous Driving: Current Challenges and Future Directions. *IEEE Transactions on Intelligent Transportation Systems* 2021; 22: 4316–4336. DOI: 10.1109/TITS.2020.3032227
6. Ning H, Yin R, Ullah A, Shi F, A Survey on Hybrid Human-Artificial Intelligence for Autonomous Driving. *IEEE Transactions on Intelligent Transportation Systems* 2021;23:7: 6011–6026. doi: 10.1109/TITS.2021.3074695
7. Arunmozhi M, Venkatesh VG, Yangyan Shi V, Raja Sreedharan V, Lenny Koh SC, Design and Development of Automobile Assembly Model using Federated Artificial Intelligence with Smart Contract, *International*

Journal of Production Research 2022, 60:1, 111–135, DOI: 10.1080/ 00207543.2021.1988750

8. Singh S, Baljit Singh Saini. "Autonomous Cars: Recent Developments, Challenges, and Possible Solutions." In *IOP Conference Series: Materials Science and Engineering* 2021, 1022:1, 012028. IOP Publishing. DOI 10.1088/1757-899X/1022/1/012028

9. Brown NE, Rojas JF, Goberville NA, Alzubi H, AlRousan Q, Chieh (Ross) Wang, Huff S, Rios-Torres J, Ekti AR, LaClair TJ, et al. "Development of an Energy Efficient and Cost Effective Autonomous Vehicle Research Platform" *Sensors* 2022;22:16: 5999. https://doi.org/10.3390/s22165999

10. Shadrin, Sergey Sergeevich, Oleg Olegovich Varlamov, Andrey Mikhailovich Ivanov. "Experimental Autonomous Road Vehicle with Logical Artificial Intelligence." *Journal of Advanced Transportation* 2017;17. https://doi.org/ 10.1155/2017/2492765

11. Koricanac I, "Impact of AI on the Automobile Industry in the US." (2021). Available at SSRN 3841426. DOI: 10.2139/ssrn.3841426

12. Ravishankaran C, "Impact on How AI in Automobile Industry has Affected the Type Approval Process at RDW." Master's thesis, University of Twente, 2021. https://appinventiv.com/blog/ai-in-automotive-industry/amp/

13. Li J, Cheng H, Guo H, Qiu S. "Survey on Artificial Intelligence for Vehicles." *Automotive Innovation* 2018;1, 2–14. https://doi.org/10.1007/ s42154-018-0009-9

14. Phogat M, Kumar A, Nandal D, et al. A Novel Automating Irrigation Techniques based on Artificial Neural Network and Fuzzy Logic. *Journal of Physics: Conference Series* 1950. Epub ahead of print 2021. DOI: 10.1088/ 1742-6596/1950/1/012088

Index

For Product Safety Concerns and Information please contact our EU
representative GPSR@taylorandfrancis.com
Taylor & Francis Verlag GmbH, Kaufingerstraße 24, 80331 München, Germany